The Four Seasons of Greek Philosophy

Dedication

To the Tilters and
the Dreamers and the
Slaves of Laurium
Past - Present - and Future
for
like the Poor
They are always amongst us

1st Publishing Paul Pavlou
Nicosia

Maureen O'Sullivan

The Four Seasons of Greek Philosophy

EFSTATHIADIS GROUP

First Published in Cyprus by Paul Pavlou in Nicosia

ISBN 960 226 334 2

Second Impression 1992

Printed and bound in Greece by
EFSTATHIADIS GROUP S.A.

Distributed by
EFSTATHIADIS GROUP S.A.
HEAD OFFICE: AGIOU ATHANASIOU ST. GR - 145 65 ANIXI ATTIKIS
TEL: (01) 8140602, 8140702 FAX: (01) 8142915 TELEX: 216176 EF
ATHENS BRANCH: 14 VALTETSIOU ST. GR - 106 80 ATHENS
TEL: (01) 3633319, 3614312, 3637284 FAX: (01) 3614312
ATHENS BOOKSHOP: 84 ACADEMIAS ST. TEL: 3637439
THESSALONIKI BRANCH: 4 C. CRISTALLI ST. ANTIGONIDON SQUARE
THESSALONIKI, GR - 546 30 TEL: (031) 511781, 542498, FAX 544759
THESSALONIKI BOOKSHOP: 14 ETHNIKIS AMINIS ST. TEL: (031) 278158

Contents

CHAPTER 1

WHAT IS PHILOSOPHY?
AND-WHAT MAKES A PHILOSOPHER?

So, what is philosophy? you ask. And what exactly goes into making-up the character of a philosopher? And who were these Greeks? Why, and how, did they invent this philosophy in the first place? And most importantly — what is the use of learning about it?

In order to answer all these questions which may now be assaulting the brain-cells of the average lay-man on first setting eyes on this book, it would probably be as well to proceed immediately to a definition of the word 'philosophy' itself; as this word was originally invented by the Greeks, and is today in common linguistic use in numerous countries, where innumerable people, seldom — (if ever) — spare so much as a thought for those Ancient people, when articulating it.

The prefix 'philo' in theGreek language means, 'to love', and 'sophia' is the Greek for 'wisdom', hence we have the word 'philosophy', which means a 'love of wisdom'. A philosopher therefore, is a 'lover of wisdom' — although possibly a better definition would have been a 'seeker of wisdom' — as seeking for truth, is really what most of the gentlemen in this book are occupied in doing. Still, this is not the time to start splitting etymological hairs, and so we may safely describe philosophers as 'lovers of wisdom', who spend all their waking hours both fanatically, and steadfastly, engaged in this long-suffering and laborious enterprise.

But what exactly makes a philosopher you ask. What induces someone to expend his brief mortal existence employed in the seeking of truth, or the loving of wisdom, anyway? Is it due to a naturally morbid disposition on his part? — coupled with bad digestion? Or, are those suffering from deep spiritual depression, and psychological melancholia, more in tune with this pursuit, right from the start? Is philosophy then, some type of affliction, or disease? Is it perhaps, a terrible raging thirst for knowledge and wisdom, which has been derived from an unduly lengthy diet of over-salted lies and superstitions having been forcibly stuffed down the throat of the victim, until he was unable to swallow anymore? Is that what this philosophy thing is? you ask. An unquenchable thirst, which never abates — and for which the sufferer can find no cure?

The philosopher Aristotle, once wrote that, "All Men by nature desire to know" — but, do they? Or, do some of them desire more than others? And even if the majority of people do decide that they want to know, many of them get bored with the experience, or tired out by such strenuous enquiry; and, after a decent interval of time, they abandon it — in much the same way as they once retired from the piano lessons of their childhood, after the tedious duty of practising daily scales, had proved too onerous. So then, are philosophers just very hard thinking people? People who persist in thought, and who carry their ideas and questions through to some general conclusion?

Or, yet again, is all philosophic enquiry simply based upon the emotions of Wonder, Doubt, and Fear? Emotions which we all experience at some time or other in our lives; and some of us, for longer periods than others.

The feeling of wonder regarding the world, we meet with most compellingly when we are children. However, the majority of us lose this questioning spirit in due time. Initially in fact, all children are natural philosophers, and they drive their elders and betters mad with their continualphilosophicinterrogation. "What is this?" "Who made me?" "Where was I before I was born?" "Why is this, this? and not that?" And so the child persists, until dissuaded by impatient and exhausted adults, and he learns that asking these questions is not considered smart, and definitely not the wise thing to do (especially just before the dinner hour, or when Dad first gets home from work), and most of all — he discovers that asking questions such as these, is not part of the normally accepted Adult Behaviour Pattern — and so he ceases.

The true philosopher, then, to some extent perhaps, always remains a child.

And the person struggling with inconsistencies in his religious, or, social systems; who cannot logically see why this thing should be considered ethical and moral, and the other, not — he is also a tremulous philosopher; dealing with his doubt, and attempting to understand; to discover the reasoning behind everything — or even if there is any type of reasoning there at all!

So the doubter is likewise a philosopher — even if he can never find anything in which to believe, and needs must stay a miserable sceptic 'till the end of his days.

The fearful and uncertain person, and the man facing old age, or death; (and generally these two states of being are to some extent interrelated), they also seek answers in order to allay their fears — and in consequence — become philosophers.

The frightened man turns to philosophy as the flower turns to the sun — he has need of it, instinctively!

And if all the above is true, and these emotions do stimulate philosophical enquiry, then this book is eminently suitable reading material for all children, agnostics, and the terror-ridden! — And nowadays, these classifications must surely apply to quite a number of people in the modern world.

In truth though, philosophy is for everyone — it is simply a matter of persistent thought. Thought which can be undertaken at any time, and in any place; and which requires absolutely no skill, or capital. The only essential element is the thought — although, the persistent character of the thought must be stressed — as it is the quality of persistence which is the most important part of this operation.

And practising philosophy is very natural to people, and it is not an abnormal activity at all; though the banal may perhaps laugh aloud at the very suggestion. To become a Thinker, is to cross the "Pons Asinorum" —or, the "Bridge of Asses", as Euclid described his fifth preposition in geometry; and, it signals the passing from the vulgar semi-ape stage of primitive Man, to the beginnings of true Human Thought and Development.

Philosophy is in fact going on about us all the time, everywhere, and we even have common or garden examples of it in the international Folk-lore and Proverbs which have been handed down through the Ages, and which are the collective wisdom and observation of the ordinary people. And even if this wisdom has sometimes come from the intuitive sub-conscious of Man, and not from his logical conscious — the philosophical movement is still at work there, and is continuing, all the time.

Philosophy may occur in any geographic area, and it may arise in any climate; although it will become more developed into institutionalised Schools of Thought wherever there is a solid economic basis to support it; and, where there are enough people anxious to follow through, and to adopt a particular trend in thought — **or**, where, the Powers that be, **throw their support behind it**! But, a Blackman who is transplanted into a cold and alien climate, and who is suffering from the weather, may become more philosophical in inclination than a Whiteman living in the same location. —The very conditions of life will force him to become so. Similarly, a Whiteman with a sensitive skin, who resides in a hot environment which compels him to remain indoors much of the time, may also turn to philosophy for diversion. So perhaps, to the previously mentioned emotions of Wonder, Doubt and Fear, which we had decided might motivate the philosophical urge in people — we might also add the emotion of Pain. Quite possibly in fact, Pain and Suffering, are the greatest drives that Man has ever had, or continues to have, towards deep thought.

The Philosopher, like the Artist, is almost certainly a person with a keen sense of the imperfection of life, and, he, or she, may also be a person possessed of a strong sense of the injustice of life, as well. On the whole, the Philosopher is searching for Harmony and Balance — for a way to make everything that much better, or purer; more in tone, or true in colour; and, more precisely correct in design. And he is searching for the key to how life works, and to the theory, or truth, behind the seemingly random happenings of every day. And as the philosopher has need of time and solitude to spend in deep contemplation, we may say then that to a certain extent, he needs to be a 'Loner', or a 'Hermit'; someone with a great amount of time, and very little company. Therefore, to the list of personality traits, and characteristics of philosophers, we might also ascribe the quality of 'Loneliness' — where-upon the Shepherd, and the Night Watchman, will now also be entitled to join this band of heavy thinkers. And if either of these individuals cares to write his thoughts down, or to draw some general conclusions on life, and to publish these, then he may in turn, be known as a, 'professional' philosopher. If not however, then he will pass from this earth, unfêted and unsung; for it is only the professional philosophers that the world ever learns of —although there are countless others existing right under our noses all the time.

Some people of course, are infinitely more aware than others of the need for a system of either divine, or, natural order, and for divine, or natural justice in this world; but most of us do question these things at some time or other in our lives — as the individual can never completely succeed in being happy with himself alone — unless, of course, he keeps himself very busy, and very mentally occupied — and very petty-minded! The Cosmic Loneliness however is always with us (whether we like to admit it or not) — a large, black Void, inexorably waiting to engulf us —and Man continually, (if erratically, and rather infrequently) raises his voice to cry, "What am I doing here?" and, "Where am I eventually going to go?"

Naturally, persistent thinking on questions such as these, does tend to make a person a little disturbed at times, and possibly also serves to interfere with the digestion; so maybe we can insert people with internal disorders, to that list of innately talented philosophers, as many of the Ancient Greek Philosophers did in fact suffer medically in just such a fashion. Therefore, if the Reader is rather worried about the state of his health, it might then be as well for him to leave the more creative and theorizing side of philosophy to others, and simply to read about what some people in Ancient Greece (two and a half thousand years ago) spent the best part of their lives agonizing over, — and then — to adopt one of these philosophical theories to suit himself.

Plato, the philosopher and instructor of Aristotle, said that, "Philosophy and Medicine constitute real knowledge, in contrast to the apparent knowledge of Rhetoric and Cooking." But Cooks and Rhetoricians need not be offended by these words, as philosophy, to some degree or other, is needed in both these Arts, and both these Arts may actually be used to develop philosophy. This is actually the most interesting facet of this subject, as people may turn to philosophy, or become involved in doing it, by virtue of the very fact that they have specialized in doing something else very well. A person may be trained in Biology, Mathematics, or Cooking, and yet eventually, he may develop into a Philosopher. He may be a Technician, a Doctor, or an Artist; who having asked many questions about his own particular field of study, then proceeds to connect between his subject and another — to comprehend the interrelationship between the various spheres of thought; and to understand the underlying, and unifying theme of life. The Philosopher makes the 'Leap' and crosses the division; sees in his Mathematics, the connection with, and the rules applying to, the Mathematics of life itself — or, in the harmony of sound, he discovers an hypothesis which will possibly hold true for the very harmony of Life, and for all living organisms. "If," says the Philosopher, "this theory holds true for this thing in Physics, then perhaps it can be applied in some other field of knowledge, and will be equally veritable in matters of Metaphysics and Ethics." And that is the 'Philosophical Leap' — a mental crossing of the barriers from one science, art, or region of thought, into another — and it is an action, which is at the same time both outstandingly difficult, and complicated; and yet astonishingly easy, and straight forward.

§ § § § § §

Each of these Ancient Greek Philosophers in our story was a fairly colourful character in his own right — (people always seem to have cared for a little 'dash' to their philosophers) — and people who make the 'Leap Forward', and who cross so spectacularly in Thought, are generally considered a little eccentric in their own day and age. So perhaps another personal quality of most philosophers is a certain degree of 'rugged individualism' in their temperamental make-up. And while reading this book you will probably also discover that certain individual philosophers, and their particular theories, are much more to your liking than are others; and the Author herself openly admits to being prejudiced in favour of those philosophies which are based upon biological studies, and evolutionary theories — simply because that is what she herself happens to believe in.

But the real joy of reading philosophy — as distinct from the arduous task of actually building a completely new philosophy from scratch by yourself — is that, unlike the institutionalised philosophy of Religion; the philosophies of the Ancient Greeks (and those of the Pre-Socratic Philosophers, in particular) are such that you can adapt them to suit yourself —and **not** have to change yourself, in order to fit in with someone else's theories on life. And, unlike the ready-made shop garment of Religion, which you buy, and whose purchase will depend to a great extent on the range of choice available, and on your economic where-with-all (in other words your national church, and whichever religious denomination you happen to have been born into), the study of philosophy is like coming upon various widths of material, which may be inspected and purchased at leisure, and then sewn together in order to suit yourself. You may simply disregard those which you do not happen to care for, and drape around your soul, the ones which you do. You may take the whole thing up in places, or let it down in others; and in general, you may design an intellectual costume in accordance with your own needs. The basic materials are there, but you are your own creator. And that is what being an 'Eclectic' means; that is to choose, (the word comes from the Greek, and means to 'select'), those aspects of a philosophy which appeal most to you. And who knows, you may even continue to build on your own, and perhaps even end up by forming an entirely new philosophy of your own construction.

§ § § § § § §

The three major strains of philosophy which were developed among the Ancient Greeks, concerned the Physical, Metaphysical, and Ethical concepts and problems of life; and in general, they proceeded from the Physical Wonder, and the Metaphysical Doubt, of the Pre-Socratic Philosophers; on to the eventual culmination in the attempted blue-printing of a fool-proof plan for dealing with the Ethical problems of Man and the Society, by the *fearful* Post-Socratics. Philosophy, like the Greeks themselves, became more institutionalised, and more systematized, as it developed. What originally began as pure questioning thought by the Pre-Socratic Thinkers, eventually wound up as a rigid religion of intellectualism with the Post Socratics, and that is why there is a quite discernable cycle of four seasons to the life of Philosophy in Greece. The Pre-Socratic Philosophers who first planted these philosophical seeds in the Spring in Ionia and Italy, laid the garden in preparation for the bursting into a thousand blossoms of the Socratic Summer in Athens. But after the death of Socrates, the short, bounteous, and beautiful Summer was over. Then with the commencement of the decline of Greece (and with the failure of Athens as an entity in particular,) philosophy passed into its Autumnal period — mellow and mature, and more highly developed than ever before; with the works of the great Classical Philosophers Plato and Aristotle. Although in the Author's estimation Aristotle constitutes something more in the way of an Indian Summer, than an Autumn, as he was always more optimistic than Plato. But, whether Autumnal or not, the time of Greece was growing shorter, and philosophy as such was dying nevertheless —Thought had become a terminal case obviously! With the rise of Epicureanism, and Stoicism, we come to the Winter of Greek Philosophy and to the Nadir of Greek thought. And to a time in which the intellectual quest has been transformed into a quasi-religious and superstitious doctrine, or is used simply as a means of intellectual escapism. And finally, with the fall of Greece beneath the Roman heel, the Peripatetics and the Sceptics appear, like the hint and promise of some new Spring of the Future — a long way off still, it is true, but certain to arrive some day.

And so as Greece rose and fell, the philosophy movement inclined and declined also — and yet certain parts of all these diverse philosophies have continued down to us to some extent in either our modern religions, or, in our contemporary social systems. That is why the Ancient Greeks are such a fascinating people to study, as even today, so much of our modern thinking, can be discerned in their ancient way of life. And so many of our new-fangled problems are in fact old-fangled dilemmas, which they faced, but did not manage to resolve either — those many years ago.

And therefore, if you are ready to begin your own Historical and Philosophical Leap, we will proceed post-haste to Greece, to observe how people were living at the dawn of Philosophy, and to ruminate upon; (and hopefully, to understand also) why it was that the Greeks became such very hard thinking people, long before the rest of Europe had even discovered how to cogitate at all!

HOW GREEK PHILOSOPHY BEGAN

At first, philosophy was divided into two main schools of thought in Greece. One was known as the Ionian (which didn't happen to be anywhere near the Ionian Sea,) and the other, was called the Italian — and was not Italian at all — but Greek!

Right now, the Reader may be scratching his head and saying, "Alright! Enough! This philosophy business is not for me! It's far too confusing altogether!" But if he will bear a little patiently with the Writer, she wll endeavour to explain how these misnomers came about.

Firstly, the Ionian Philosophy School began on that piece of coast line in Asia Minor which runs along the Aegean Sea from directly opposite the island of Chios in the north, to the island of Leros in the south.

This area became the territory of the Ionian Greeks from the Greek Mainland who had been pushed to emigrate there, due to pressure from the advancing Dorian Greeks then arriving in the Greek Mainland during the period of Great Migrations in 1104 B.C. As these invading Greeks in Asia Minor were known as Ionians, (due to their tribe being descended from the mythological Ion) so the area which they colonized was named Ionia, after them.

There was in fact a whole lot of movement going on about this time, as the Achaean Greeks (i.e. the Greeks associated with Homer and the Heroic Age) had originally come into this Mediterranean area, and had conquered, slaughtered, and settled quite comfortably upon the aboriginal Creto-Pelasgo-Myceneaen civilizations in Crete and Mainland Greece, and were just beginning to feel at home in the area when the Dorians (the Greek tribe which eventually organised the Spartan State) from Thessaly slaves, and discontented and impoverished mainlanders, were continually being sent off in order to open up some new territory or other. Italy in fact had the dubious distinction for being the most popular choice for 'enforced' colonization in the 5th and 6th centuries B.C. Most Greek colonies however, became autonomous rather rapidly, and in consequence, were never as unified or tied to the Mother-Land, as were the colonies of the British Empire at a later date. The Greeks fanatical love of independence was however always their greatest attribute while at the same time being their Achilles' Heel, and they could absolutely never work together for any length of time — except in cases of dire emergency —such as when the Persians attempted to invade and conquer them. It really did seem that there was nothing the Greeks really enjoyed so much, as indulging in vicious battles amongst themselves; and so their various colonies were actually only united in a common language, an Olympian God System, and, a desire for trade. Perhaps in fact, they secretly preferred fighting with each other simply because they were the only people they could really respect? But I digress, with these cryptic comments on the wearisome war-faring nature of the Greeks, and we must return once more to philosophy, as that is after all, our subject.

Anyway, these are the two main schools of thought which began the philosophy movement in Greece. The Physical Ionian school was built upon the official Greek myths, and it was influenced from the East; and the Mystical, or Metaphysical, Italian school, developed from the Resurrection Cults, and it was influenced by the land and the people of the North and the West of Europe.

By 462 B.C. however, Philosophy had moved its centre to Athens, because that city had finally decided to grow-up and to become 'Glorious'; or, in other words, Athens was by then, the wealthiest and most powerful centre of the Greek world following the Persian Wars. From then on Philosophy was to become increasingly institutionalized, and [illegible] certain extent it began to form a type of new religion for the educated Greek who no longer seriously believed in either the Myths, or, the Cults. Philosophy in Athens was also developed due to the competition and an[illegible]onism between the various power groups there, and some schools of p[illegible]osophy started to arise which protested at the authority of the State, [illegible] others arose under the direct encouragement and indirect auspices of [illegible]ate, and began to be used as a form of political control by the System[illegible]osophy is after all a form of religion, and religion has almost never be[illegible]wn to be without a political tinge for any length of time. Philos[illegible] [illegible]gain, like religion; may start out as a pure form of the aspirations[illegible]eople, but sooner or later come what may, the Powerful take over, [illegible]ed to bend and to shape it to their own designs, and specificatio[illegible]

and Illyria, (all tall, warlike and illiterate upstarts in Achaean eyes) began driving southwards in 1104 B.C. and commenced scattering people around the Mediterranean, like so much confetti at a church wedding. From North West Greece the Aeolian Greeks fled to Asia Minor, and there began the Aeolian League of Twelve Cities in the region of what had once been Troy. The Ionians meanwhile, left the Peloponnesus to the Dorians, and set up new areas of influence in Attica, Euboaea, the Cyclades, and the Ionian Dodecapolis in Asia Minor. The Euxines also packed their bags from wherever they were residing all over Greece, and moved on before the Dorian tide, to stake their claim to land in Thrace, the Hellespont, Propontis, and around the Euxine Sea. Still other Greeks left for the Ionian Isles of the Ionian Sea, and for Southern Italy, Sicily, Gaul, and Spain; and henceforth these particular Greeks will be known as the Italians, or as the inhabitants of 'Magna Graecia'; and we will be hearing quite a lot about them in philosophy.

It is worth noting also, that during this period of strife and bustle, even some of the Dorians were forced to move-out themselves, and quite a few of them not only caused a lot of bother to the other longer established Greeks, but they also over-flowed into the Cyclades, Crete, Cyrene, and Rhodes, as well as to the Dorian Hexapolis just south of the Ionian area in Asia Minor.

So even the Dorians suffered during this period of transition, although most of the other Greeks just looked on them as insensitive trouble-makers!

The Ionians, due to their fortunate position in Asia Minor, became one of the most developed Greek centres, and they founded the richest civilization in the Ancient Greek World; and, in consequence, produced famous Architecture, Music, Poetry, and Philosophy. But their new polity after 1104 B.C. was built upon the ruins of other much more advanced civilizations in the Middle Eastern area, and they were in due course, to be further influenced by Egypt, with its advanced learning in Astronomy and Mathematics. And the Ionians even imbibed a certain amount of Egyptian religious ideas, and in particular, the ideology regarding the Resurrection Cults, which were then very popular there. Then, from the Phoeniceans, the Ionians derived the rudiments of Trading, and the all important Alphabet; and from the Assyrians they discovered the art of Statuary. Lydia and Mesopotamia instructed them in Banking and Trade also, and the Phrygians gave them Music, and the religious goddess Cybele to worship. Hence the Ionian civilization grew as a result of all these influences. But possibly, the most gratitude for their achievements, should be given to the Persians, who created so much conflict and competition in the region, thereby spuring the Ionians on to the accomplishment of much greater things. It was actually the Persians; the most bitter foes of the

Ionians; who really made them into the foremost civilization which they were to become — rivalry is a great motivator of men; and hate is possibly a stronger driving force than love. While Athens was nothing but a miserable village, the Ionian Greeks in Asia Minor were already busy, pouring forth an abundance of music, literature, and ideas upon the Mediterranean World. And that is why Philosophy was born in this region of the Greek World, rather than in any other.

The Ionian School of Philosophy was also considerably influenced by the Homeric Myths, and by the Legends concerning the origins of the world, and of all forms of life. The Cosmogeny, as it was known, stated that the world had been born from nothing but Chaos, and that gradually there had been implemented a co-operative venture of a type between Night, and Death; which had then managed to bring forth Love; and that from Love, had eventually come Light and Day. It was definitely a very pretty and poetic interpretation of the beginnings of Life, but, to the questioning person, this story left a lot to be desired, and the intellectuals of Ionia didn't really feel that the Cosmogeny held the answers to all their queries. This early Bible of the Greeks, which attempted to give some type of basis for all animate and inanimate matter in the world, and which traced the origins of the Greek people back to a group of twelve supreme deities who ruled both the World, and the Greek citizen's life, completely — was not a sufficiently rational, nor a satisfying enough explanation for these early Ionian intellectuals, and they wanted to discover exactly **what life was**; and, what the physical nature of the dratted thing was also! Therefore they were more interested in a rather materialistic philosophy, that is to say, they were searching for the truth, in order to gain an idea of the actual material of life itself. In consequence therefore, these philosophers were the first Scientists, or Physicists, of Ancient Greece.

§ § § § § §

The Italian School of Philosophy however, was born in Southern Italy and Sicily, (and of course it was not really Italian, as Italy did not actually exist as a nation at that time although inPhilosophicalterminology this Greek area is called Italian). But this geographic location, which had been first colonized at the time of the Great Migrations, was then subject to yet another large influx of Greek immigrants around the year 700 B.C. These later settlers from the Greek Mainland, like the Ionian Greeks; built a very flourishing civilization in this new colony of theirs — a civilization based mainly on trade with the northern European barbarians, (that means the ancestors of the Writer, and probably of the Reader also!) and on extensive agriculture and commerce between the other Greek City-States and themselves. Their jurisdiction began to really achieve an eco-

nomic prominence around 500 B.C. just as Ionia's influence was diminis ing, and this territory which was also known as the 'Magna Graecia', 'Big Greece' area; rich and powerful though it was, developed after Ioni and was not able in consequence, to benefit from the older centres c civilization in the Middle East and the Far East. Therefore, the 'Italian Greeks had a quite different attitude to life in many ways and this differ ence can be perceived, in their development of philosophy. (We are all of us, after all, the products, or the victims, of our environment!)

This School of Philosophy in Italy began with Pythagoras who was himself an emigrant from Ionia, and it was influenced not so much by the official Greek myths and legends of the birth of the World, but, by the Cult of Orpheus, which had descended into Southern Greece, and Italy, from Thrace in North Greece. And it is of this important religious diversion that we will speak now.

In Greece, from the time of the development of the City-State, there existed the recognised Olympian God System of the famous twelve deities, who were headed by Zeus the Captain of the Gods; and these Gods represented Beauty, Order, and Justice, in the Greek Civilization System. They also represented the Rulers, and the City Dwellers; the Aristocrats, and the Achaean Greeks; and of course, the successful New Rich Merchants. **But**, they did not really represent the peasants, the slaves, the under-dogs, or, the losers. Therefore the Olympian Religion left much to be desired in the eyes of the majority of people. Hence the Cults sprang up in Italy and elsewhere, in answer to the needs of the people — and in Chapter Three, the Reader can learn what these Cults were, and how these Cults influenced the Italian Philosophy Movement. Suffice it for now to state that the Cults always had a higher degree of spiritual content in their ideology, than did the official State Religion; and they were very concerned with the 'Soul', and with Life after Death. Therefore this Cult of Orpheus which found its way down to Southern Italy, or 'Magna Graecia', affected the philosophers there, who in turn became more Metaphysical in their attitude and philosophical thought, rather than remaining merely Physical. And the Italian Philosophers asked questions regarding the State of Life, and the spiritual aspects of Life; rather than merely querying the physical qualities of the world itself.

Also [illegible] be observed that Magna Graecia never did attain the decadent sp[illegible] of Ionia. It was rich, but it was also always abundant in troublesome [illegible]onists and runaway slaves, as Italy had become a very fashionable [illegible] ground for convict settlements in the Greek World around 500 B.[illegible] Greeks naturally, had worked out the original blueprint for that [illegible]ctory scheme of killing two birds with one stone (i.e. getting rid [illegible], and building an empire at the same time!) long before the Britis[illegible]d to using it, in Australia! — and shipments of

So, philosophy born in Ionia and Italy, came to town (i.e. Athens) with the Sophists, upset the official Olympian religious system terribly; was given a martyr, and therefore made sacred and established, by the death of Socrates; became institutionalised under Plato; was used to build an Empire under Aristotle; revolted somewhat with the Cynics and the Hedonists; and progressed (or regressed) into Christian Theology with the Stoics — It evolved into Intellectual Detachment and Spiritual Escape with the Epicureans — into Scholarship and Modern Science with the Peripatetics; and finally; devolved into the lone voice of the Satirical Dissident minority — with the Sceptics. Therefore, Philosophy played its part in the development of the historical process in Greece, and it also affected the historical process and the growth of thought, in the whole of Western Europe. The most truthful and pure philosophers (the most keen, if naive searchers, in fact) were those who came before Socrates, because following that period, philosophy became a political instrument to be of use in the hands of the power-hungry. But all of the Thinkers in this book are worth reading about — if not for their theories, (which might have sometimes been formulated in order to please a particular clique, rather than the spirit of truth) — but for their life stories, which are full of interest and colour, independent of their philosophy — or possibly even dependent upon it.

Philosophy of course, (like everything else) was the product of the Socio-Economic environment of the times, and so, though the degree of love for wisdom might have remained the same throughout the years, the particular wisdom that was loved — **varied**; according to the conditions pertaining to Greece in those particular days.

And eventually, all these philosophies, (parts of them at any rate) plus the various religious ideas, and the cults; were later fused into one conglomerate Christian Creed by Saint Paul and the Church Fathers. Christianity neatly tied up all the loose ends — and every myth, and every individual philosophy, (whatever was not detrimental to the State naturally) was brought together and amalgamated under the Roman umbrella of unity, by the Third Century A.D., — as Civilization in Europe was then in great need of a *new universal and cosmopolitan faith*, in keeping with the new conditions of life then prevailing.

But the Birth of Christianity inevitably spelt the Death of Greek Philosophy, and though the mass education and thinking level of people rose — the actual quality of thought, to a great extent — deteriorated.

But, we are running too far ahead in our story, so let us therefore, retrace our steps to the Springtime of the Greek World, to the purity and freshness of those naive Greeks in Ionia and Italy, and let us see just what made them actually start to think in the first place. And our Cycle of Four Seasons, will follow not only the history of the philosophy movement in

Greece, but also the history of the Greeks themselves; because the Greek Civilization, and the Greek Philosophy, are so interconnected, that neither one can really be considered without the other. And ironically, it is from the moment that the Greeks first began to think, that they became their own worst enemies. Their very civilization weighed so heavily upon their shoulders, that they probably never enjoyed even one moment of their era of glorious achievements; and quite possibly they were rather relieved to eventually take a backseat to the Romans in the winter of their declining years — and to retire from the conflict of Ape versus Human; and, Animal Instinct versus Logic. The ability to think was a wonderful evolutionary development in Man it is true — but it certainly did tend to give him a headache!

Spring

Spring-time in Ionia and Italy and the Birth of Thought.

The Pre-Socratic Philosophers

The Milesians — Thales,
Anaximander,
Anaximenes

Pythagoras

Heracleitus

Xenophanes

Parmenides and Zeno

Anaxagoras

Empedocles

Leucippus

Democritus

CHAPTER 2

WHAT IS THIS THING CALLED LIFE?

The Milesian Meteorologists and the Cosmogeny.

Miletus in Asia Minor was the birthplace of Greek Philosophy in the 6th century B.C. according to all reports — and the Greeks responsible for this early flowering in thought — were the Ionians.

Both the Ionian and Aeolian Greeks had originally come from the Greek Mainland, and driven before the tide of land hungry Dorian invaders, had begun arriving in Asia Minor from, between 1100 to 850 B.C. The Aeolians, (as described in the Homeric Odes regarding the Trojan War) had defeated the older civilizations which had been flourishing along the northern area of the Aegean coastline, and had then established a colonization area known as the Aeolian League of Twelve Major Cities which included the island of Lesbos in their territory. Directly south of them, the Ionians set-up their own area of influence known as the Ionian Dodecapolis, or, the Ionian Twelve Cities, which included the island of Samos.

Samos, of Ionian influencebecame famous for Aesop, the Founder of the Morality Fable; and Lesbos, of Aeolian influence, became infamous for Sappho, the Founder of Lesbianism.

It might be noted however, that Sappho was actually an ancient poetess of great talent and ability, but who nowadays unfortunately, seems to fascinate the average scholar and layman for far more prosaic reasons, and many and varied are the heated exchanges and discussions regarding her. Was she really beautiful? — or was she really plain? Did she really prefer to pour forth her affections physically upon members of her own sex or not? All these issues though seem totally irrelevant somehow, as surely it is her poems which should be under scrutiny, and **not** her sexual diversons. And one cannot help wondering whether this is not another case of mere male chauvinism, because in serious conversation regarding Socrates and Plato, little is ever said regarding THEIR sexual inversion. However, Sappho and her poetry, (whatever the truth regarding her sexual persuasions), along with Alcaeus, (who invented the "alcaic" metre in poetry) contributed to making the Aeolians famous for their lyricism in both verse and music — while Thales of Miletus, and his philosophical descendants, made the Ionians famous for their mental ruminations. The Aeolian Twelve gave birth to the Arts, and the Ionian Twelve gave birth to Science; and Athens in Motherland Greece witnessed the graduation of both these babes into adulthood — and eventually, she made a good profit from both of them as well!

At the time of the Great Migrations, the City-State of **Miletus** had actually been colonized in an extremely satisfactory and efficient manner. At least according to the Ionian Greeks it had been most satisfactory and efficient, and it had been accomplished with an almost perfect assimilation of both the aboriginal population, and the incoming colonizers. The Ionian Greeks had simply moved into the area; killed off all the males; married all the females; and bred a new hybrid race of Ionian Greeks. A similar experiment was more or less attempted by British colonists in the 19th century A.D. when they wiped out the entire Aboriginal race in Tasmania, and only the few women who had been captured and forced to co-habit with some Whalers in the area, were then able to continue the indigenous blood-line up to, and including the present day. The Hybrid of course, is a common biological feature in Life, and genocide, is a common Strategic feature in Empire Building.

Miletus was the centre of the Ionian Big Twelve, due to its having eighty colonies of its very own, and these colonies furnished it with the raw materials necessary for trading with the East, and in particular with Egypt, North Lydia, Babylonia and Phoenicia. Like all the other City-States of Greece, Miletus had begun its life by being ruled by Kings — had revolted, and taken up being ruled by Aristocrats — revolted again — and then fallen under the rule of a class of Tyrants, who had evolved from a Middle Class of very wealthy merchants.

Due to the richness of trade and the passage of peoples through its ports, the city began to grow in culture (as culture can only grow when people have enough time and money to devote themselves to things other than the compulsory and basic grubbing for filthy lucre), and this affluent entrepôt developed literature, history, early science, mathematics and philosophy. As the Greeks had very little to occupy themselves with, (most of the slaves were actually doing the work it must be remembered!) the more scholarly, or intellectual of them, turned to consider the world, and began to question what it **really** was — and how, it had **really** come into being. These gentlemen viewed with scepticism the various stories in Greek Mythology, concerning the creation of the world in which it was stated that the world had been born from Nothing, and that Night and Death had also come out of Nothing, and that eventually between them had formed Love — which in turn had formed Light, and then, Day. And thus began the world, according to the Cosmogeny, or Creation Myth of the Greeks.

"Nothing comes from Nothing," muttered these ancient sceptics, "and Nothing goes into Nothing either," they said. "And whatever this Nothing is, then it must be Something, and we're going to find out what that is!" And so they set about their task, and, although they didn't believe the Cosmogeny Myth anymore, (they saw travellers coming through their ports everyday, with equally weird but differing versions of the Creation of the World). They **did** believe that behind these pretty stories there might exist a rational explanation which Time, and the Imagination of Man, had distorted, and so the first philosophers sought to re-evaluate the Myths, and to analyse them more thoroughly.

As every Disadvantage creates, and is in turn, responsible for every Advantage (a little homily of which the Writer is exceedingly fond, as the Reader will no doubt realise on proceeding through this book) or, to put it more simply, "For every cloud, there is a silver lining", so the decadent wealth of Miletus (and it was decadent as you shall see), led to leisure; and leisure in turn, led to the development of an Aristocracy of Thinkers. These early philosophers were cultured people who were economically independent, respected, (or if not respected, at least tolerated) and who were allowed to continue their thinking (for the most part) undisturbed. Wealth, and Leisure, are both absolutely essential requirements for all philosophers, which is why we do not generally see the harrassed housewife and mother of six children emerging as a leading light in the scholastic world. Very probably she, (the housewife) often has quite brilliant mental insights into life, but, due to the nature of her work, can never find the time to write them down, and moreover, can **never** manage to get **even** her husband and children to listen to her; due to their being more interested in getting something hot, into their stomachs, and something clean, onto their backs. And the above, are some of the reasons why **all** the philosophers in this book are Male Scholars, and none of them Female House-Keepers (like the harrassed Author of this book!)

Besides the Homeric Myths, and the mixture of religions and ideas from both East and West which were churning inside the mental melting pot of Miletus, the rudiments of Astronomy, Astrology and Mathematics had also entered from the East, and so Greek Thought and Reason were built upon this intermingling of superstition, speculation, and scholasticism — both domestic — and, imported.

These early Milesian Scientists were also very preoccupied with clouds, mist, fog, and water, in all forms in general; so it leads one to suppose that besides being naturally depressed, due to bad digestion, (universally purported to be the cause of developing a philosophical disposition) they were also bothered badly by the weather conditions then prevailing in Ionia. If this was not the case, then one cannot, for the life of one, imagine why they didn't just apply themselves to **enjoying** life in their luxurious city; and forget about the miserable business of addling their brains in order to come up with the TRUTH — Truth being a relative matter anyway — even at the best of times! However, the Milesians were not weak fleshpots like the rest of us, but were most persistent men, who dedicated their lives to the pursuit of knowledge — and we are indebted to them for initiating this stream of Greek philosophy which was to grow into the mighty river of Western Thought; and therefore, a little background on this thoughtful trio, might not go amiss.

Thales, the Father of Philosophy, was born about 640 B.C., although another source has it that he was born in 624 B.C. and that he died in 546 B.C. Quite possibly he came from Phoenician parentage; and quite definitely he was educated for a time in Egypt and the Near East. He supposedly said, "For these three things I am grateful to fate: first that I was born a man, and not a beast, second that I am a man, and not a woman, and third that I am a Greek and not a barbarian". — But don't let this put you off him! Despite this example of overt racial bigotry, and Male Chauvinism, he was a remarkably fine thinker.

In his youth (that is the first forty years or so, as Philosophers generally enjoy a more protracted adolescence than do the rest of us) he was a business man who became quite literally star struck one evening when he is reputed to have fallen into a ditch, (much to the amusement of a passing slave girl) while he was walking through the countryside and gazing at the heavens above. (This may well have been the first recorded physical example in history of anyone making the 'Philosophical Leap' —if that is what Thales was actually up to in the ditch!) Anyway, whatever he was doing, it was following this 'Leap' that he then turned from business to Philosophy . Thales it was who introduced the study of both Mathematics and Astronomy to Greece, and who first demonstrated the geometric theorems which were later to be collected and compiled in book form by Euclid. His actual fixation with triangles seems to have come about due to his intense study of the pyramids in Egypt. And as well as being enamoured with geometry, he was a successful predictor of solar eclipses. Besides all the above, Thales was also a Statesman, and an Engineer, and he was deemed to be one of the "Seven Wise Men of Greece". How did he ever find the time in order to philosophize, you wonder? And well you might. But he did! And I should add that he was a very good business man on top of all his other achievements; however, he was philosophic enough to retire from business, before the love of money as a commodity in itself began to get to him. Thales in fact, typifies the statement of Francis Bacon that "Knowledge is Power", and there is a nice little story by Aristotle concerning his abilities in this direction.

One dark Milesian winter, this wise old man (knowing from his study of astronomy that the weather conditions predicted a rich olive harvest in the summer), hired, at a very low price, all the olive presses in Miletus and Chios. Then, when summer came, and the olives were dropping in abundance from the trees, and the people were desperate to pound the juice from them, he rented out his hired oil presses at exorbitant rates, and made a killing on the oil market. In this way he raised a huge amount of money to finance his meditations, and managed at the same time to convince the hoi polloi, that Philosophers **could be rich**, if they **CHOSE** to be, but that the majority of that noble profession, just didn't see the sense in pursuing wealth for its own sake! One supposes anyway, that after this little incident, the Milesian populace, very wisely, kept well away from Thales, and left him to do his thinking in absolute peace!

Having cunningly earned himself both money and time, Thales then turned to considering the world at large, and after due deliberation, he decided, that Water was the primary and basic element of life. (Perhaps he was more influenced by Greek Mythology than he thought, because according to the Myths, Oceanus was the father of all life!) And, Thales also decided, that this moisture, or water, "to hugron" in Greek, was the very seed of life itself; from which everything came; and to which everything returned.

His view of the world was that it was a hemisphere, resting on an endless expanse of water; and that the Earth, was a flat disc, floating on the flat side of the interior of this hemisphere — all of which sounds rather confusing; but still and all it can be said that Thales was right about the water side of things, because it certainly is an inherent part of all forms of matter; and it is absolutely essential for the maintenance of life.

Thales also held that there was some type of life force, or 'soul', in every particle of every plant, and animal, and metal, and man; that this vital power never died; but simply changed form; and that therefore, there was no difference between life or death! Having heard this extraordinary theory, some person (possibly his wife, or some other relative hoping to inherit), asked Thales, why, having such views on the innocuousness of the state of 'rigor mortis', he didn't then elect to be a corpse immediately forthwith, and to get the death factor over and done with right away? Fixing his pert questioner with a steely gaze, Thales explained patiently that he didn't intend to precipitously leave life for death, simply "Because there is no difference!" And with that, he put paid to both the questioner, and to the claim on his property!

Thales in fact, was never known to find himself short of a pithy answer or two, and when once asked what the most difficult thing in the world was, he replied, "To know thyself". And on another occasion, when he was asked what the easiest thing in the world was, he answered, "To give advice".

The Father of Philosophy finally expired in 546 B.C. (one hesitates to use the word 'died', since according to him there was no such state, or at least it didn't make much difference one way or another!) and this non-event occurred while he was enjoying himself as a spectator at a gymnastic contest.

According to the ancient historian Diogenes Laertius, Thales was, "worn out with heat, thirst, and weakness." All Olympic Games organisers reading this book, should take careful note, as it seems that the general conditions at public games have remained more or less the same over the last two thousand years or so.

What I should like to know though, is what a philosopher was doing at such a ridiculous time-wasting event as an athletics meeting anyway? —; when he quite obviously should have been at home working on his wisdom!

Anaximander 611-549 B.C. (or, 610-546 B.C.) was the student of Thales, and he also hailed from Miletus. He progressed beyond his teacher (some of course, might say instead that he retrogressed!) by defining the origins of the world not, as "water", but as, "something".

According to Anaximander, the basis of Life was a boundless mass; an indefinite, infinite, "apeiron", or endless mass of something; which possessed no specific qualities, but which developed by its inherent forces into all the varied realities of the universe. All of which sounds even more confused and confusing than Thales' view of the world, but at least Anaximander was moving towards the idea of gas, and combustion, and the "Big Bang" Theory for the birth of the Cosmos. Also it shows that Anaximander was neither a dogmatist nor a liar, and what he didn't know, or didn't understand, he simply admitted, and left it alone, to be whatever it was. Which was really very courageous of him, but hardly comforting for those of you sitting perched anxiously on the edges of your chairs, and earnestly reading this book in the vain attempt of discovering and obtaining some wisdom. However, what Anaximander lacked in precise knowledge or definitive language, he made up for in other spheres, and like Thales, he was an astronomer as well as a philosopher, and having a great interest in geography as well, he was the first man (along with fellow Milesian Hecataeus) to draw a world map.

To return to Anaximander's 'something'. (Do we have to? I hear you sigh). He believed that from this Primordial Infinite , new worlds were born in succession, which evolved, and then died; and that all the opposites i.e. hot/cold; moist/dry; develop from this 'something'; and that they finally dissolve into it as well. And he concluded with abit of wary wisdom which bears deep meditation upon. "Things perish into those from which they have been born." (This statement can probably be interpreted in many ways, but which ever way you do choose to interpret it, the words portend most ominously.)

As regards the world itself, Anaximander advanced on Thales' conception of it, and said that he had decided that it was a cylinder, hanging freely suspended by fire filled misty hoops, in the centre of the universe;

and that the sun, moon and other stars, revolved around the Earth. (More than likely there are a good many bad geography students in the world today who wouldn't find anything untoward about this description, and who would probably consider that Anaximander's theory was as good as anyone else's anyway!)

But Dear Reader, before you begin to scoff too much at poor old Anaximander, let me add that both the Sociologist Herbert Spencer A.D. 1860, and the Biologist Charles Darwin A.D. 1859, were indebted to this ancient Greek gentleman for his revolutionary views on evolution, and without whom they would neither of them have been able to publish their works — in order to make themselves so famous with their progressive doctrines in the 19th century.

Way back in the 6th century B.C. Anaximander it was who first propounded an amazing theory on the evolution of the world, and he stated that the Earth had been in a fluid state (the boundless 'something', 'apeiron'); that some external heat had dried some fluid into land, and evaporated other fluid into clouds; and that the variations in heat had caused the winds. Living organisms had then arisen, Anaximander said, and they had arisen in various stages, and water animals i.e. fish, had later moved to the land — and still later in time, these landed water animals had then become men.

One of the reasons that Anaximander hit upon this world shaking hypothesis was that in his free moments he used to sit watching the fishermen in Miletus pulling in and cutting open the bodies of sharks, and he noticed that the Mediterranean Artan Sharks hatched eggs inside their bodies in the same way as Mammals did. Therefore he deduced that all life forms originated from the same source as it were, and that different species were simply variations on a main theme.

If there had only been some large printing companies around at the time of Anaximander, then he could have made a fortune with his theory, instead of having to content himself merely with writing down his ideas for his students; and with spending his leisure time sitting on the beach watching the Ionian fishermen at work on killing Man's ancestors. Unfortunately for Anaximander however, he was born just too far in advance of his time.

The world's first evolutionist also had something significant to say on Life itself, and on the concept of natural Law or Justice. "Everything returns to its origins, as is ordained," he said, "for they give satisfaction and reparation to one another for their injustice according to the ordering of time." In other words, "Every dog has its day", and "As you sow, so shall you reap"; and personally speaking, I find this a most satisfying philosophy, and lick my lips in gleeful anticipation thinking of all the afflictions about to break forth over the heads of all those who have ever harmed me.

Definitely Anaximander will be enjoyed by all those suffering from having been scorned or ill-treated, and who are, or who have been unable, to fight back in any way. It is a very comforting thing to know that there is a type of Natural or Divine Retribution (which was originally **vaguely** mentioned in the Greek Mythology System with the personifications of Dikes as Justice, and Nemesis as Revenge). Unfortunately Anaximander cannot be read in abundance today because the major part of his work exists now only in 'fragments'. (Which is the Scholarly way of saying bits and pieces). But his ideas can still be lovingly savoured nonetheless. In point of fact we can't really say too much in favour of Anaximander, Biologist, Physicist, Astronomer and Philosopher extraordinaîre — because he single handedly invented both Science and Philosophy (as we know them today), and he put rationalism on such a firm footing, that it took a 1,000 years before the Dark Ages could extinguish the flame which he had initially lit.

Anaximenes, the last in this trilogy of Milesian Thinkers, 585-528 B.C. (N.B. Please do not get very pernickety about the dates — none of my sources agrees with the others, and in truth, the writer of this guide to Philosophy has come to the conclusion that no one is very sure exactly when these Pre-Socratic Philosophers came onto this earth, nor, when they left it!) Anyhow, Anaximenes, (born sometime or other in the 6th century) was a pupil of Anaximander, and he decided that his teacher's 'something', or the basic principle of Life, was actually 'AIR'.

As Anaximenes saw it, "that which is our soul and constitutive principle, also holds the universe together." So this 'air' of life was also the 'air' of the 'Soul', or the 'Psyche' or the 'Pneuma'; which terminology I shall now endeavour to explain.

In the ancient Greek thought, this 'Psyche' was something akin to a butterfly which dwelt within man and which was the very essence of his true self. The word 'psyche' in Ancient Greek means, 'butterfly', and the idea of a butterfly soul giving life to an organism is a very pretty and lyrical conception — if a trifle unscientific. The word 'pneuma' in Ancient Greek means "air", or "wind", and it referred to the actual function of respiration in the human body; so that when it was written in Homer, that the 'pneuma' left somebody or other, it actually meant that this person had breathed his last. Nowadays, in most European languages we have the word 'pneumonia', which refers to the inflammation of the 'breathing', or 'air', or 'wind apparatus' of a person or animal — and so we see this early tie-up in Greek thinking with the various organs of the body, and the endeavouring of these early scientists to try to discover exactly which organ was **most responsible** for Life itself; and whichever organ that was, they then decided was quite possibly the 'Soul' of the person also. Anaximenes really wanted to discover exactly what the most necessary element was for maintaining this 'Life', or 'Soul', and after long consideration he decided that 'Air' was really the most essential; and that all other elements were produced from it.

Rarefaction of air produces fire, he said, and condensation of air produces wind, cloud, water, earth, and stone. From this he concluded that the Soul, which is also air, holds us together, so that the 'air' or 'pneuma' of the world is its Spirit, or Breath, or God. And with this theory, Anaximenes really established the 'Soul' as something solid (if we can actually say such a thing about *such* an airy substance) and this Soul, which had been only a type of generally accepted but unimportant matter and substance to Thales and Anaximander, now became a most important matter and substance for all future philosophers. Anaximenes decided that there was definitely some type of Soul in Man, and that also there was definitely some type of Cosmic Presence which was ruling the Universe. And this little piece of information was eventually seized upon with glee by practically every philosopher following in the footsteps of the Milesians, and some groups, like the Stoics and the Christians, would especially put this theory to good use at a much later date.

As regards the physical realities of our world, Anaximenes finally came to the conclusion of doing away with Anaximander's fire filled misty hoops, and instead, he announced, that this cylinder Earth was held up by Mist (or Air) itself, and that no hoops were necessary. Apart from this statement however, he did not essentially differ from the general theories previously developed by his teacher.

In these discoveries and thoughts of the early Milesian Philosophers we can perhaps, almost detect the hand of the Far East, and denote the hot fiery breath of the Chinese Dragon in particular, because in the Chinese Philosophy of Tao, or, "the Way of Life", there are similar ideas, regarding the basic principles of life; and in the oriental T'ai chi exercises, the Five Elements of Fire, Water, Wood, Wind, Metal and Earth, are parts of a harmonic system of mental and physical gymnastics. So it may be assumed therefore, that the Milesians quite possibly had some type of contact with the Orient, in order to develop their theories; although a great many historians of philosophy refute this idea most emphatically.

On the whole, the choice of these principles (of air, water and fire) for being the basic matter of all life, and for having formed, or caused, the creation of the world, seems logical enough; as everything in the world, is, to some extent or other, derived from them. So we must admit that the Milesians were pretty far ahead in their thinking — especially for those times!

Between them, Thales, Anaximander, and Anaximenes, established the following:-

1. That there was a single natural basis for everything in the world (although they were not in agreement on what that basis actually was), and that there was no Supernatural basis for the Creation of the World and Life.

2. That a simple or single force was better than a complex system of separate spirits (and so much more convenient for all those wishing to believe in the Monic Theory!)

3. Ex Nihilo Nihilfit — Nothing comes out of Nothing (or you can't get blood from a stone, or money from a bankrupt, as the less philosophic members of Miletus had always known!) Correspondingly, and comfortingly, (especially for agnostics and atheists) it also proves that nothing real can, or ever will, disappear.

4. The Milesian Philosophers were practical observers of Life, and curious about natural Phenomena, and their philosophy was mainly dependent on, or based upon, their other studies in astronomy, geography, geology and meteorology. They were in fact, Physical Philosophers, or, philosophical physicists — and most of all, they were Greece's first pure Scientists.

Just at the birth of this philosophical movement, the City-State of Miletus, unfortunately, began to decline (as did the whole of Ionia) due to its addictive love of luxury, and due also to the invasions of the Persians which began in 546 B.C. and which continued almost uninterruptedly until the absolute destruction of Miletus in 494 B.C.

During the latter part of the 6th century, and following this Persian destruction of Miletus, the majority of the intellectuals (being unable to contemplate and theorize in safety and peace, without the annoying disturbances of loud martial music, and fast flying javelins), decided to emigrate to the Greek colonies of Italy, or Magna Graecia, and so the philosophical Movement spread to the West in the Greek World; although Miletus kept throwing up hard Thinkers, and Scientists, every generation or so, for centuries to come. But as Ionia had lost its economic and military power, its intellectuals could never exist there for very long, and accordingly had to emigrate to make a living elsewhere. Hence a 'Brain-Drain' developed, and Ionia and Italy contended for the position of chief breeding ground for the supply of Mental Trail-Blazers and Pioneers of Ancient Greek Thought.

Of course, in Miletus, internal decay had begun long before the destructive Persian invaders broke through the City Walls. This decline or decay had begun almost simultaneously with the rise in her luxury and wealth, and with her love for same — to the exclusion of all else. A well known and popular ancient comment about the Milesians was that, "Once upon a time, the Milesians were brave", and that about summed the situation up. There had always been a continuous Class Warfare between the rich and the poor (a condition which existed in all the Greek City-States and which could have been termed a type of chronic social illness among the Greeks) and this Greek Social Disease weakened Miletus, and left her wide open to invasion.

In 546 B.C. Cyrus conquered Lydia and took the Ionian cities into the Persian Empire, and it was a long and weary time before Miletus ever again, enjoyed her former prestige and affluence. The Spring in Miletus had definitely come to a close; but, philosophically speaking, — what a beautiful Spring it had been!

Delphi: Theatre and Temple of Apollo.

TOP: *Olive harvest.* BOTTOM: *Ploughing and sowing.*

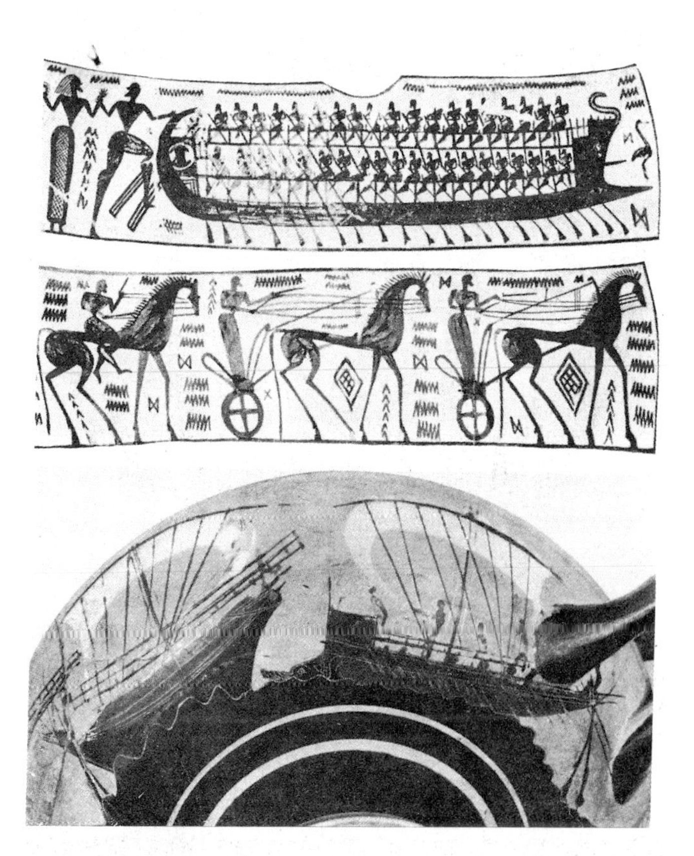

TOP: *A large ship,* CENTER: *Chariots and horsemen (both from an Attic geometric mixing-bowl).*
BOTTOM: *Merchant ship and long boat.*

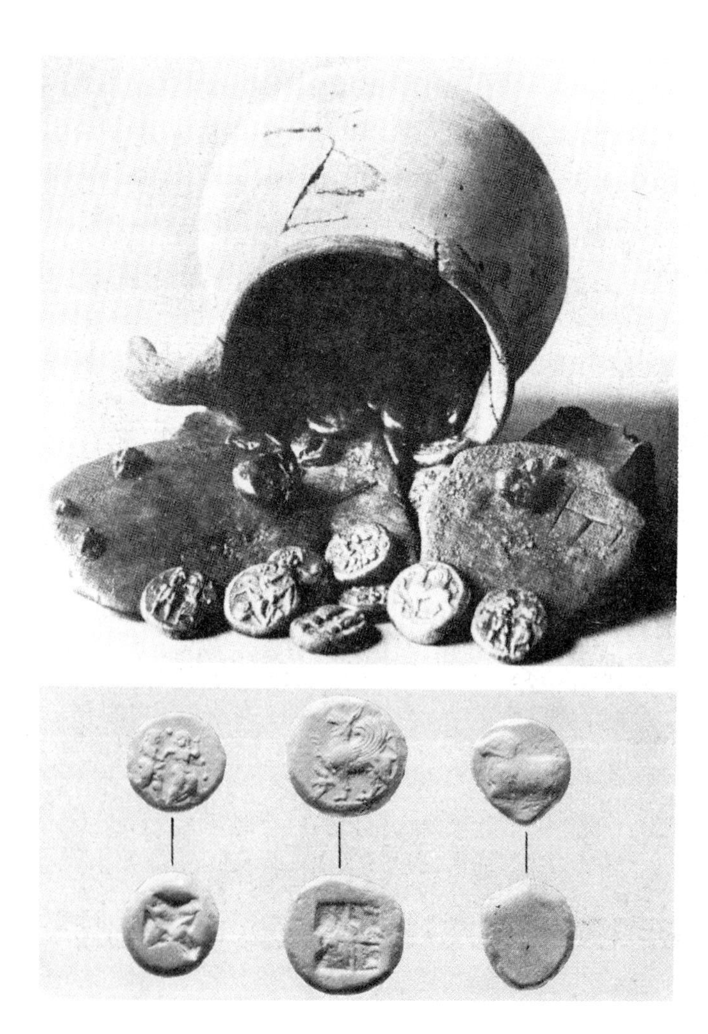

TOP: *Hoard of Greek coins.* BOTTOM: *Coins of the type found in this hoard. From left to right: Macedonia (Lete), Thrace (Abdera), Cyprus (Euelthon of Salamis); all c. 530.*

Maenads.

Bronze head, 1 Ft high, Cyrene, probably mid fourth century.

Athenian Scool.

LEFT: *Alexander the Great, from the bust in Louvre.* RIGHT: *Aristotle.*

CHAPTER 3

LOOKING FOR THE LOST CHORD

Inner Harmony and the Cult in Italy.

As stated in the last chapter, (and as the attentive Reader will no doubt have noted), following the decline of Ionia and Aeolia, in the latter half of the 6th Century B.C., many intellectuals emigrated to other City-States in Greece, and one of these emigrants was none other than Pythagoras of Samos (571-497 B.C.)

Pythagoras arrived in Crotona, Italy (located near the instep of the Big Boot) around 530 B.C. and there he founded the Pythagorean Brotherhood and School of Philosophy, which was based upon the then fashionable Orphic Cult. Pythagoras, incidentally, is the gentleman who discovered that the square on the hypotoneuse of a right-angled triangle, is equal to the total sum of the squares on the other two sides. This of course might not possibly seem very enthralling to those of you who experience utter revulsion at the mere mention of the word Mathematics, but wait awhile; because there were other interesting aspects to this old fellow's character, which might yet take your fancy.

Firstly though, a few words should be said about Crotona itself, and even more importantly, about the Orphic Religious Cult which was then raging through Southern Italy like an epidemic of influenza; and which was striking down all the poor, enslaved, questioning — or just plain miserable, people of the day.

There were three main elements apparent in the Religious Life of Ancient Greece, and the first was the Chthonian Religion which originated from the Minoan, Pelasgo-Mycenaean Civilizations, and which had been in vogue in the pre-Homeric period. The Minoans and the Pelasgo-Mycenaeans had been fore-runners to the Greeks in the Mediterranean area, before the Achaean Greeks first began arriving in the 13th and 14th centuries B.C. These very ancient people (nobody seems exactly sure who they were) had built towns in Crete and Mycenae and other parts of mainland Greece, and mainly worshipped Subterranean or Vegetation Deities i.e. the Natural Elements of Life; the plants, the Sun, the Moon, Mother Earth etc. After these aborigines of Greece had settled in the area, the Achaean Greeks then invaded and conquered them. Unfortunately nobody seems very sure exactly who these ancient Achaean Greeks were either! — in fact the archaeologist Sir William Ridgeway suggested in 1901 that they were Celts — which is not really as crazy an idea as it may seem — as we shall explain later. Still enough of this racial theorizing for the moment, and back to the subject at hand. When these Achaean Greeks, and later, the Dorian Greeks, started settling in this Mediterranean area, they began liquidating the original inhabitants (as is always the way in history), by the simple process of assassination; or, by pushing them away up into the hills. Then the Greek invaders set about introducing their own Homeric Myths and Celestial God System, (which was composed of the Twelve Olympians captained by Zeus) on top of the chthonic religion of the Minoan, Pelasgo-Mycenaean people. This then was the second Religious element in Greek life, and the Olympic Gods became the "Official" Greek City-State Religion, and this completely satisfied the middle and upper classes; but it was not such a source of consolation to the poor and the dispossessed. (And we may include the dispossessed ancient peoples in this category, as a change of national religion always signifies a change in the socio-economic life of a people!) However, the old Subterranean religion did not become extinct, but only remained dormant; and it continued to hold sway in the country areas. (An analogy may perhaps be drawn here with the stories concerning the "Leprechaun" in Ireland, as those fairy folk really represent the Subterranean, orchthonic,religion of the original people of that land mass, who were living there before the Celts invaded.)

But somewhere along the line in Greece, a new religious mode came into fashion, with the importation of the Egypto-Asiatic Mystic Cults, which believed in Resurrected Gods; and which, then combined with the old Subterranean Vegetation Religion in order to form the basis for new Mystic Cults that suited the pockets of the poor and the troubled. And so here we have the third main element in Greek Religious Life — the Mystic Resurrection Cult, with a Vegetation background.

The Orphic Cult which affected Italy so strongly was one of these Cults, and we will turn to examine it in greater detail now. If, however, the Reader is seriously interested in learning about the other Cults which were all the rage in 5th Century Greece (at the time of Pericles and the Golden Age), then she/he, must avail her/himself; of the "Greek Gods", a previous book by this Author, and one in which a larger coverage is given to these religious movements.

The Orphic Cult though was really an off-shoot of the Dionysac Cult; rather as the High Church of England is an off-shoot of the Roman Catholic Church; or as various Protestant Churches are variations on the Calvin and Lutheran themes. (Just as most philosophies are variations on other older philosophies in fact!)

Dionysos the God of Wine, was the half-mortal son of Zeus the supreme Patriarchal God of Olympus, and he was worshipped by countless wine lovers (and possibly even vine lovers) in many parts of Greece. He was worshipped even more strongly in Thrace in the North Eastern area of Greece, where the people were reputed to be the most aggressive and war-like Greeks. However the Thracians didn't really need to drink wine to worship Dionysos, because they had already developed a liquor brewed from barley (probably the original whiskey), and being a hard-fighting, hard-drinking people, they had then decided that Dionysos, or, "Sabazius", as he was more familiarly known to them, was just about the only God worth worrying about — and the only one from which they could get their money's worth. "If you have to believe in anything," said the Thracians, "then you might as well believe in something that makes you feel good." So the Dionysos, or Dionysac, Cult swept from Thrace into the rest of Greece, drowning the inhabitants in alcoholism, and dragging the Orphic Cult just behind it. (N.B. With all the characteristics of the Thracians as evinced above, it might be well worth investigating as to whether **THEY** were the ancient Celts whom Ridgeway referred to as the first Greeks!)

According to Legend incidentally, this Orpheus of the Orphic Cult had also been one of the Argonauts in the Quest for the Golden Fleece, but then everyone seems to have been pretty busy in those Homeric and Heroic, Golden days, and, to have lived two or three lives at the same time, with great ease and nonchalance. The Ancients were obviously made of sterner stuff than we Moderns! Anyhow, Orpheus, in this Cult story, was a Thracian who was very cultured, and very musical (the Thracians were in fact well-known for their music, along with their fighting, their drinking, and their red-hair!) and he was a priest of the Dionysac Cult, and was a most ascetic fellow. He is reported to have wandered the countryside of Greece, playing his lyre (as Pan did with his pipes) and to have unceasingly administered solace, and music, and words of wisdom, to the miserable —and, to all those too poor to buy a radio! Then he met Eurydice; fell madly in love; and married her. And he almost broke his lyre in anguish when she died. But nothing daunted, this intrepid musician plunged deep down into Hades (the Underworld) to retrieve his lost better-half.

Once in the palace of death, he musically charmed Persephone the unwilling wife of Pluto into returning Eurydice to life and to him; and she consented simply because she was so charmed by his playing. **But** Persephone warned him, that he must start moving back up, and out of Hades, and that he **must not** look back to see Eurydice who would be dutifully following in his footsteps. Here we have the origin of that famous saying "Never look back!" and it is obviously an infallible commandment, and there are numerous examples in history of the wisdom of this instruction and of the catastrophies which befell those who did not heed it! For example there was Lot's Wife who got turned into a pillar of salt for disobeying the self-same directive at Soddom and Gomorrah! And in Orpheus' case, he could not restrain himself either, so Eurydice was lost to him forever, and he had to wander through life alone; inconsolable in his grief.

After this, so some ancient writers say, Orpheus turned to pederasty, in an attempt to comfort himself in his loneliness, but I think this is a vicious slur on the character of such an artistic man. What is obvious is that no other woman could take the place of Eurydice in either his bed or in his heart — and in consequence, he drove the women of Thrace wild, because he steadfastly, and unhesitatingly, repulsed all their advances.

Hell hath no fury like a woman scorned it is said, and seemingly the Thracian women were no exception to the rule in this matter, for one night they leapt "en masse" upon their Pop Idol at a Dionysac Festival, and then tore him into a million pieces. (This method of removing someone from life may seem savage "in extremis" to us in the 20th century, but it was quite commonplace among the peoples of those days when stainless steel knives were not so plentiful as they are now, and even in A.D 415 the practice of hacking people to pieces was still going strong when the Pagan Philosopher Hypatia fell prey to some obstreperous Alexandrian Christians who insisted on scraping her flesh from her bones with mussel shells; and then burnt her rather messy remains; in order to be sure! There was a political motive for this murder of Hypatia of course, and it really had nothing to do with religious doctrine as such, and probably Orpheus was also 'done in'; for reasons other than his self-ordained celibacy.) Following his untimely and grotesque demise however, legend has it that Zeus placed the lyre of Orpheus up in the sky as a constellation among the stars, and his severed head (still singing!) was buried at Lesbos the Aeolian city in Asia Minor — which no doubt accounts for the remarkable artistic spirit, and the creative achievements of the Aeolians in ancient times. The place where Orpheus' head was buried also became famous as an oracle, at an even later date, and the area was always filled with the song of sweet nightingales so it is said.

After the death of Orpheus, a Cult grew up around the supposed sacred songs which he had supposedly left behind, and this formed the basis for a mystery cult more advanced in doctrine and ritual than the Dionysac Cult — and much more moral in influence also. (After what had happened to Orpheus at the hands of members of the Dionysac Cult one cannot help observing that this lot obviously **NEEDED** a more moral influence!) In a way though, it may be supposed that the Orphic Cult was only rather a reformed version of the Dionysac Cult, and in general it had much the same ideology, although it was more cultivated and progressive in theology.

The main creed of the Orphic movement was firstly; an affirmation of the passion, suffering, death and resurrection of Dionysos the Divine Son of God (Zeus), and secondly; a belief in the resurrection of all men after death; and of their eventual reward in the after life in Heaven; or-of their eventual punishment in Hell.

The followers of Orphism (like the followers of Dionysos) believed that Dionysos had been slain by the Titans (the wild forces of Nature in the Cosmogeny or Creation Story) and that these Titans were the ancestors of all Mankind; and that therefore, all men had carried a type of original sin from that time on; and that they were in fact born **already guilty** of the death of the Son of God (Zeus). They also believed that within the body of Man, lay his imprisoned Soul, which at death, was released to face trial by the Underworld Gods; and that if found guilty of misdeeds in this life, it would then undergo eternal torture in Hell.

There was also another Orphic belief which concerned Soul Transmigration; and the devotees of Orphism held that after death the Soul transmigrated and was reborn into another Life, more pleasant or less pleasant, depending on what was necessary for salvation, and on the amount of virtue or vice sustained in the previous life. Therefore, if a person had been a thorough going rapscallion in one life, he would be reborn in such conditions, and in such a form (e.g. animal, insect) that he would suffer excrutiatingly and unceasingly in another; thereby becoming purified from sin; and **eventually**, he would become **good enough** to pass over into the Islands of the Blest; that is, Heaven.

There was even a third alternative (The Orphic Cult certainly tried hard to please, and had something for practically everyone, in much the same way as did Saint Paul with his early version of Christianity on his missionary journeys) and this third option was, that after death (and in order to end the sufferings and torments of Hell punishment), a person could be redeemed by the penances performed by friends, or by the atonements paid (the operative word here being 'paid'), by friends, to the Orphic Priests. (Well and all! everyone has got to make a living, and Orphic priests had appetites like anyone else!) **Or**, redemption could be achieved by a guilty person **in advance**, simply, by buying atonements on Earth; **BEFORE** his trip to the Final Judgement. And this method probably best suited those advocates of the 'Be Prepared' Motto, and all those people who happened to have layed aside a sizeable enough cash allowance for such transactions. Plato though, in his writings of the fourth century B.C. was exceedingly scornful of these Orphic mendicants who wandered from door to door, selling remission of sins in advance, like our modern Life Insurance Salesmen. Possibly though, the whole concept of Insurance as such, began with the Orphics; and Western Capitalism, and Directors of all such security conscious commercial establishments, should perhaps pause at this point in their reading, and give three minutes silence, in respectful homage to these mystics who originally founded this profitable business for them!

The Orphic Cult enthusiasts also believed in a ritual form of communion with their God. They believed that as Dionysos had been devoured by the Titans, they, the people, as the descendents of the Titans, **not only** carried the stain of original sin for this act, **but also**, **carried** within their bodies, some of the **Divine Spirit** of Dionysos. Therefore they used to meet in solemn ceremonies in which they ate the raw flesh of a bull. (Why a bull should have been selected for this honour I have no idea, unless it was because the bull symbolised the brute strength of animal nature which had at one time been worshipped by the Pelasgo-Mycenaean civilization in their Chthonic religion. And of course we must remember also that King Minos in Crete was likewise rather fond of this particular species of livestock!) Anyway, eat this bull raw, they did, and they seemed to feel that the slaying of the bull commemorated the slaying of Dionysos; and that, by eating the bull's flesh, they were absorbing once more and anew, the Divine Essence of their God.

So this was the Orphic Cult which had appeared in Greece most forcefully, and most fervantly, about the 6th century B.C., and it was the Cult which had equally fervantly and forcefully affected the philosophy of the Mathematician and Musicologist, Pythagoras of Crotona.

And now, at last, for the long promised few words about Crotona itself.

Crotona (you have finally discovered it on your map, I trust) was founded by Achaean Greeks mostly, who came from the Mainland around 710 B.C., and who had also founded the colony of Sybaris a little earlier in 721 B.C. Unfortunately Sybaris no longer exists, but at one time this town was the talk of the Mediterranean World, and the Sybarites themselves coined a new word in the language of every country in the world, as their name became synonymous with extreme wealth and idleness — and with the passionate love of same! And even those money loving Milesians could not compete with the Sybarites in their passion for pleasure. The Sybarites became the wealthiest, laziest, and most scandalously hedonistic of all the Magna Graecia colonies; and were in consequence, jealously hated by every other City-State. But they were especially hated by their particular trading foe, Crotona.

These Sybarites controlled the land trade routes in Italy, and grew so rich in this way, that it was nothing unusual for your average Sybarite to have a retinue of around 1,000 servants. Their roads were covered with awnings, in order to protect the heads of the inhabitants from the sun and the rain; and all trade workshops were located on industrial estates well outside the city, so that the ears of the Sybarites should not be troubled by the vulgar clangings and bangings of hammers, and such like noisy instruments. Most of the time however, the Sybarites stayed indoors, reclining on couches; and consuming delicacies concocted by the various cooks of the town (who worked very hard at creating new recipes; and who were then able to patent these recipes for the time period of one year.) Fine living was an art form in Sybaris!

The Crotoniates, their trading rivals, who depended on ships stopping in their port (instead of going round into Sybaris), were so green with envy, that they could not even **stomach the word Sybaris**, and in 510 B.C they managed not only to destroy the city, but to RAZE it completely from the ground and from the map, so that today Sybaris exists only in ancient cartographer's drawings of the period. Later on however the town was founded again, but this time under the name of Thurii (sixty-five years after the original date of destruction, to be precise.) But today even Thurii has gone, so it seems that the sin of Sybarism, or Sybaritism, lingers long.

From this little story we can deduce that Crotona itself was a remarkably covetous city and a not terribly affluent one (but not exactly impoverished either.) It was also known for its healthy climate; its athletes, such as Milo (the famous gentleman who involuntarily leant his name to a well-known health drink, and who alsohappenedto have been a follower of Pythagoras) and Crotona was also the centre for the greatest School of Medicine in Magna Graecia, and it produced Alcmaeon, the REAL Father of Greek Medicine, who came on the scene before Hippocrates, and who, incidentally, (like Milo) was yet another disciple of the Pythagorean Philosophy.

Now let us at last begin to examine what this Pythagorean Philosophy — which began around 530 B.C. when Pythagoras landed in Crotona — was really all about.

As we have observed; originally, Pythagoras hailed from Samos the Aeolian island in Asia Minor situated up the coast from the City-State of Miletus, of Ionia.

After getting himself born, around about 580 B.C., he then spent the next 50 years travelling through Arabia, Syria, Phoenicia, India, and Gaul, and he finally arrived back in Greece with a truly wonderful piece of advice for all travellers (including the Tourists of Nowadays) "When you are travelling abroad, look not back at your own borders." So, if the Tourist reading this book, happens at this particular moment in time to be suffering from a lack of communication, an internal disruption due to a difference in either water or food; or, an overdose of hostility on the part of the natives; then he, or she, may care to bear these words in mind and to ponder soulfully upon them in his/her homesickness.

Besides trotting about abroad and discovering the secrets of having marvellous vacations, Pythagoras also studied Astronomy and Geometry, and painstakingly checked into the various Resurrection Myths then prevalent in the East. He then returned to the island of Samos, but decided that the middle class dictatorship in vogue there at that period, was not to his liking, so he immediately emigrated to Crotona in the West.

Once settled in Crotona, Pythagoras thence began his school, in which he accepted women as well as men (although the female students devoted most of their time to studying maternal and domestic arts, and only gained a smattering of philosophy and literature), and according to all the reports of the day, Pythagoras turned out the most eligible brides and house-wives in all Greece, and ancient bachelors were mad keen to get their hands on one of them! The male students, on the other hand however, studied mostly philosophy, literature, mathematics and music, and didn't bother about cramming their heads with any domestic rubbish, because they had deeper matters to concern themselves with; and, because there was much more to this school of Pythagoras' than mere book learning.

Pythagoras actually instituted a Pythagorean Brotherhood in his school, which was run rather like a monastery, and in which the novices (that is the new students), were required to preserve the 'Pythagorean Silence' for the first five years, during which time they were instructed in the religious side of Pythagoras' philosophy, and presumably, learnt not to 'answer back', or to annoy their teacher with any obscure questions, or smart remarks.

Many teachers today, I am sure, would be only **too happy** to be able to impose a "Pythagorean Silence" on their classes, but alas, such devotion to duty, and to the desires of teachers, has long since passed away from our society! Anyhow after this trial of mute discipline for this awesome period of time (indeed, maybe after five years, the student had even **forgotten how to speak**!) the aspiring Brother was finally admitted to the inner circle of wisdom, whence all things immediately became clear to him.

The Pythagoreans had special views (different from those held by the orthodox Orphic Cult), about the purification of the Soul, and about its return to life; and especially, as to the exact nature of its Divinity. But it is rather difficult to know precisely what Pythagoras thought or taught (as distinct from that which was taught by his disciples), because the Pythagorean School (like most philosophical groups), had more of a love for Wisdom, than they had, for **Truth**. And consequently, after the death of Pythagoras, his students forged his writings, or altered them in many ways in order to have them fit in, with what THEY THOUGHT, he should have said, or thought. This of course is not a sin known only to the Greeks, but it is a practice which has been, and still is, popular **everywhere** in the world. Quite possibly, academic scholars and historians, are guilty of more perjury and fraud in their daily work, than any mere salesman in a Used Car Mart, and this thought is rather an awesome one! A lie told in order to sell an object, and to thereby earn some money, is, if not admirable, at least understandable! But, a lie told, in order to give credence to some erroneous idea or theory, is a far more reprehensible act. But why, one asks, do they do it? I suppose the easiest (perhaps not the correct!) answer to come up with, is that actually searching for the truth is such a wearisome business, and so very unrewarding most of the time, that certain individuals take it upon themselves to circumlocute the problem by simply inventing an answer to suit the question — and themselves!

Anyway, from what can be deduced about the theories of Pythagoras, he believed that Man had a Soul and, that this Soul was Divine because of the intellect of Man, and because Man had the power to know the eternal unchanging Truth. This Truth, according to Pythagoras, was manifest in the elements of form, order, proportion, limit and harmony in the Universe; and above all, this harmony was represented by musical harmony, with the fixed proportions of the Tonic Scale; and this harmony was also observable in the order of the Heavenly Bodies in the Galaxy. The Stars in the Sky, and the Musical Notes on an instrument, were both evidence of this inner harmony of life to Pythagoras, and he made his 'Philosophical Leap' (one hopes you remember what that is!) it is recorded, when passing a blacksmith's shop one day, and hearing the regular musical intervals which were being wrung from the striking of the anvil. He then conducted experiments with various lengths of twine in the classroom, made rapid calculations in mathematics — and eventually came up with his theory of fixed order and harmony in Music, Maths, and Space.

"Things are numbers," declared Pythagoras, and forever after, wedded the study of Music to Mathematics, and thereby created a lot of trouble and needless misery for musical (but not necessarily mathematical) people!

By contemplating perfect harmony, Pythagoras believed that the Soul was purified, and was returned to a god-like state; and he decided that the study of Maths and Physics could also bring about this euphoric tranquillity. (Personally speaking though, the Author of this book, finds this **very difficult** to swallow!)

He also held, that form, order, limit, light, and rest, were good things; and that indefiniteness, darkness, disorder, motion and change were bad things, (which seems a rather dogmatic and static view of Life!) He also believed that Form was a Male Principle, and was good; whereas Matter, was a Female Principle, and was bad, which theory shows Pythagoras up to be not only a reactionary Puritan, but a Sexist, as well! In fact, Pythagoras had a strong aversion to change as such, in any shape, or form, and he seems to have inaugerated this rather static attitude in philosophy which was to prevail in Italy long after his passing.

Pythagoras' view of the cosmology (world) was that it was composed of a dark indefinite vapour (rather like Anaximander's theory on the Primal Stuff), but that this vapour had been drawn into a geometric order. The Universe was a living sphere, whose centre was the Earth, so he said, and the Earth was also a sphere, revolving like the planets in the direction of West to East. The Earth was divided into five zones: the Arctic, Antarctic, Summer, Winter, and Equatorial — and if all that seems a little strange to you, at least it must be allowed that Pythagoras was the first recorded person to actually decide that the world was round, and give the word 'Kosmos' to the Greek Language, and from which the rest of the world received the word 'Cosmopolitan', meaning, 'a citizen of the round world'.

This musical mathematician was also the first person to create the word 'Philosophy' (the Love of Wisdom), for, when asked to define what his actual objective was (doubtless, people had observed him running around the place with armfuls of cat gut, and measuring rods!) he declared, that his search, was for a love of Wisdom; but, that he was not absolutely sure that he had actually attained that Wisdom; **only**, that he **loved it**. Incidentally it might be noted that Pythagoras' ideas regarding the harmony of music, and the peace of the Soul, were generally believed in and applied by most doctors of the day in Greece, who argued that if they couldn't cure people by any other means, then they could at least authorise a bit of music to be played at their bedsides. So the ancient medical fraternity decided that in some instances, music actually effected a cure, and in others, well, at least the poor unfortunate died more pleasantly!

Pythagoras believed that the Soul was composed of three parts:- Feeling, Intuition, and Reason. The Feeling section was centred in the heart, and Intuition and Reason were located in the head. Feeling and Intuition were found in animals, as well as in Man, said he, but only Man possessed Reason, and in consequence therefore, he was immortal. After death, according to Pythagoras, the Soul underwent a period of purgation (cleansing) in Hades (Hell), and then returned to Earth to enter an entirely new body in a chain of continuous transmigrations which could only be ended by the pursuance of a completely virtuous life.

Pythagoras informed his students meanwhile, that in his previous lives he had (among many others) been a courtesan, and a Hero at the Battle of Troy. One imagines that it was just as well that the 'Pythagorean Silence' was in force, otherwise the poor old gentleman might have been laughed out of his own school! Also it is said, that on one occasion, he picked up the hem of his spotless white robe, and tore out of the classroom, in order to rescue a dog which was being beaten. He announced to the astonishment of both the *Animal Beater,* and his own students, that in the frantic yelps of the dog, he had immediately detected the vocal notes of a recently dearly departed friend, who obviously must have been considerably wicked and licentious in his previous life in order to have been so demoted in form in the one under discussion. (Owners of dogs might care to bear this story in mind though, and people in general, might be advised to look to their consciences a little, if they wish not to transmigrate in a quadrupedal figure in a future life!)

This re-incarnation theory of Pythagoras' was not only derived from the Orphic Cult in Greece, but it was also strongly influenced by the Hindu Philosophy of India, and there was a good deal of the Hindu pessimism in other Pythagorean ideas as well. The main purpose of life in the Pythagorean System was (as has been disclosed) to gain release from re-incarnation; and the method of achieving this, was by virtue; and **virtue**, was the **harmony of the soul**. Harmony was induced into a soul, not only by music, but by wisdom; and Harmony itself equalled Wisdom, Truth, and the Golden Mean (i.e. everything in Moderation, and nothing in excess!) The opposite path of vice and cacophony led to discord, excess, sin, tragedy, and punishment. Justice, that quality which seemingly everyone is looking for and which hardly anyone finds — at least not to their own individual satisfaction! (rather like the abstract quality of Truth!) well, this Justice, according to dear old Pythagoras, was a square number — NOT an odd one! And he believed that sooner OR later, **everything** would be **SQUARED** — which sounds a very ominous proposition, and pictures of fiery Creators with slide-rules, and pocket calculators fly before the mind's eye. (This is an especially horrifying idea, if, like this Writer, you are **NOT** a mathematically inclined person, for how then is one to know if one has ended up with an odd, or even number!)

But in Crotona these ideas were perfectly acceptable, and people flocked to join Pythagoras' ranks (perhaps some of them were runaway slaves from Sybaris, hoping to get an education in this life, and some type of franchise in the next!) and the big question burning in the hearts of all these students of philosophy was, "How may I deliver myself from this body of death, from this sorrowful weary wheel of mortal existence; and become again a God?" And Pythagoras supplied the answer with his Brotherhood, in which on entering, students took a vow of loyalty to both the Master, and to each other, and then consented to live a life of monastic simplicity, with a communistic fellowship in the sharing of all their goods and possessions.

The Brothers were also restricted in their eating habits, and could not (under pain of expulsion!) partake of flesh, eggs, or beans. Why exactly beans were forbidden, is still rather a mystery to this Writer; and whether it was on the grounds of religious belief, or in the cause of good digestion, she could not ascertain. Meat, naturally was forbidden, as the Pythagoreans believed in the transmigration of souls, and therefore did not wish to be cannibals, and to eat their late Grandfathers, and such. Wine was not forbidden them, but water was preferred in its stead, and encouraged; and Pythagoras himself, like many other philosophers, seemed to have been most strongly attracted to a diet of honey, bread, and vegetables.

The members of this sect were also prohibited from killing any animal; or from destroying any cultivated tree. They were admonished to dress simply, and to behave modestly. And most of all — to refrain from excessive laughter or weeping — (in fact both joy and sorrow were frowned upon.) They were not to swear to other Gods (the Olympians), or to offer victims as sacrifices on their altars, and at the close of each day, they were to examine their collective conscience, in order to see just how well they had fared in the battle against vice, during that particular twenty.four hour period.

Pythagoras as their leader, was deemed to be a model of good behaviour himself — **Never**, (according to all reports) drank wine by day, (does this mean that he was swilling it down his throat at night?) — **Always** wore a spotless white robe, (especially when rescuing dogs!) — **Never** hit a slave, (why hadn't he emancipated all of them, the Democrat of Today might ask?) — **Never** laughed, jested, or told stories, (a real Puritan, and obviously a very difficult man to live with) — **Never** made love, (although he had a wife, Theano, and a daughter, Demo) And all in all, Pythagoras must have driven the drunks and libertines of Crotona mad with unrighteous indignation and anger! All of which he most certainly did; and in consequence therefore, he paid for this obnoxious display of virtue, at a later stage, as we shall soon see. Indeed, Pythagoras should have remembered his own good advice about the 'Golden Mean'. And he should have realised that a little goodness goes a long, long, way — and that too much virtue, is almost as bad as too much vice, and, as the ancient Greeks used to advise, 'Moderation' is desirable, in everything!

For their initiation into the Brotherhood, the disciples had to undergo a purification of the body by abstinence and self-control, and to purify the mind by scientific study. The 'Pythagorean Silence' which has been mentioned (time and again, you sigh!) lasted for five years, and after that, one supposes, the students were just too tired and too confused to think of arguing, or of making any smart rebellious remarks. Mathematics was a subject deemed most important as an abstract theory in order to help in training the mind to think clearly, and the Pythagorean Brotherhood were the very first people to actually classify numbers into odd and even. And when **not** doing their geometrical exercises, they concentrated on trying to discern the harmony, or music, of the spheres, which they said was inaudible to the ears of most men, as most men were not wise enough, or 'tuned in' enough, to hear it.

As we have seen, Pythagoras was a total reactionary, and being a member of the Aristocracy, or Decayed Gentry class, he found the whole idea of Democracy abhorrent. It is necessary though, that the word 'Democracy' not be confused with what is meant by this terminology today. To the ancient Greeks (who, incidentally, invented the word) Democracy meant a system whereby a City-State was ruled by the wealthy Middle-Class Merchants and Citizens. In this system, the Aristocrats were tolerated, (only just!) or their families were married into, (on account of the blue blood running in their veins) but **none** of the New Rich Merchants actually took them seriously; nor were any of these Merchants prepared to listen to these poor "passe" fools mouthing off any advice on the running of things, and the affairs of the State. Likewise, the poor, and the slaves had no vote, nor rights of any kind, in this democratic system, and as for the women, why they were requested to please stay in their homes with the doors shut, and their mouths closed! Consequently, Democracy had a rather limited appeal. But, it was championed by the wealthiest sectors of the society, and therefore it held sway, and was the political system that controlled most of the City-States of Greece, for most of the time.

Pythagoras, like most teachers (after all, who would choose to teach if he had the capital to become a Merchant?) was descended from a bankrupt, noble, landed-gentry family, and he hated the Democrats of Samos (from whom he had escaped by emigrating), and he equally detested those of the same political persuasion in Crotona (whom he was now irrevocably forced to endure) — and his soul eventually became filled with a fiery fervour of revolution against them. Therefore he began instructing his students in the political idea of a "philosophical élîte" ruling the State (something which Plato was also to advocate at a later stage in Greek history) and in between humming; and calculating; and saving canine lives; he plotted; and planned — and in general stirred up a real hornet's nest against himself. And these hornets — the Bankers, and the Merchants, and the respectable people of the town — one day descended on his communistic intellectual aristocracy, and burned his Commune down; killing several inmates in the process; and driving the rest away from the City.

Thereafter the Pythagorean Liberation Movement moved its revolutionary headquarters to Thebes in Boeotia, and concentrated all its energies into the over-throw of Democratic States like Athens, and into the most vocal and vituperative opposition to the Ionian Philosophers, the Sophists — and all other supporters of that pernicious "equality theory". Naturally enough, Plato was most impressed with their ideas, and he took many of their theories to mould into his own Oligarchic Philosophy in the Autumn of Greek Civilization.

There are two conflicting stories concerning the quietus of Pythagoras — one being, that he was slain while attempting to flee, as he wouldn't, (even though in flight for his life) step over a field of beans. This gentleman and scholar obviously carried his beliefs to absurdity, or, as Tertullian later remarked, "Credo quia absurdum." The other story however, has it that he escaped to Metapontum, where he abstained from food for forty days; starved himself to death; and (hopefully!) entered into a more pleasant form and station, in his next life! It is recorded anyway that he died at the age of eighty years, which was not much, considering the longevity of most ancient philosophers, but it was considerably longer than the usual lifespan of the inmates of the Laurium silver mines!

Many of his ideas (excluding his mysticism of numbers) were adopted by many of the philosophers who followed him, including; Plato, Aristotle, the Stoics, and others; and whether truly wise or not, Pythagoras gave Philosophy its name, and introduced it as a science, and as an art, to the Magna Graecia area. And one of the greatest disciples of Pythagorean harmony (musically speaking!) was the brilliant composer Stravinsky, so therefore the world of music lovers owes Pythagoras a great debt, even if the Modern Scholars do not think too highly of him. And, most of all, Pythagoras introduced the Spring of philosophic thought into Italy, and so began the thinking process there.

CHAPTER 4

KINETIC VERSUS STATIC

The Flux of Heracleitus of Ionia confronts the Rigidity of Parmenides of Italy.

The Ionian and Italian Schools of Philosophy now entered a new phase of development, in which both areas came into conflict with one another. In Ionia there arose the philosopher Heracleitus, with his theories on the Kinetic quality of Life with the perpetual movement and continuous change of all things; in order to create an order — **out of disorder**. "Strife is the Father of all things". "All things flow — nothing abides."

Whereas in Elea, in Italy, Xenophanes and Parmenides formulated a monic doctrine on the Balance of Nature and Life, which involved absolute rigidity, and **an absence of change of any kind**; and in which **all movement** was suspicious, and was to be disparaged at all costs. "That which is, is impossible not to be." "It abides the same, remaining in the same place, by itself." And what, the Reader may ask, is **it**? And who cares if **it abides** or if **it doesn't**? Well, let us go a little more deeply into this matter and see what this whole controversy between Ionia and Italy was really all about.

Personally speaking, the Author finds the theories of Heracleitus the more comforting of the two Schools, and she would advise anyone living in depressing circumstances, which are beyond their capability of altering, to definitely give Heracleitus a read. A person so afflicted will surely find Heracleitus and his ideas on the continual changing nature of life, to be of great solace to them. Unfortunately, like most of the Pre-Socratic philosophers, Heracleitus' wisdom has only survived in 'fragments', but as they are such strong, pithy messages, Heracleitus, like 'caviar', goes a long way! The Reader may of course snort derisively and mutter darkly that the love of 'caviar' is an acquired taste, and that perhaps Heracleitus is another! Be that as it may — Should there be a Heaven? And should the Author ever get there? One of the people she would most like to sit down with, over a cup of tea, is — Heracleitus! And that is her highest form of praise. It might be worth mentioning that Henry Ward Beecher, the Famous American Divine said almost the same thing about that dreadful sociologist Herbert Spencer whom we mentioned in the chapter before last. Still and all, there's no accounting for taste, and I'm sure Heaven will be large enough to contain all those wishing to have cups of tea with various personalities, obnoxious or otherwise! But enough of Tea, and Heaven, and let us turn to an 'in depth' study of these diverse Philosophies — and we may as well begin with the more pleasant of the two.

Heracleitus and the Flow of Life

Heracleitus was born about 504 B.C. (or 530 B.C.) the son of a noble (but probably decaying) family in Ephesus, Ionia; which was one of the most important cities (after Miletus), and which was located up the coast a little way from the birth place of Thales, and across the Caystrian Gulf from the island of Samos. Ephesus, (some say it was Ionia's **most famous** city, and even more important than Miletus) was founded about 1000 B.C. by colonists from Athens, and was, like Miletus, a successful trading city, with a very developed artistic, religious, and cultural life. Around about 540 B.C, a large temple to Artemis was begun, which at that time was reckoned to be the largest temple in the Greek World, and which was in consequence therefore, one of the Seven Wonders of the World — and this temple was finally completed in 420 B.C. A useless piece of information and mere trivia, you may say, but it does show that the Ephesians had money; great tenacity of purpose; (one hundred years is a long time to persevere with a public building) and an enormously large number of slaves; all of which assets it was ready, willing, and able, to expend on this undertaking. In other words, Manpower was no problem, and a City-State and its wealth, were measured in terms of the quantity of readily available captive workers at its disposal. And the next time you behold some ancient edifice, you might care to meditate on the number of workers who slaved on the building of it; and as a matter of interest, in the modern Ephesus of today (which is now part of Turkey) there still stands, a very large and multitudinously-breasted Mother Goddess statue from those ancient times — the construction of which, must have given quite a headache to many a bonded labourer. But, besides abounding in these civic inferiors, Ephesus was also very well known in Greece, for its poets; philosophers; and expensively gowned women. Heracleitus however, could not stand the sight of any of them. "The Ephesians ought to hang themselves, everyone who is of age," he said, "and leave the city to the boys."

Naturally the Ephesians took no notice whatsoever of what Hercleitus thought, and they just went merrily on cultivating the senses, and accumulating money in trade, until the Persians came down and taught them all a lesson in the 5th century B.C.

Heracleitus, as a member of the old aristocratic class, which was appalled at the "Neo Plutoi" (New Rich) Democratic faction, which was then ruling Ephesus, could not tolerate the majority of his fellow citizens. "One man to me is 10,000, if he be best," said Heracleitus; and in order to press home his point more thoroughly, "There are many bad, but few good." So saying, he spat upon the bright lights of the City, and took to the mountains, and commenced (unlike the other philosophers in Greece), to seek his wisdom in solitude, and to keep himself to himself, without attempting to begin a school, or to change the tide of popular opinion in any way whatsoever. Heracleitus possessed a truly detached personality, and he was a wise man in the tradition of the East, living alone in contemplation, and bothering not at all about the State.

This sarcastic old sage had also despaired of any of his contemporary thinkers, as well as discounting the theories of the preceding philosophers in Greece. "Abundant learning does not form the mind," (most students would agree with him on this point; and teachers also — if they were honest!) "If it did, it would have instructed Hesiod, Pythagoras, Xenophanes, and Hecataeus." "Polymathy" — meaning many lessons, or, much learning, he despised, and so he turned (as the 20th century Fench philosopher Bergson, at a later stage also did) to the quality of "Intuition", in order to understand the truth. "For the only real wisdom is to know that idea which by itself will govern everything on every occasion." And he stated that in order to understand the truth, "I searched myself". In Heracleitus' eyes, the failure to understand the 'Logos' or the Reason of Life, was the root of all evil. Sometime later, Socrates was also supposed to have advocated much the same principle, with his theory that Knowledge is Virtue, and that in order to be Courageous, for example, all one had to do was to understand exactly what Courage was, and then one automatically had it. (An interesting idea certainly!)

From his hermit home high in the mountains, Heracleitus observed Nature; wrote on these observations; and propounded a theory of evolutionary process and change in life, which (like the Milesians') anticipated the works of both Spencer and Darwin. And when he was not observing Nature, he roundly and loudly cursed the stupidity of the Ephesians down below. Originally, he had been disgusted with them because they had expelled Hermodorus from the city, and Hermodorus in Heracleitus' opinion, had been the only decent person in the place. The philosopher stated that the Ephesian attitude towards people of value was, "Let no one of us be the worthiest, but if there is one, then let him go somewhere else among others." (Unfortunately, there are many places in the world even today, where people think in exactly the same way as did those City Fathers of Ephesus.)

Since the Ephesians had no desire for excellence or truth, Heracleitus decided then to leave them to their ignorance; and up in the hills, he formed his theories on the Unity of Opposites; the Harmony of Strife; the Changing pattern of Energy; and the Underlying Order of the World — which order was built upon Action and Re-Action.

Let us examine firstly, his theories on the Unity of Opposites. As Heracleitus saw life, everything was in fact its very opposite. Life was Death; Good was Bad; and Waking was Sleeping — it was simply a matter of looking at the subject from another angle, or point of view. The environment of the Sea, equalled life for the Fish, but death for Man; so therefore, everything was subjective, or, as we say nowadays, "One man's trash is another man's treasure", or even, "One man's fish is another man's poison." Good and bad were relative things and subject to our personal views. Furthermore, he held that there was actually a polar attraction between these opposites, and that they had need of each other in order to show their own individual qualities. So, Sickness was needed in order to appreciate Health, and Winter was necessary in order to create Summer. (One might suspect of course that Heracleitus was rather something of a rationalist, who was trying desperately hard to accept his lot in life — rather like someone saying, "Well, if we must have evil in the world, then let us make the best of it, and try to find some use for it!") But his theories are quite logical if you think deeply enough about them, and as I said before, they do constitute a comforting creed for all those in affliction of any kind — even for those suffering toothache! After all, if you had never experienced toothache, then you'd never know how marvellous it was to be free of it; and the toothache itself serves the purpose of sending you to a dentist to repair your rotten teeth; and, it also provides a living for your Dentist, so that he can feed his wife and fourteen children! — therefore everything is necessary, or, 'for the best', as my grandmother used to say; (and I really don't know if she ever happened to have read Heracleitus —or, just worked out this wisdom for herself!)

This misanthropic philosopher also decided that there was a regular sequence of succession with all these opposites, for example; — hot became cold; cold became hot; the living, were in fact, **dying** — and so one must suppose then that the dying were in consequence going towards some new life! As all opposites were actually the same as each other, or to put it grammatically, every antonym was really a synonym; and, as they were **unified** by their **interdependence**; so were they also in **constant strife** —which Strife actually created the Harmony of Life. Heracleitus likened the warring opposition between class and class, man and woman, and summer versus winter, to the tension and interplay of the bow against the harp. He reasoned that as the bow is drawn in opposition against the strings of the harp (or violin) and thereby creates music; so the warring factions of life, strike against each other, and in their very opposition, create the harmonic balance of Life, and the necessary Change of Life. "War (Strife) is the Father of all things," said Heracleitus, and we may say that he was a fore-runner to Hegel and his Thesis, Antithesis, Synthesis, Theory — as well as having provided inspiration for Darwin's evolutionary theory of constant change and biological adaptation. The Good needed the Bad, and the Male needed the Female, in order to create the whole: and unlike the Italian Philosophers, he did not demand a monic theory and plan to Life. Light was necessary for there to be darkness, and vice versa; and **all things in life were subject to perpetual change**. "While we enter the same streams, other and other waters flow by us." "All things flow." "We are, and we are not." Hence his famous saying, "You cannot step into the same river twice." The change itself might be minute and imperceptible (infinitesimal even) to our eyes, but it had occurred, and was occurring all around us, all the time. (And changing for the worse! I hear the pessimist mutter — but wait awhile! Because Heracleitus has a hopeful message even for the Professional Defeatist!)

This continual flux and flow of life and its changing patterns meant that everything in Nature died into **the Life of Something Else** — everything was changed, absorbed, and evolved — but **never actually disappeared**. And this all came about due to a 'Logos', or Universal Principle of Life, which, to Heracleitus, was FIRE.

Now the Milesians had looked for a basic primary source of life, or universal principle, and they had come up with Water, Mist, and 'Something'. Heracleitus however thought that Fire was the answer, and he probably meant this not only literally, but metaphorically as well. Fire was the Absolute — it was both evolving, and alternately, kindled, and quenched. (Fire after all, had been very important to Man, and essential for his escape from a primitive animal life, on to a more civilized existence with hot dinners, and warmly washed clothes etc. If the Reader does not believe me, let him consider what would happen in the jungle should animals ever get round to using matches! How, for instance, could one possibly hope to deal with a lion who knew how to roast a chop, and heat water for a bath? In fact, probably the only thing that keeps Man in a superior position to the other animals is this very use of fire — without it we'd all be fetching and carrying for a nation of Hyenas; or a World Government of Apes!) But, departing from this tone of levity, it must also be noted that the Greek Myth regarding the origins of Fire, and of how it was given to Man by Prometheus, was well known and loved amongst the people, and therefore Heracleitus was very much aware of the various ramifications of this combustive substance, and of the importance attached to Fire, as an object in itself.

The Fire of Life, he called Divine, "Fire will judge and convict all things," — which statement might have meant that Heracleitus believed in some type of Last Judgement, of Final Cosmic Conflagration. And this Fire equalled Energy; which was in a constant changing process on a Downward Path to condensation, moisture, water and earth; and on an Upward Path to water, moisture and fire. And this theory actually fits in quite well with the modern hypothesis on the beginnings of the World, with the energy, heat, and fire contracting to form gas and moisture; and the chemical residue of water being left to finally form solid earth. This fellow from Ephesus was certainly way ahead of his time!

This Fire (which was later borrowed by the Stoics, and the Christian Church with their remarkably similar doctrines of Final Judgement and

Hell) was an "Everliving" fire, but **not** an "immortal" one, for it (the fire) was in turn transformed into all things — and all things were transformed into it. The Logos or Reason of Life was the Fire, and it was a cyclic, ever-recurring process, and this idea hints that Heracleitus believed in either a process of continual evolution (and we may include Man in this), or, in some type of re-incarnation. And he had something to say on the Soul of Man as well, (as did most of the philosophers), and he defined it as the "Psyche" and added, "You could not find the ends of the soul, though you travelled everyway, so deep is its logos." (Which leads us to think that **even he** wasn't quite sure where it was!) And again he stated, "The soul has a logos which increases itself," and this may mean that the Soul can be developed, and can grow, and that it is up to a person to take good care of it, just as Socrates advised later on in history. The Reader had best make-up his own mind on this point!

To sum up — we see that Heracleitus believes in a law of constant change in the Universe, with everything in flux; that Opposites themselves constitute Unity; (just as within the living cells of a body, opposite processes are continuously building-up and breaking-down in order to form the whole); and that the Order, or Balance of the World, though ever changing, is created by Strife, and by a form of continual revolution, with the competition of various groups creating Justice — by their very competition! "Through Strife, all things arise and pass away." That a Logos or Reason rules the World with a wisdom of orderly energy (the flow of Life); and that the main constituent, or principle ruling feature of Life, is FIRE.

Heracleitus was also known as the "Obscure", though whether that was because he was rarely seen in beautiful Down-Town Ephesus, or whether it was because scholars found his work difficult to understand, is not disclosed to us. He developed most of his theories in solitude, while reflecting on nature, "The things of which there is sight, hearing, knowledge: those are the things I prize." And in seeking to explain living Nature, Hercleitus made much use of metaphor and allegory, and leant upon the stories from Greek Mythology and the Cosmogeny, in order to underline and illustrate his points, using references such as, "The Thunderbolt which steers all things" — meaning the Fire of Life; and yet also making this symbol analogous to the "thunderbolt" of Zeus, the Captain of the Olympian Gods. But although he used the myths as a form of illustration in his writing, he contemptuously dismissed both them and the religious blood sacrifices in the temples to the various deities, which were then a common practice of his day. "They 'purify' themselves by staining themselves with different blood, as if one who stepped in mud should wash it off with mud. But one would be thought mad, if any man should see him behaving in this way." And his final condemnation of his fellow citizens was short but sweet, "Donkeys would choose garbage rather than gold!" — which seems to sum the situation up quite neatly on the feelings of Heracleitus for Ephesus and its inhabitants.

I could go on quoting many more pertinent comments by Heracleitus, but possibly the Reader feels he's already had more than enough, and that his head is reeling under this onslaught of Divine Fire, Perpetual Change, and Constant Strife. This remarkable philosopher single-handedly supplied enough grist for the combined mills of Plato, Zeno, Hegel, Bergson, Darwin, and Nietzsche; and possibly many others besides — not to mention what his theories may give rise to in the future. The circumstances regarding his final expiration are in some doubt, but, according to the historian and chronicler, Diogenes Laertius — having lived most of his life in the mountains; and having gained most of his nourishment from grasses and plants; he developed the disease of Dropsy, and was forced down into the city, in search of medical advice. (Vegetarians need not become disturbed at this point — The Author has checked out this theory with a medical practitioner of her acquaintance who has assured her categorically that there is **absolutely no truth** in this story at all! Heracleitus may indeed have developed Dropsy, but he **did not develop it** from eating only vegetables!)

Well anyway, once down in Ephesus, Heracleitus did the medical rounds, and just couldn't resist setting the doctors a riddle — instead of simply explaining his symptoms in the ordinary way. "How can you produce a drought after wet weather?" he asked them, and it seems that they just couldn't understand that he was referring to his condition. (They must have been a very stupid lot in Ephesus!) So, the philosopher went off to a stable full of oxen, and lay down and covered himself with cow dung, in the hope that the warmth emanating from it, would cause the water in his body to evaporate. This was quite a scientific, and a really unique idea for dealing with his particular problem, but unfortunately it didn't work, and his odorous blanket simply asphyxiated him instead.

Heracleitus departed from this troubled world in his seventieth year, so it is said, and I personally hope that he found his next existence to be composed of more understanding people than had been the case in Ephesus.

We shall leave Heracleitus with one final and very wise statement on the condition of drink in general, and of drunkeness in particular: "It is a delight for a man to be Wet (i.e. drunk) but a Dry soul is wiser, and **is best**."

And that, I think, should be adopted as the motto of Alcoholics everywhere. Cryptic but to the point!

ITALY AND THE ELEATIC SCHOOL

The Static Viewpoint.

Parmenides of Elea, the great opponent of Heracleitus, actually began his theorizing at a new school of philosophy in Italy, which had originally been founded by a gentleman called Xenophanes, of whom we had now better say a few words.

Xenophanes was born in Colophon, a town in Ionia just north of Ephesus, and he emigrated to Elea in Italy, around 510 B.C. Previous to this, he had (like Pythgoras), been a world tourist for some 67 years. The love of travel was a characteristic of displaced Ionians it seems! Elea itself appears not to have been particularly remarkable in ancient history, and is un-note worthy apart from itsphilosophyschool which was begun by this gentleman, and Xenophanes could perhaps better be described as a wandering religious teacher rather than a philosopher. But then again, to depict him as a religious teacher is rather erroneous because he ribaldly attacked all the Greek Mythology, scoffed at the works of Homer and Hesiod, and preached a type of Pan-Animism.

From the fragments of his work which have survived, (this has begun to sound rather like some poor old woman's collection of bone-china after a bull has been through the living-room!) he purported to have believed that all things, and all men were derived from earth, and water, by natural laws. And he also announced to all and sundry that water had once nearly covered the whole earth; and he knew this, he said, because he had observed marine fossils far inland on the tops of mountains. This fact had also been hinted at in the Creation stories of Greek Mythology, as the Greeks (like many other peoples) had a popular saga about Floods, and about the Human Race continuing on with the aid of a type of Floating Box, or Ark. But Xenophanes also insisted that one day in the future, water would **again** cover the entire earth. So it behoves those impressed by his prediction, to tear out and buy themselves some type of sailing gear as soon as possible.

But for all his modern evolutionary ideas, Xenophanes was a Monist, and he held that all change, all history, and all separateness were artificial and superficial phenomena, and that beneath the flux and variety of forms there was only one unchanging unity which was the innermost reality of God. Xenophanes therefore, with his rigid form Monic doctrine, was in direct antithesis to Heracleitus; and his disciple Parmenides of Elea developed this motionless theory even further.

Xenophanes, it is recorded, lived to the age of one hundred years, but how and why he then passed away, is not set down for us. Possibly he felt in need of a rest after all his travels, as even the most seasoned tourist is often tempted to call it a day, no matter how much he is enjoying himself! However, his ideas were carried on by Parmenides who actually began the Philosophy of Idealism, which later still, Plato would build upon, and which philosophy of Idealism, would wage war against the philosophy of Materialism in all future centuries.

Parmenides the next Thinker on our list, was a distinguished citizen of Elea in Italy, and even more than a distinguished citizen, (for in truth, this description could be equally applied to the local grocer!) as he was a highly respected Statesman in his home town, and he even drew up a code of laws for his city. He was in his prime, as they say, about 475 B.C., and he was a younger contemporary of Heracleitus, and a most antagonistic contemporary as well.

He started his philosophical life by studying with the Pythagorean School in Crotona, and it could be said that he developed his style of writing from Pythagoras, and his way of thinking from Xenophanes. He wrote prolifically, and profusely (a sin common to many!) and his philosophical ideas were contained in verse works such as his "Way of Truth" and "Way of Opinion". His writings also include a magniloquent book of "Revelations", where a Goddess of Truth conducts the poet through the Gates of the Sun, which portals are zealously guarded by lofty Justice. All this spendidly lyrical loquacity however, contains the kernal of rigid dogmatism that, All Reality is One; that All Appearances of Change and Motion are Illusory; that All Change is Impossible; and that Reality is Eternal and Indestructible. Not a very comforting philosophy, and definitely not one to be dwelt upon at length, or while languishing in a prison cell! In the Author's humble opinion, Parmenides should be consigned to the fire (Divine or otherwise) as an intensive reading of his works is liable to lead to a heavy depression settling on the human spirit — not to mention putting one off philosophy for life!

This rigid doctrinaîre stated that nothing comes from nothing; nothing disappears into nothing; and nothing is divisible. (On this score one might almost agree with the gentleman when considering the actual buying power of the £ Sterling nowadays!)

In the History of Philosophy however, Parmenides is acclaimed as the Father of Modern Logic, because he spent so much time and effort proving, persuading, and convincing everybody of the truth of his views, (with his arguments concerning what was, and what was not), that Plato, for one, was very impressed with him — but then Plato was also an Idealist, and an Anti-Materialist, like Parmenides. He is likewise classified as a Metaphysicist, as he entirely rejected the evidence or experience of the senses, and even made a distinction between 'phenomenon' (meaning unreal seen) and 'noumenon' (meaning unseen real)

Having begun his studies in Astronomy under Pythagoras, Parmenides then went on to write a philosophical poem "On Nature". (Although how he managed to observe the 'Old Girl' when he wouldn't even trust the evidence of his eyes, I don't know!) And he stated that beneath appearances (which are merely superficial), everything lies in an homogenous, unchanging, indivisible, indissoluble, and motionless unity — (one might care to add the adjective **Boring** also!) There is only One Being, One Truth, One God, One Birth, and One Death. Beginnings and Endings are only forms. The One Real (he never does seem to get around to telling us what that is!) Never Begins, and Never Ends. There is only **Being** (which sounds very much like someone using the present Continuous Tense too often!) and his despairing, passive theories are quite similar to the pessimism and anti-sensationism of the Hindu belief, and perhaps both these philosophies developed from similar socio-economic conditions and possibly due to regressive life-styles.

It seems that Parmenides had been so aroused by Xenophanes' statement that there was only One Reality, which was both the World and God; that having decided this was tne absolute truth, he then had only to commence constructing a theory in order to prove it. His monistic attitude covered even physical things, and as regards the 'Stuff' of life, that the early Milesians had been investigating and trying to locate as the First Principle; Parmenides announced smartly that whatever life was made of — be it fire, water, mist, or whatever — it was definitely made of one kind of substance only. And that shut the book on that! He then went on to say that this 'Stuff' — whatever it was — was Eternal, and could not be destroyed, changed, increased, or diminished in any way whatsoever. And that shut the book on that problem as well!

He also made a pronouncement on the nature of 'Phenomenalism', and said firmly that there was absolutely no distinguishing between the qualities of things, and the things themselves; that, for example, heat and brightness were not qualities of fire, but constituted fire itself. All of which I find rather bewildering, and secretly feel that Parmenides never attempted to do any cooking in his life, for if he had, he would have discovered that there is a great deal of difference between heat and brightness, when one is trying to coax something to fry with the last fumes of a gas bottle gone dry.

As Parmenides categorically threw out all observation with the senses, so this student of philosophy is inclined to throw out Parmenides as a complete waste of time! His static theories denying motion and change were in direct antithesis to the Kinetic metaphysics of Heracleitus, and his depressing monism was later refuted by the atomists Democritus and Leucippus. In a nutshell; in a word; Parmenides is Pah! ---- and definitely not a philosopher to take to bed with you on a long winter evening!

It is reported that Parmenides and his disciple Zeno of Elea (not to be confused with Zeno of Cyprus, the Founder of Stoicism) came to Athens about 450 B.C., and baffled the Athenians, but delighted Socrates, who was impressed with Zeno's ability at argument and paradox. There is some disagreement as to whether it is Parmenides, or Zeno, who is the father of Modern Logic, but in my estimation, there is not much (good that is!) to choose between either of them.

A typical example of Zeno's paradoxical skill is the following:- A flying arrow is actually at rest; for at any moment in its flight it is only one point in space i.e. motionless. Its motion, however actual to the senses, is logically and metaphysically unreal.

And if you like that sort of thing, then the Authorwould advise you to buy the complete unexpurgated works of Zeno, and to peruse them at your leisure. Personally speaking the whole thing makes me shudder — although I do acknowledge that pardoxes and riddles are very popular with the average thirteen-year-old school boy.

Zeno however, impressed his dialectical ability on Socrates, who then began turning it loose on the average citizen in the Agora (market-place) and in consequence made himself most unpopular. I only think that it is a pity that when they asked Socrates to drink the hemlock in 399 B.C., they didn't include Zeno and Parmenides in the invitation.

Maybe there was something to be said for the Spartan attitude after all, and for their refuşal to allow public consideration of philosophical problems. According to Athenaeus, a grammarian of the 20th century; the Spartans banned philosophical debates "on account of the jealousy and strife, and profitless discussions to which they give rise"; and considering all this nonsense flying around from Parmenides and Zeno, perhaps they were very wise to do so. Being Laconic, was very possibly, a philosophy in itself!

CHAPTER 5

NOUS AND EROS — THE COSMIC MOTIVATORS.

Anaxagoras of Ionia and Empedocles of Italy.

It is now that the Ionian and Italian Schools of Philosophy merge into a marriage of minds; a marriage of both materialism and idealism; with the advent of two new bright lights on the philosophical scene — Anaxagoras of Ionia, and Empedocles of Italy.

We shall consider Anaxagoras of Ionia first, as this truly remarkable intellectual managed to wed Heracleitus' pluralism to Parmenides' monism; and by trying to please all the people, all the time; he inevitably succeeded in pleasing none of the people, none of the time! — and let that be a warning to everyone!

Anaxagoras had the dubious distinction in Greek History of being the first philosopher to have been publicly persecuted, and he was born in Clazomenae in Ionia, (a town north of Ephesus and across from the Island of Chios, of modern chewing-gum fame), in the year 500 B.C. He was a student of the Milesian School (or what was left of it, after the Persians had gotten through with this area), and on reaching middle-age (or some say when even younger) he went to Athens to explore Truth, and to then propound it, and to advertise it to the Athenians-who most certainly didn't thank him for it-as they hadn't even asked him for this product in the first place!

Anaxagoras (at whatever age he was) arrived in Athens around 480 B.C. in the time of Pericles and the Golden Age, and he was a friend (for a short period) of both that famous gentleman, and his equally famous mistress Aspasia. Naturally we shall examine the more interesting aspects of this relationship later —but first we must do some serious work.

This new representative of Ionian philosophy also appeared on the Athenian scene only slighty prior to the philosophical season of the Sophists and Socrates, so therefore his ideas tended to influence a great number of people contemporary to himself. His main hypothesis was that the ideas of Anaximander and the Ionian School regarding Change and Development WERE correct; but that the rigid doctrines of Parmenides and the Eleatic School could also be successfully brought into agreement with them. He believed that there was a constant physical evolution in the world, but that it was controlled by a kind of Divine Reason; which reason he gave the name of 'NOUS' — and the Athenians, not very impressed with his ideas, gave Anaxagoras the same appellation — and catcalled him 'Nous' very derisively as he passed them in the streets.

Firstly we will examine his Change Theory.

Like Heracleitus, Anaxagoras saw Change as a basic essential of existence. He believed that there were an infinite number of First Principles, such as smell, colour, temperature etc., but he was equally convinced that Change was constantly at work in nature, combining and recombining these basic elements. He also noted that Change was just as obvious in Society, and that Institutions were not permanent structures, but were continually altering. Oligarchies developed into Democracies, which in due course developed into something else. (This theory did not warm the hearts of any of his listeners however, as people have this strange, and quite illogical desire, to see their own particular political faction in power, **all the time**!) So Anaxagoras gave credence to the Kinetic Flux theories of Heracleitus, but decided that there should be some type of Order, or Reason in charge of this Flux, and therefore he came up with 'NOUS'.

This 'NOUS', Anaxagoras held, was a force producing 'stuff' (back to Anaximander again!) which introduced order into the Universe, and dominated the interaction of the basic elements. This 'NOUS' was purely mental, and from it came world order, regularity, and the development of things to definite ends. This 'NOUS' was present in everything in life that moved; in Man, animals, plants, and material objects. It was a type of spiritual reason, or could be likened to Aristotle's First Mover, or Biological Force (which we are yet to meet officially); or to Bergson's Life Force or Élan Vital. And this 'NOUS' permeated **everything**, and one can imagine how worried the Athenians became on hearing this — after all, this damn thing which they couldn't see, was **even** in an empty wine bottle!

Having made a courtesy bow to Idealism, with 'NOUS', Anaxagoras then reverted to Materialism, with his other pronouncements on life; and in particular, with his interest in Astronomy which he had learnt from having read the works of Anaximenes. When asked one day what the object of his life was, he replied, "The investigation of the Sun, Moon, and Heavens", and with such a ridiculous statement, he immediately branded himself as strange in the head, for everyone else in Athens knew perfectly well that the **only object** worth pursuing in life, was the almighty Drachma! The Sun and Stars, he announced, were glowing masses of rock, and the Sun was nothing supernatural, only a red hot mass — and furthemore it was many times larger than Peloponnesus. (Naturally this didn't make him popular with devotees of Apollo the Sun God, nor with the people living in this mountainous area, who, like the Texans, used to brag that everything of theirs was bigger than anyone else's! — and here was this long-haired creep from Ionia, refuting their proudest boast!) He also explained (though nobody asked him to, and few wanted to hear) about the reasoning behind the eclipses; and then foolhardily he went on to mention that there were other celestial bodies as well, which were inhabited like Earth. "Men are formed", he told them, "and other animals that have life; the men dwell in cities and cultivate fields as we do." All of which goes to show what a bright lad Anaxagoras was, but how dumb he was also! Pronouncements such as this, did not make him popular, and his name was not high on the list of dinner invitations in the best circles of Athens — and in consequence, he courted wisdom in poverty.

It must be admitted that really and truly, Anaxagoras just didn't know where and when to stop, for he informed everyone that Thunder was caused by the collision of clouds, and that lightning was due simply to the friction of same. (This was a dreadful shot at the Captain of the gods old Zeus himself, as he was the **owner** of the Thunderbolts!) And he also told them, (anyone who hadn't yet put their hands over their ears in desperation and in order not to hear these blasphemies), that the quantity of matter never changed, but that **all forms** begin, and then pass away; and that in time; even the mountains would become sea. (The folks living up in Mt. Pindus must have been terribly upset, and really, one can understand their apprehension — Anaxagoras was causing the very earth to tremble under their feet!) All organisms, continued Anaxagoras gravely, were originally generated out of earth, moisture, and heat, and therefore had developed one from the other; and Man had only advanced beyond other animals because his erect posture had freed his hands, and therefore enabled him to grasp things. And with this evolutionary bombshell Anaxarogas really drew the wrath of the Gods down on his head. How could anyone feel comfortable knowing that he was only just a slightly bit smarter than his dog? And only more smart because he had managed to balance on two limbs instead of four! In fact Anaxagoras was both the Copernicus and Darwin of his age, and while Darwin was fortunate enough to get away with it — Anaxagoras, like Copernicus, (and a certain teacher in an American school some time later in history,) paid the customary price for being more intelligent than his peers; and for allowing them to know it!

This clever lad from Clazomenae sought natural explanations everywhere and at all times, and when a single-horned and sacred, (supposed sacred that is) ram was brought as a gift to Pericles, Anaxagoras insisted on cutting open the animal's head in order to show that it wasn't sacred at all. That it simply had only one horn because the brain of the creature **only filled** one side of the head. Naturally nobody but himself was very happy about this little exhibition, as the donor of the sheep was insulted; the ram was mortified, due to the loss of both status and life; and the slaves who had to clean up the mess from the operation, and who were forced to work on their half-day off, were the most put out of all!

When he wasn't scandalizing the Athenians, or entertaining Pericles, Anaxagoras worked in poverty stricken privacy on his book "On Nature".

Every philosopher appears to have written a book entitled "On Nature" at some time or other, and it seems that producing a work on this subject was the necessaryrequirementfor being regarded as a philosopher in those days, and in order to be taken seriously by everyone — in fact it was rather like the compulsory Doctoral Thesis of our days. In reality Anaxagoras was merely developing, and expanding upon, the theories of the Milesians and Heracleitus; and one suspects that he was actually an out and out philosophical materialist, who only invented the idea of an idealistic 'NOUS' in order to save his own skin. Idealist Philosophers were of course always more popular among the masses, and generally they were more affluent also, and this theory of a Divine Brain running the Cosmos, was possibly developed in order to cover up his true materialism.

In this version of the Creation of the World, Anaxagoras proclaimed that the World was originally chaos, (just as the Mythology had described it) and composed of diverse seeds of life, which were all pervaded by 'NOUS' (the Divine Reason, Mind, or Life Force) and which was akin to the source of life and motion in us. As the mind gives order to the chaos of our actions, so the World Mind gave order to the seeds of life by setting them in Rotary Vortex (similar again to the Cosmogeny). This Rotation then sorted the seeds into four elements, Fire, Air, Water, and Earth (Chinese or Milesian influence again!) and separated the world into two revolving layers; an outer one of 'ether', and an inner one of 'air'. Because of the whirling motion, the surrounding fiery 'ether' tore away stones from earth, and kindled them into stars. Perhaps Anaxagoras was attempting to explain the qualities of 'Hydrogen' here; and perhaps he was even more advanced that we will even admit nowadays. Anyway, he was definitely continuing the Ionian Physicist Tradition, and he was truly an astoundingly progressive thinker for his day and age.

In 432 B.C., two years before the outbreak of the Peloponnesian War between Sparta and Athens, the Athenian toleration for intellectuals completely gave way; and Cleon (a rival of Pericles) decided to get rid of three birds with one stone, by bringing Pericles' mistress Aspasia, (a 'Hetaerae' i.e. a concubine and a close friend of many Athenian philosphers) to trial, on a charge of impiety (not immorality mark you, but impiety!) Pheidias, the Sculptor, was also accused on a charge of embezzling (he was at that time decorating the Parthenon, but as with the case of the Sydney Opera House, that construction also failed to appeal to everyone, and people immediately began to resent having to pay for it!) Anaxagoras was indicted in the same clean-up campaign for both impiety, and irreligion; and most of all — because he had described the Sun (at that time a God in Greece) as a glowing piece of rock! Cleon naturally figured to himself that by getting rid of Pericles' favourite mistress, favourite sculptor, and favourite philosopher all in one fell swoop; it would not be long before he would manage to get rid of Pericles himself! And so it came about. Within three years of losing all three, Pericles lost his hold on life itself, and left this earth, a broken, philosopherless, sculptorless, and mistressless, man!

And what of Anaxagoras? Well, he fled Athens to Lampsacus on the Hellespont in Ionia, and continued teaching philosophy there, according to one story. Another tale has it that he was imprisoned and offered the customary cup of hemlock, but that having decided that the taste of the brew didn't agree with his digestion, he arranged with Pericles to effect an escape for him. (Pheidias however, so the same story goes, was not as lucky, and had to rot in gaol until he died. Can this possibly mean that artists are more expendible than philosophers? And why didn't Pericles help Pheidias, as well as Anaxagoras?) Whatever the truth of the matter though, Anaxagoras definitely ended up in Lampsacus, which, like most areas outside Athens in those days, was much more progressive, and much more liberal in its ideas and attitudes. Athens in the 5th century B.C. in fact, was still only a poor little backward country town compared to the older Greek City-States, and people there just weren't ready for modern ideas on evolution and the like. It's the same old story today, and the economy and age of a place always decide its social and political policy; and all the Prophets, Philosophers, Thinkers, and Artists etc., would be better off migrating to decayed old cities, where a tradition of culture has already been sown; than in attempting to stay and instil knowledge and love of beauty, in hearts too barren, dry, and ignorant to receive these seeds.

They say that when news of his condemnation and death sentence reached Anaxagoras in Lampsacus, (the Athenians persistently continued to condemn him even though he wasn't anywhere around for them to get their hands on!) he remarked of the Athenians, (their ears must have been burning!) "Nature has long since condemned both them and me". Which words of wisdom should give pause to many a person — I know they have, the Author!

Anaxagoras is supposed to have died about the year 428 B.C., at the relatively youthful age of seventy-three (youthful for philosophers anyway, because they were generally a rather hardy bunch!) and this early demise was likely as not due to the great proverty he had been forced to endure at the end. Pericles, before his own death in 429, remembered that his philosopher friend was still kicking his heels in Lampsacus, and he decided rather belatedly to send him a drachma or two, in order to tide him over. But Anaxagoras, having not heard from Pericles for a number of years, was not highly impressed with his ex-benefactor's generosity, and he returned the gift with the curt message that, "Those who have occasion for a lamp, supply it with oil." And those of us who would like not to lose our friends, should also bear this in mind, and make sure that we keep the lamp of friendship continually alight, and continually filled with the oil of social communication!

From Anaxagoras and his 'NOUS', we shall now promptly proceed to Empedocles and his 'EROS'. This gentleman, like Anaxagoras, was another Pluralist, but instead of giving order to the world through Reason (NOUS), he invented, or discovered, a system of order through 'EROS' —i.e. Love, or Feeling; or, the Spirit of Love. In the Greek Mythology, Eros was the God of Love personified in the figure of a small baby, who with blindfolded eyes, and clutching poisonous darts, wandered the world causing emotional havoc in areas which had hitherto been tranquil and serene. In the earlier Greek Cosmogeny, Eros had also been mentioned, but there he was depicted as the force which ruled the world, and which brought Order to everything-after the original period in which Chaos had ruled supreme.

Empedocles the originator of this Love Theory was born in 493 B.C. (the year of Marathon), in the City-State of Acragas in Italy. Acragas is found in Sicily if you look attentively enough at the map, but, (just in order to confuse you!) it is marked under the Roman name of Agrigentum — and in the 6th century B.C. it was the largest and richest city in Sicily, and produced the affluent merchants who became the multi-millionaires of their time. And one of these old rich families in Acragas, with a positive passion for horse-racing, gave birth to Philosophical Empedocles — a surprising fact but true, as one can hardly credit that a clan of gamblers could manage to produce a philosopher between them; but they did! And obviously there is hope for the world even yet — and no matter what is said — Truth is definitely stranger than Fiction!

This astonishing Sicilian, who beautifully balanced Anaxagoras, was well known as a Statesman, Poet, and Quack, or, in more polite terms, a Spiritual Healer; as well as being acknowledged to be an outstanding Philosopher. It was also rumoured about (the source of the story being Empedocles himself) that he was, in addition to everything else, a God! This deification, in consequence, entitled him to great fame during his day and age in the Greek World, and there were legends connected with his name. He is remarkable most of all, in having managed to wed Myth to Logic; and for having discovered, not one main cosmic motivator (as was the case with Anaxagoras) but for having kindly provided the world with Two Principal Movers. Empedocles stated that there is Aphrodite or Love, which is the Principle of Unification; and Ares (the God of War) or Strife, which is the Principle of Division; and that the cosmic process is an ever-recurring cycle of confrontation between these two; in which each prevails for a period, and then each gives way to the other. And with this little packet we now have a nice mixture of Heracleitus' flux and change theory, plus the Italian ideas concerning a Higher Spirit, and Divine Intervention.

Originally, Empedocles had studied in the Pythagorean School, but (the real reasons are unknown!) had been expelled for divulging some secret esoteric doctrine supposedly, and consequently his views were a little of this, and a little of that, and rather like a pot-luck casserole on washing day. — But they were very interesting nonetheless.

He believed in a world sphere, (the Orphic World Egg idea), with the elements of Life being Fire, Air, Earth, and Water; all perfectly interlaced, and bound together by Love. This composition equalled complete Harmony and Perfection, said Empedocles; but then Strife always arose, and got the upper hand, and divided everything, and separated all the components or elements, until Love took over once more, and again balanced everything up. With this theory Empedocles himself managed to combine all the ingredients of the Orphic Doctrine, (the belief in the Soul and its Divine Origins; its fall and successive re-incarnations; and its final return to the company of the Gods;) with the physical manifestions of life easily discernible to any half intelligent observer. And hence he concocted a cocktail of Cosmology, Biology and Astronomy. Quite a drink! And this heady brew definitely packed a punch for everyone who happened to imbibe it, or even to sniff at its bouquet. But, unlike Anaxagoras, Empedocles had more sense than to stay around and make himself unpopular, so he hopped in and out of Athens more rapidly and more irregularly than an international representative of a 20th century Monopoly; and in order to doubly insure his life, he kept the natives in their places by the simple method of practicing a little voodoo, (his Faith Healing activities!) in his spare time.

Empedocles believed whole-heartedly in the Pythagorean transmigration of souls, (or so he said anyway!) and he announced that in previous lives he had himself been a youth, a maiden, a flowering shrub, a bird, a fish; and much, more. (These pronouncements definitely impressed people and helped to keep the hemlock from his door.) Like the Pythagoreans, he also thought that eating meat was cannibalistic, and furthermore, he stated, that he believed that ALL MEN had once been Gods (this was very much in keeping with the Greek Myth regarding the first men being made of Gold), and that they had fallen into a lower life form, due to their impurity and violence. (And if the Reader finds any of this confusing then he must simply acquire a copy of the Author's book, "The Greek Gods", in order to read up on the Cosmogeny!)

So Empedocles wandered Greece, sighing and mourning his past Divinity, "From what glory, from what immeasurable bliss, have I now sunk to roam with mortals on this earth." And probably, almost identical thoughts are often expressed by the urban house-wife, when up to her armpits in greasy dish-washing water (and by any other people brought low in life!) And doubtless the first convicts in Sydney Cove in 1778, said more or less the same thing when they first landed in that God forsaken place.

As this philosopher was convinced of his divine origins; or at least, desirous of convincing others of them; he dressed in purple, the symbolic colour for the royal or divine; placed golden sandals on his feet, like Hermes, the God of Commerce; and adorned his brow with a wreath of laurel leaves, like Apollo. It was to his friends that he first confessed the secret that he was really a God incarnate, and of course in no time at all, the story had done the rounds of all the coffee shops, and Empedocles (unlike Anaxagoras) was viewed, not so much with derision and suspicion — but, with reverence and fear.

One may be forgiven for thinking that this lad from Sicily was one of the greatest 'Con Men' of Athens, (shades of the gambler blood coming through!) for, having claimed Supernatural Powers, he then commenced trotting around, and performing magic rites; and healing the sick — and generally, with extremely good results, strange to relate. Perhaps the sight of him all togged up in his violet splendour was enough just to cheer up the patients and to give them new heart. How many illnesses are simply brought about by depression and boredom, anyhow? And maybe Empedocles was more advanced in medicinal psychology than is realised, and **possibly**, a good, (or at least, **interesting**) bedside manner is the best medicine in the world, and way and above any other type of treatment! Actually he was quite skilled in herbal medicine in his own way, (everything about Empedocles was highly individualistic, and more than likely, he was the sort of person you either loved, or loathed, on first sight), and along with his other virtues or vices, he was an excellent orator, who taught Gorgias the Sophist of Italy, a thing or two. Like everyone else with an education in Greece, he also wrote a treatise, "On Nature", and then hawked it round to try and make some money; as well as penning another work entitled, "On Purification".

Everywhere he went, Empedocles the Divine, was the cynosure of all eyes, and when he attended the Olympics, the spectators never knew whether to rivet their attention on the contestants, or on him. Doubtless there were a lot of people suffering from Spasmodic Torticollis (Wryneck, to the Layman!) on those occasion, and Empedocles probably collected quite a large number of new patients after having spent a day at the Stadium.

An eclectic, (meaning one who chooses — 'eclectic' is from a Greek word meaning to choose; therefore we have the word 'election' in the English language) Empedocles discerned a little bit of wisdom in practically everyone's philosophy, and accordingly he adopted various ideas. Unlike Parmenides he believed in the Senses, and quite often fed his own as well! He also believed in a theory of hermaphroditic people, and thought that at the beginning of the world both sexes had been contained in the one body (Hermes the Male God, and Aphrodite the Female Goddess —therefore Hermes + Aphrodite = Hermaphrodite) and that they had then become separated into Male and Female, and in consequence each longed to be re-united with the other — A unique and definitely interesting explanation for the Sex Drive, and one rather similar to that which Aristophanes, (according to Plato) also later gave credence to. In Empedocles' eyes, Love and Hate, and Good and Evil, fought and balanced against each other in a vast universal rhythmic dance of Life and Death and that dreadful man Herbert Spencer also later brought out the same theory in the 19th century. (Spencer must have done a great deal of reading of the Ancient Greek Philosophers!)

In his twi-light years, Empedocles became more of a preacher and prophet, than a philosopher; rather like a combination of Buddha, Pythagoras and Schopenhauer. (They do say of course that our early religious training always gets to us most strongly at the end of life!) Schopenhauer was that extremely deep, and extremely pessimistic German philosopher A.D 1788 - 1860, and Empedocles, like Schopenhauer, grew very disgusted with people and warned the guilty human race that they should abstain from marriage; (probably quite a popular suggestion) procreation; (a trifle difficult to enforce, or to convince some people on this score); and beans! Why everyone should have been so dead set against this miserable legume, I don't know, but it seems to have definitely been 'de rigueur' to most Hard Thinkers, to go through Life without them!

Legend has it that Empedocles finished his life by jumping into Etna's volcano; and Legend adds that although the volcano accepted the philosopher, it didn't take kindly to his footwear — and exploding viciously, it regurgitated his golden sandals; leaving them to rest on the rim of its fiery mouth. So, in a typically dramatic fashion Empedocles removed himself permanently from the Stage of Life, bequeathing his only valuable possessions (apart from his theories of course!) to the customary ingratitude of posterity.

CHAPTER 6

THE MATERIALIST MAVERICKS.

Leucippus and Democritus the Atomists.

Before Philosophy really came of age and set Athens completely in a whirl with the arrival of the Sophists; two gentlemen appeared in Greece with a completely materialist view of things, and, what is more; an Atomic view of things as well! These two were Leucippus of Miletus, in Ionia; and Democritus, the Laughing Philosopher, (why laughing, I have no idea!) who came from Abdera in Thrace, in the north east of Greece. Between them, these two mavericks of thought, built the Atomic Theory, which was indirectly based upon (everything in life is based upon, or derived from something else, don't you know!) the latest Pythagorean decision that all things were composed of numbers in the sense of individual units; plus the statement by Philolaus of Thebes, that, "All things take place by necessity and by harmony." They were also strongly influenced by the plurality of motion theory, which had been brought out by Zeno of Elea, and the Author is indeed glad to know that anyone was actually able to squeeze any wisdom at all out of Zeno's paradoxes — personally speaking she would have found it extraordinarily difficult to do so herself!

Leucippus, the first of the Atomists, is a rather shadowy figure of the 5th century B.C. who went from Miletus to Elea, about 435 B.C., in order to undertake a period of study under Zeno. He survived the experience; learnt about the latest numerical atomist theory of the surviving Pythagoreans; combined this with Zeno's crazy plurality of motion idea; muttered wisely in his beard; and then departed for Abdera, a flourishing Ionian colony (settled by Ionians from Asia Minor that is) in Thrace, where he immediately began teaching, in order to make a living. The idea of anyone trying to actually live on a teacher's wage is quite a ridiculous notion of course, and really one wonders why the philosphers didn't exhibit more commonsense. However it is a paradox of life (and not one of Zeno's) that the wisest of men are also the most foolish, and that, may possibly account for it! Also, if one has education, but nothing else, very probably there is not much else that one can do — except teach!

Anyhow, regarding the financial situation of Leucippus we know nothing whatsoever, nor do we know exactly what it was that he was cramming into their wooden heads in Abdera. All we do have on record about this character is one fragment of his golden thoughts which goes as follows — "Nothing happens without a reason, but all things occur for a reason, and for necessity." And this seems an extremely logical supposition, so I must admit that I find Leucippus to have been a very wise man about life in general, (even if he wasn't so smart in his choice of profession,) and this statement of his is quite a good thing to murmur to yourself whenever things go wrong in life, because pain which serves a purpose, always seems easier to bear than pain which does not.

Like Heracleitus, Leucippus is an admirable person to read when in trouble and despair, and it is a great tragedy that we don't have more of him to indulge in. But besides being a comfort to those in trouble, Leucippus also discovered, or developed, the notion of "The Void", or "Empty Space". The Universe, he contended, contained atoms and space, and nothing else. These atoms were continually tumbling around in the 'Void' and perpetually attracted to each other, and furthermore, all things were composed of them, including the Planets; the Stars; and even the Human Soul — (which by now, everybody had finally gotten round to accepting as being a definite problem which had to be dealt with somehow or other!) So from Leucippus in his penurious position in Abdera came the original blueprint for today's modern advances in medicine and nuclear warfare; proving conclusively therefore that for everything **truly good — somebody, somewhere, can always manage to convert it into something truly evil**! And I wonder exactly where in "The Void" was Leucippus; when they were attempting to split the atom, in order to bomb Japan during the 2nd World War — and more importantly; what did he think?

Now, Democrtitus of the dimples, or the smiles, or whatever it was that earned him the name of laughing boy; was a pupil (some say an associate) of Leucippus, and he was born in Abdera in 460 B.C. Adhering closely to Leucippus' theories, he pronounced, "There are only Atoms and the Void", and he proceeded then to develop an Atomist concept which henceforth became the world's first materialist Philosophy. (Perhaps the reason why Democritus was always laughing was because of the dismay and consternation which his theories had caused; and because of the pained expressions visible on the Idealist Philosophers' faces!) One wonders in fact how much Democritus might have influenced the German Philosopher Nietzsche A.D. 1844-1900 because that gentleman was always warning people regarding the danger of falling into the 'Black Pit of Despair', and this sounds remarkably like Democritus's 'Void'. But, while this chasm of Cosmic Loneliness may have worried poor dear, unhappy Nietzsche, it didn't really appear to have unduly upset Democritus.

This cheerful philosopher was actually born lucky, (perhaps that's why he was always laughing!) in the fact that like Empedocles, he sprang from a very wealthy family in Abdera; and he was even luckier in the fact that he inherited about 100 talents (a considerable fortune in those days), from his kith and kin, and which then enabled him to go off in order to broaden his mind in travel. This leads me to suppose that travel (like leisure) is another "absolutely necessary" pre-requisite for those wishing to become practising philosophers, and if the reader wishes to start in on this occupation, then he/she had better book him/herself in on the next available charter flight, or package deal, to somewhere or other at once. First you see the world; and then you write about it!

Democritus himself did the grand tour of his day which included Egypt, Babylon, Ethiopia, Persia, and India; and at Thebes, he stopped for some time and took in the ideas of Philolaus. Philolaus, incidentally is not particularly important in philosophical spheres, but it should be noted that this clever fellow was the first to discover (and to announce it aloud as well) that the Earth **was not the centre of the Universe**, but only one of many planets, and quite possibly, not a very interesting one! Doubtless this statement didn't make Philolaus very popular, which is why he doesn't figure much in the general run-of-the-mill philosophical history books!

Having spent all his money, Democritus then returned to Abdera, and reviewed the situation most philosophically(here the meaning of the word PHILOSOPHY is, without despair!) There was nothing else for it he realised calmly. He was too poor to go into business for himself. — He would just have to pull in his belt, to live simply; and to call himself a philosopher! Poverty could be classy he probably decided, **IF**, it was accompanied by an intellectual attitude. So accordingly he retired to a modest establishment, hung up his shingle, and announced to all and sundry that he was now in business. (Rather like a doctor in a Frontier Town in the Wild West of the U.S.A. in the pioneering days!) The tradesmen who approached him, quite naturally shook their heads sadly, for they realised that he would never be able, (even if he **were willing**) to pay them. "You may be able to get blood from a stone," said the Athenian grocers wisely, "but it's for sure you'll never be able to get money from a philospher." So you see Dear Reader, how wondrously life works, and how even the unpaid bills of the philosopher may actually cause philosophy (i.e. truth and wisdom) to flourish, and to burst forth in blossom from that stoniest of ground, from the possessor of the sternest of soul; and the hardest of heart — the Trader!

Our lad Democritus, although a Materialist, (as distinct from an Idealist), was far from being either vulgar or crass, and he proclaimed seriously, and meant every word of it I am sure, "I would rather discover a single demonstration in geometry, than win the throne of Persia." Darius of Persia (558-486 B.C) would have found this pronouncement rather unsettling, if, he had been around at the time to hear it! — after all, what was the use of sitting on a throne, if nobody else wanted it?

Besides being a lover of poverty and truth, Democritus also sought privacy and peace, and he shunned dialectical discussion; founded no school of his own; and holidayed in Athens without even calling on any of the philosophers there, or ever wasting his time in argument. Like the modest violet of the woods, Democritus stayed in his own backyard, and grew, (philosophically speaking) and produced publication after publication, on:- Maths, Physics, Astronomy, Navigation, Geography, Anatomy, Physiology, Psychology, Psychotherapy, Medicine, Philosophy, Music, and Art. And so we see that Democritus must have been one of the most dedicated and greatest Thinkers of all ages, and possibly best deserving of the title of Philosopher Extraordinâire!

Unlike the Monism of Parmenides; the Atomism of Democritus stated that the Senses **are to be trusted** to analyse things of the exterior; and, he added, in very logical and down to earth fashion, (which is most appreciated after all the confusion we have had on this point) that **Sensations are correct**; that sweet is sweet, and that cold is cold; but that actually, everything, is only Atoms and the Void; and that all the senses are really only variations on the Form, or Sense of Touch. Basically, the sensations are caused by the Atoms being discharged by the object concerned, he said, and then these atoms fall upon our sense organs, so that the atoms of Sound, touch our ears; and the atoms of a Sight, touch our eyes; and the atoms of a Smell, touch our noses. Bearing all this in mind, the next time your noisy next-door neighbour is having a party, and you can't sleep, simply tell him that his atoms of Sound are touching your ears too much — Unless he knows something about Philosophy or Atomic Theory, he will not understand a word you are talking about, and will become convinced that you are mad; **possibly dangerous**; and that it would be better for him to turn the racket down at once.

Only necessity rules everything, said Democritus. There is no 'NOUS' as in Anaxagoras' theories, and no 'Love and Hate', or 'Eros and Strife', as in Empedocles' hypothesis. All matter quantity remains the same, but the atomic combinations change continually. Necessity is the cause of absolutely everything in life.(Even my dear old Grandmother used to say that "Necessity was the Mother of Invention", — who knows, perhaps she was a disciple of Democritus!) And according to Democritus there is definitely NO CHANCE! (Gamblers who believe in Lady Luck please take careful note!) Chance is only a **fiction** which is used to cover **our ignorance of circumstances and conditions** said Democritus. (Very strong words here indeed!)

In his supposition regarding the beginnings of Life, Democritus decided that Organic Beings arose from a moist earth; and that everything in Man was, and is, composed of Atoms; including, as we have already stated, the Soul. And in fact, **Everything in Everything, was; and is; Atoms.** BUT! (here a discreet glance in the direction of idealism) the Atoms of the Soul, are the best Atoms of Man, and a wise man will cultivate thought, and thereby free himself from passion, superstition, and fear. And in this statement of Democritus' we can dimly discern the origins of Cynicism and

Stoicism. Happiness does not come from without, insisted Democritus, and it does not come from material goods. (So take back that video-set, and diamond tiara immediately!) But happiness does come from, and is found, **within Man**, in his atomic depths. (Rather like the deeps of the 'Logos' in which Heracleitus was searching, perhaps.) I must admit that while this does seem to be a very wise philosophy, the thought does also occur to sceptical me, that it would possibly be a rather nice little philosophy to circulate amongst the Poor; in order to direct them on a search of their inner selves; and away from conspiring to create the perfect Revolution! — Probably though, this philosophy (like most unpleasant and difficult things) is true, and we should all turn our backs on material wealth, and direct ourselves to the gathering of mental and spiritual affluence instead.

"Culture is better than Riches," said Democritus, and I am forced to agree with him here, but I do wonder how one manages to build the culture of a country without a good economic foundation. After all, the Happiness Kid from Abdera, inherited a sizeable sum in order to allow him to spend freely on his journeys around the world, whilst engaged in putting a little cerebral spit and polish on himself! "No power, and no treasure, can outweigh the extension of our knowledge," he thundered; beginning to sound rather like a moralist (and all moralists are always most uncomfortable folk to live with) and it is really small wonder that the Athenians had no time for Philosophers. They poor souls, (the Athenians) plainly got tired of being criticised, (and who can blame them?) and Democritus was obviously quite sensible, not to announce his presence in the City any time he passed through. The Athenians, most likely as not, would have promptly evicted him from Piraeus immediately, if they had known — and without the benefit of boat or life-jacket either!

As regards Sensual Pleasure, Democritus admitted that it was pleasurable, (we all know to which particular sensual pleasure he was probably referring, I am sure) but he warned that this pleasure was only fitful, and that it was better to have peace and serenity of soul, and most importantly, to have good cheer. (Hence the laughter, and a jocular stab at the miserable Pythagoreans!) And to have Moderation, (Aristotle would also come to this same conclusion) and Order; and Symmetry, in Life. Man, declared Democritus, should learn from the Animals; and here the wiseman of Abdera has captured my heart entirely, and I couldn't agree more. How often have I sat, and watched the cat of my next-door-neighbour, and thought quietly to myself, that, on the whole, the cat, was a far more cultivated and intelligent creature that its owner. This doesn't say much for my next-door-neighbour, I know, but then she doesn't say much for me — except something bad! However, it is true that animals seem to possess an inner tranquillity far surpassing that of man, and as regards Direct Behaviour, Logic, (based on Instinct) and Good Manners; why, they really leave absolutely nothing to be desired! Your average dog for instance, knows immediately what he thinks of the other dog that he meets in the street, and after a compulsory sniff (rather like our handshake) he goes straight on into the act of telling him. While Human Beings prevaricate, and vaccillate, and can never seem to understand whether they like each other or not. And we Humans continually get frustrated, and repress our natural feelings, and suffer from ulcers and nervous breakdowns, because we simply **must** pretend to be polite; even when the other person is walking all over us, and is being covertly aggressive. But the superior canine just lifts his leg, and marks out his territory quite calmly, and if the other dog comes over the line, why then they fight it out, and immediately solve the dispute without any unnecessary palaver. Obviously (or so it seems to me at any rate), animals are much more logical than Man, and definitely they are worth our closest study and observation.

But enough of these flippant thoughts of mine on the subject of Man's inferiority to Animals, and back to some heavy moralising from Democritus. "Good Actions," he said, "should be done not out of compulsion, but from conviction, not from hope of reward, but for their own sake..... A man should feel more shame in doing evil before himself than before all the world." And it might be a good idea and a good action if some philanthropic and philosophically inclined millionaire would offer to set the above words on billboards and to display them boldly throughout the city centres of the world. Think what a break-through it would be if we took to advertising goodness and philosophy, instead of only food, drink, vehicles, and clothing. And furthermore, the idea might even catch on and actually become fashinable; as most Lost Causes do; (one hundred years **too late**!) — and the world might manage to produce a harvest of happy, peaceful, good-living souls — and Television might take to advertising and to attempting to persuade people to have a smile and a good thought — instead of a caffeinated or carbonated drink!

The most cheerful philosopher on record, and the least demanding of men, Democritus lived to either ninety, or, one hundred and nine years of age — (there is some disagreement on the number of years he actually chalked up), and he received a grant for his work "Great World", from the City of Abdera, in order to tide him over his hungry senescent days. In fact his longevity was the marvel of many, (after all the grant from the City had not been that big!) and he was asked to disclose the secret for his obstinate endurance. Democritus replied to all enquiries that the elixir of life was quite obviously **Honey**, which he ate daily. (I do hope the price of that commodity doesn't rise with the sales following the publication of this book!) And that he also believed in the efficacious practice of frequently bathing the body with oil. (Whether or not he used soap and water as well as the oil, I regret to say, I could not discover.)

Having come to the conclusion that he had lived among the Atoms and the Void of this life quite long enough, Democritus finally decided to starve himself to death. Therefore he set about this activity in a most practical, purposeful, and light-hearted manner; as was his wont in all things. His sister however was most upset with his plans. **Not**, mind you, because she was overcome with consanguineous love, (as Democritus' family seem on the whole to have been a rather cold-blooded lot, and perhaps that is why he was always laughing — in order to cover up the inner pain!) BUT, because she (his sister) had worked it out on her abacus, or whatever it was that she used; that her brother would fade away at the beginning of the Festival of Thesmorphoria; and in consequence she would miss out on all the fun. This festival, incidentally, was one of the sixty or so held annually in the Greek world, and it was a strange phallic-cult ceremony celebrating Demeter supposedly, and which was based upon the ancient chthonic vegetation beliefs. In actual fact it was probably just an excuse for everyone to run around in the city streets being lewd and ribald — And Heaven knows **what** Democritus' sister was thinking of, in wanting to attend it! Anyhow, Democritus, as tolerant and complaisant and agreeable as ever, decided to hold some small loaves of bread dressed in honey to his nostrils, in order to breathe in the food. (Or as he would have put it himself, to allow his nostrils to touch the atoms of smell!) And to try, in this way, not to break his fast — (because it is extremely aggravating if you are setting out to kill yourself, to have to post-pone it and then to start it all over again!) but to make himself last out the festival — so that his stupid, selfish, and totally lacking in sympathy sister, might get a chance to wear her new dress; or to show off her new hair-style — or do whatever it was that she wanted to do!

Unfortunately, this experiment of breathing in atoms of food (rather reminiscent of Heracleitus in the stable with the dung) was destined to fail. And Democritus broke his sister's heart, by dying in the middle of the festivities, and thereby denying her the chance of dancing wantonly in the main thoroughfares of the town. She was obviously so put out by the whole thing, that it was probably just as well that the City of Abdera paid for the philosopher's funeral, because it was quite clear that his sister would **not** have bothered to have put him respectfully under the ground **at all** — So wrathful was she about the missed carnival!

Democritus passed away in 370 B.C. and as they say in Ireland; we will never see his like again!

Summer

Summer Time in Athens — and the Living was Easy.

The Sophists come to town.

Socrates is murdered by the State.

CHAPTER 7

PHILOSOPHY GOES COMMERCIAL WITH THE SOPHISTS

The Thinking Shops open up in Athens.

Athens grew exceedingly rich in the time of Pericles 463-431 B.C., and historically speaking, the 5th century became termed the 'Golden Age' of the Athenians, who built up great economic wealth from trade; on top of the initial nest-egg of loot which they had commandeered from the defeated Persians after having finally put paid to any Eastern threat at Marathon (on land) and Salamis (on sea) in 480. Along with this fiscal wealth, Athens now began to develop a tremendous political power in the Greek World, and by a series of treaties which they forged between, (or forced upon) other Greek City-States, they had soon become the 'Big Brother' of the Hellenic World and the leading light of Hellas. Athens in fact, was all set to begin the Peloponnesian War. The bit was already between her teeth. She had dealt with the Persians — Now she would deal with the Greeks! She would show them which City-State was superior to all others, and which City-State deserved to rule supreme. The time for Greek Unification was now at hand; as far as the Athenians were concerned.

From all over the Greek world; from Ionia, Thrace, Italy, and even Sparta; people flocked to Athens. They had to. Their own areas had been bankrupted in the recent wars, and Athens was the only place where the money was and the jobs were. Athens had finally grown-up, and had developed a new mercantile economy, and because of this new economy, a new class of wealthy merchants also began evolving. A new class who were in need of education, or at least the veneer of cultivation and learning. — And in the rest of impoverished Greece there were scores of well educated young men from *decayed* Gentry families, who could, and would, supply just this product. It is the same old story the whole world over, and it continues 'ad infinitum' to this day. We have numerous examples in history of the enlightenment of the rude new conquering class being undertaken by the enfeebled and dying old former elîte. From 146 B.C. onwards the cultivated Greeks would educate the barbaric Romans; and after A.D. 1917, the Russian emigres (sporting diamond tiaras, and lengthy titles) would have to earn their living by teaching languages and the 'niceities of etiquette' to the less cultured, in lands other than their own. These are but a couple of instances.This education process is happening all the time, and has been happening all through history; because no matter how distasteful the task; the struggle for survival must go on; and the fallen aristocrats have no other choice but to pin up their fraying skirts and to hop to; and to make the best of it among their crude, New Rich, masters.

So, into Athens came the Sophists, (the word means the 'Wise', and at that time it was not thought a derogatory title, until Plato saw fit to inject some venom into the pronunciation of it), and they were educationists, or nomad teachers from the once great, but now eclipsed Greek colonies of Asia Minor. And they looked ever so slightly down their noses at their richer and newer kith and kin, and felt no compunction whatsoever in setting the morality of the Athenians on its collective head. The Sophists were not worried about how their teachings would pollute the pure bucolic air of Athens, nor of how their education might attack the traditions or morality, (whatever that word **really** meant — as the Athenians were far from puritanical!) of the State. They opened up their Very Hard Thinking Shops as Aristophanes was to describe them in his play "The Clouds", and in which he mercilessly attacked the new philosophical movement; the Sophists in general; and Socrates in particular. — And their Athenian students became sceptical, and cynical about life; due to this new knowledge now being imparted to them; and they proceeded (as all the youth do), to mock their elders; to kick over the traces; and to Challenge the System. A long standing argument now began to ensue between 'Nature' on the one hand, and 'Convention' and 'Morality' on the other; and the worship of the Olympic God System was rejected as mere superstitious rubbish by these young Athenian students. The Athenian grey beards and presbyters however, charged that the Sophists taught unscrupulous individualism. All of which is a load of unmitigated rubbish, as education does not produce this, or any other mental attitude, if the political, economic, social, and, moral conditions of a State, do not encourage it as well! And anyway, how much influence does the average teacher hold over a student? Almost none, I hear all the teachers of the world chorus fretfully. And it is unfortunately true that no matter what morality a teacher tries to pound into a child's head, either the parent, or the society, always manages to destroy it, or, to tear it out! But then, it is a favourite theory of the populace that everything wrong with the current younger generation has its roots in the school room — People need Scape-Goats — all the time!

The Sophists became the Athenian Scape-Goats also, and they were charged with causing their students to adopt a Broad Cosmopolitanism, along with Unscrupulous Individualism — which really meant, among other things; that the youth became tired of fighting wars for their Elders and Betters, and therefore decided that it was much more sensible to stay at home like the presbyters, and to make some money selling their country out to the highest bidder. It is interesting to note (and it may be instructive as well!) that at **no time** in Athenian history was there ever a **lack** of Traitors. Someone, somewhere or other, always had some particular axe to grind, and he then invariably and resolutely ground it, by bringing invading troops through the secret mountain passes, or by speaking on behalf of some other acquisitively intentioned out-sider. Truly, the Athenians didn't need the Sophists to teach them how to betray their State — they had already been using the recipe for treachery, (and with much success) for donkeys years!

The Assembly however, decided that the Logic and Rhetoric of the Sophists (the two subjects taught most assiduously by them) were being used for legal chicanery, and political demagogy, and that philosophy had become a danger to the State; and a threat to the new urban residents of the Athenian Democracy.

Naturally this worrisome social movement and unrest which was beginning to shake Athens, really had its roots in the topsy-turvy social conditions following the Greek Persian Wars, with some people growing rich very quickly; others growing poor — equally rapidly; and refugees; and the dispossessed; widows, orphans, slaves, and bankrupts; thronging the City. Take all these factors into consideration and you will immediately find the ingredients necessary for a political bonfire. Education now became a 'must' for everyone, and education became the means to free oneself; or at least, to enable oneself to carry out more pleasant and congenial work if one happened to be a slave; or, to avoid the decline into poverty and bankruptcy if one were free. It was a common custom in Greece at that time for Freemen who went bankrupt, to sell themselves into slavery, in order to pay their debts. (And don't we do the same thing ourselves nowadays when we work for others? Slavery still exists; but in another guise!) The Sophists supplied this much needed education, and they supplied it on a grand scale with mass production and assembly line students, and it was an education to suit all tastes, and all pockets. And they enhanced Athena with an entirely new commercial process, with the creation of their Thinking Shops; when hitherto all knowledge and cultivation had only been for the very rich and old — the jealously guarded province of the Establishment "Eupatrid" Families.

But the majority of leading citizens condemned the Sophists, and commenced blaming all the immorality and violence, and sexual libertariaism of the society on their teaching. This is quite a ridiculous proposition if you think about it — Could the rise in Fascism in Germany prior to the 2nd World War, be laid at the door of the teachers — rather than at the portals of the Political and Economic Leaders of the Society? Is it really in our schools that the moral climate of a nation grows? Speaking as a teacher, I think not. But Socrates condemned the Sophists as "prostitutes of Wisdom" and for selling education; and Plato thought that they were opportunists who contributed to the delinquency of the Athenian minors; and Aristophanes thought that they were all intellectual elitists and humbugs, and described Socrates as a hypocrite, also, because Aristophanes said, that **that** saintly gentleman was no different from a Sophist himself! So, everyone seems to have been against them! All in all though, it appears to me that what was really riling everyone, was the fact that **Some** of the Sophists, seemed to be **making money** — and a rich school-teacher is a universally disliked individual, and obviously a strange anti-natural hybrid which is an abomination to all normal people! In truth though, this must surely be a unique period, **and**, the only time in history, when teachers anywhere, **ever managed** to gain a little filthy lucre! Socrates however, held that education should be entirely free. Which is all well and good, but how were the teachers to stay alive when the State wasn't paying them? And anyhow, Socrates wasn't short of a crust of two himself! And it is truly amazing, that whereas everyone acknowledges that they must pay, or work, for food; somehow or other, they seem to feel, that education, (being an abstract, and not something which they can put into their stomachs) should, on the contrary — be handed to them on a silver plate, and 'gratis'.

Plato also criticized the Sophists and their propensity for making a buck, (but then he was another independently wealthy person), and Isocrates (another Thinking Shop Merchant who began an institute for Rhetoric in 391 B.C. and who looked on himself as a King-Maker or Producer of Politicians) also commenced his great career with a speech severely castigating the Sophists. He thereby earned himself a certain degree of fame and popularity which helped launch him on his way. In fact, he (Isocrates) publicly reproved the Sophists so much, that in no time at all, he was charging 1,000 drachmas for a course of instruction in the "Art of Rhetoric and Public Speaking" —probably a Greek version of "How to Win Friends and Influence People!" Truly, some people will jump on any band-wagon, or horse, in order to win the race, and Isocrates was hardly an impecunious beggar, or impoverished ascetic, himself!

Later still, Aristotle defined the Sophist as a person who is "only eager to get rich off his apparent wisdom", and he accused Protagoras, one of the leading Sophists of "promising to make the worse appear the better reason".

So, everyone decided that whatever it was that was wrong in the State of Athens (not Denmark — apologies to Shakespeare!) it was wrong because of the Sophists; and they started sharpening up their blades in order to cut the throats of their Scape-Goats on the altar of public opinion. Unfortunately however, the knives fell down on Socrate's wind-pipe instead; and the Sophists, on the whole, escaped unscathed.

And what was this pure and punctilious Athens like, which the Sophists seemed so hell-bent on contaminating? Well! In Athens the Free Citizens numbering about 43,000 (mostly men of substance, and some traders and artisans as well) had the vote, and life was **very democratic** for them; while the women, metics, (foreigners — the word 'metoikoi' meant "sharing the house", in Greek) and worker slaves, numbering 315,000 (28,600 Metics, and 115,000 Slaves, and the number left over equalling the women and children) **did not have the vote**; and life was not so democratic for them of course! And the section without the franchise was growing!

The number of new born UNFREE citizens kept increasing because of the 451 B.C. Law which had been passed allocating the right of citizenship **ONLY** to those born of both an Athenian Father and Mother; therefore 'mixed' marriages, automatically debarred the resulting progeny from Citizenship, and this applied not only to the contemptible *barbarians,* but to Greeks from other City-States as well! Interestingly enough, in 415 B.C. the inverse date, there was a law passed allowing Men to have more than one wife, because after a disastrous war campaign in Sicily against the Carthaginians, the male ratio of Athens was so depleted that the State needed to have the women rounded up and put under **some kind of control** or other. (The women in Ancient Greece were **always** causing trouble!) So they (the City Fathers) arranged for lawful Polygamy in order to keep the Females quiet, and even Socrates availed himself of this opportunity to indulge his patriotic duty to the State by marrying and keeping a second Better-Half!

In Athens, The Father, or Patriarch of the family, also had the right to voluntarily limit his house-hold as well, and this he often did by exposing (that is putting the new-born babe outside to die from the elements) his unwanted children, and by automatically and invariably exposing the children of his slaves. Nobody expected to feed an extra mouth for nothing! Generally the poor mites were left in the grounds of the temples and the romantic night air of Athens must have been continually rent with the howls of starving and protesting babies. History has mentioned that the Spartans practised 'Exposure' as a State Collective Idea, but it tends to over-look the fact that the Athenians practised it just as readily as an Individualistic Form of Economy, and to prevent social pressure arising from the undesirable members of the group. It must be noted however that Nature definitely hates a vacuum, and often these left-over, and left-out children were picked up by some enterprising gentlemen who then brought them up in order to sell them as slaves at a future date. In Life there are always some people who can turn up money under any circumstances, and with any unpromising type of material as well! — and make a profit from anything also!

So in the Athenian Patriarchal Society, this Father (Patriarch indeed!) of the family, might take a couple of wives; discard his undesirable seed; (and the seedlings of his slaves) and if he still felt in need of diversion he might visit the cheap "Pornai" of Piraeus (generally these were Oriental prostitutes who were reserved for Sailors and the Lower Social Orders) in their rather common and vulgar brothels which had Phallic Symbols outside the doors — in place of our modern red-lights in windows. Or, he could hire some "Auletrides", or flute-players, who were rather like the "geishas" of Japan, or the "Entertainers" of the modern Stag party. (History does not bother to inform us whether the "Auletrides" also leapt out of tops of cakes!) Or, better still, he could take home a couple of concubines or so, in order to warm his feet in the cold winter months, and to fan his fevered brow in the summer. On top of all this Consumer Delight and wide range of choice, the Athenian Man about Town could avail himself of the services of the "Herairai" — or Companions; who were also prostitutes, but slightly more sophisticated versions of this ancient product — with a little more education, (sometimes a whole lot more!) and possessed of much more expensive, and discriminating tastes! Indeed the Man of the House-hold might stay out all night; drink and carouse with the boys; and make love to them as well, (for sexual inversion was not despised!) But it was a different matter for his poor unfortunate wife, or wives; and in the words of Thucydides, an Historian 471-399 B.C. "The name of a decent woman, like her person, should be shut up inside her house." And furthermore, Thucydides added, that "a woman's best fame is to be as seldom as possible mentioned by men, either for censure or for praise". So that put the lid on that! And woe betide anyone standing in the path of the magnificent Lord of the Manor. And God help the woman who so much as thought, of crossing her thresh-hold! There was segregation of the sexes everywhere anyway, and the majority of women were both uneducated and miserable, and occupied mainly in sitting in their own quarters at the back of the house. They hardly ever went out — except — to visit relations. When this did occur, they were always heavily veiled so that nobody could actually see them. And all in all, the Lot of Women, in the Athenian Golden Age, was **not** a happy one! Also they were generally married by arrangement, and even had to supply a dowry, in order to get a husband; and in the words of Medea, in one of Euripides' plays, "A Woman has to buy her Master". But the system worked perfectly well for the Men, (as of course it was supposed to do, for they were the ones who had invented it; or devised the whole scheme to begin with!) And as Demosthenes said, "We have courtesans for the sake of pleasure, concubines for the daily health of the body, and wives to bear us lawful off-spring, and to be the guardians of our homes."

In comparison with the virtuous women, the "Hetairai" at least led exciting free lives, and they even took courses in philosophy from the Sophists, and some of them were also able to indulge in mental activities which were not deemed fitting, for a **good woman**. The Hetâirai were naturally bound by law to distinguish themselves from their worthier sisters, and so wore special floral robes, and generally they dyed their hair blond; and at the theatre, or in the festivals, they sat in specially reserved seats. They drank, and talked, and got paid for having to amuse and to tolerate the men, and one of the most capable "Madams" of the period was Aspasia, (the Mistress of Pericles) and she became a leading political and educational figure in Athens. Meanwhile the goodly matrons sat home alone, bleaching their hair in private, (copying the Hetairai you notice!) trying on various primitive forms of corsetry; and attempting to reconcile themselves to their boredom, while experimenting in cosmetics, (kohl for the eyes, white lead for the skin and rouge and lipstick as well!) plus a little sexual inversion on the side! Most women in Athens in fact, seemed to prefer each other, for love-making — perhaps, due to the lack of men, (or, **interested men**) they had to! We should all remember what it was that Democritus said, regarding Necessity etc........ And incidentally, female inversion was not regarded as something monstrous, either! Homosexuality was the "IN" thing, in Athens, in those days.

And what about the slaves? Well, they poor things worked unceasingly from sun-up to sun-down. And in the Laurium silver mines they never saw the sun at all! But, not to worry, most of them never lasted more than a couple of months anyway! In fact the turnover in slaves in the silver mines was quite fantastic, and 20,000 or so, worked continuous 10 hours shifts day and night, as the Greeks were very keen on maintaining High Production Levels! — And other slaves in the City and country areas had sixty or so days (Holy Days) of Festivities to look forward to each year, when, if they were especially **unlucky**, or, **lucky**; (depending entirely on how one viewed the situation of the slave) they might actually become an **integral part** of these festivities, and might be fed to the Gods in some obscure and brutal fashion — in order that they should atone for the sins of their masters! (Human Sacrifice in the Classical World actually continued in Arcadia up until the 2nd century A.D. — but before the Birth of Christ, the number of scape-goats executed during times of plague, war, or crisis, was positively enormous. One account in fact of the martial campaigns of Hannibal, has a description of him building a pyramid fire of burning bodies which was kept alight fiercely, and continually, up until the very end of the battle!) And Aristophanes in the Golden Age complains of the streets of Athens being crammed full of people and animals, all marching to their deaths at splendid efficiently arranged public executions. After all, as the average Athenian thought, there was no sense in keeping a dog unless you whipped him everytime you were in a bad temper; in order to release your frustration; as it were. Actually though it must be recorded that the Athenians were, on the whole, very kind to their animals; and in fact they thought a great deal more of them — than they did of their slaves. In this respect the Athenians could be likened to another race of people in our days whom the Author has in mind, but whom she thinks quite possibly she might be wiser not to mention; and therefore she will leave this matter for the Reader to figure out for himself!

And if these slaves were lazy or rebellious they could be punished, and tortured; but **not killed** — not privately anyway — only, in a Public spectacle; or, by order of the State — when they would then be cudgeled to death; or thrown over a cliff; or suffer something equally spectacular and active. Death by Hemlock was reserved for the 'People of Means', and it was considered far too pleasant and passive a way for the base unfortunates of society to go! Slaves were also seldom imprisoned, as they were far too valuable an asset to be wasted in a life of idle contemplation behind bars. And, as it was taken for granted that all slaves lied, (or **would** lie, if given the opportunity) when they were called as witness in legal cases; they were automatically tortured; in order to wring the truth from them. No matter what the Slaves said, it had to accompanied by blood on their brows, and tears in their eyes — otherwise it wasn't considered worth hearing! Their breeding was also carefully regulated as we noted earlier, and they could not give evidence, or bear witness against their owners, either, in Court; or, at Judgements. Speaking up for themselves; or, against, and down for their Owners; definitely brought on the Death penalty, every time! Their only 'out' was to flee to a temple and to offer themselves there for the use of the particular God or Goddess. But in the case of Males, that generally meant castration; in order to join the priesthood. And that little operation was carried out under exceptionally bloody circumstances. In the case of runaway Female slaves however, they were forced to join the 'girls' of Aphrodite, and to supply a little "erotica" in the State Prostitution scheme.

So all in all, the fate of the slave was definitely not something to be envied; and in this writer's eyes, it left much to be desired. And I cannot for the life of me see why they were all complaining about the Sophists having destroyed the morality of Athens, when it seems quite obvious that the Democratic Athenians couldn't scrape up a cent's worth of virtue between them.

And now, after all this criticism of those 'Sacred Cows' of History, the Athenians; let us finally get down to a close look at the Sophists themselves.

As education had become the 'established thing', and the Rich, in the Assembly, as well as in the Trials, **needed** to speak well; to be able to use logic; and to look intelligent; there was created therefore, a demand for Oratory, Letters, Grammar, Logic, Science, Philosophy, and Statesmanship. The Sophists; this group of wandering gypsy-like scholars; equalled 'Instant' Knowledge in applying all the above. They actually referred to themselves as "Sophistai" i.e. teachers of wisdom, and they guaranteed to turn a sow's ear into a silk purse, every time! The cost of their services depended on their individual skill and reputation, and no doubt, **their self-confidence**! Most of all however, it probably depended on how much they could manage to squeeze out of the pockets of the new self-conscious and new rich merchants of Athens.

Two of the most famous Sophists of this period were Protagoras of Abdera, Thrace, (481-411 B.C.) and Gorgias of Leontine, Sicily, in Italy (485-380 B.C.) Both of these gentlemen charged approximately 10,000 drachmas per student, per course of instruction; while less famous teachers of the period charged more modestly. Prodicus another Sophist, for example, was known to let people in to pick up the pearls of wisdom which dropped from his lips, for as little as one to five drachmas admission, (poor fellow!) — and slaves, Hetairai, and **even Good Women**, all ventured through his doorway. He must have been something like the modern chain-store, in this production of cheap education for his day and age, and was truly in advance of his time — poor 'five and dime' Prodicus!

Protagoras also was a regular education machine in himself, and was well known and influential in Athens, which he visited frequently and systematically, teaching courses in the following:-

1. Prudence in Private and Public Matters (whatever that might have meant)
2. Orderly Management of Home and Family (obviously aimed at the Female members of the audience)
3. Rhetoric and Persuasive Speaking
4. The Ability to Understand and to Direct Affairs of State (probably useful for everyone — and what's more we could maybe do with this nowadays as well!)

And along with these he offered the usual subjects such as:- Grammar, Logic, Philosophy etc. One might even say that Protagoras was running a masculine and mental version of the Charm School for Debutants, and obviously his 'Finishing School' was a big hit with everyone — at the beginning that is!

When pupils were very poor, Protagoras said that he would agree to take them for a lower fee if they, (the students) would swear before a sacred shrine that they could not afford to pay more. This seems to have been a rather dangerous idea however, because Protagoras' main contention was that there **were no Gods**, and that Sacred Shrines were therefore **not sacred**! He is described; this atheist; as the first teacher in Greece "to arm disputants with the weapon of Sophism", that is, to instruct in the ability to out-argue one's opponent, irrespective of whether one's argument is honest or not! And he was also the "first to invent the Socratic Argument" in logic, which good old Socrates simply plagiarised, and which even later, Plato used self-righteously for his own benefit, while all the time loudly denouncing it.

This very same Sophist was the first to found European Grammar, and Philology; to distinguish the three genders of the noun, (Male, Female and Neuter) which in consequence made all English speaking students of European languages develop headaches in confusion and frustration. (I hear a chorus of sighs throughout the world from failed linguists, do I not?) And he also defined certain tenses and moods of the Verb, such as the Present, the Past, the Accusative, and the Subjunctive. Doubtless everyone was using these verb tenses long before Protagoras came on the scene, but after he had finished telling them what they were in fact actually doing, (albeit unconsciously!) they became so confused, that they could never get a sentence out of their mouths after that, without muddling themselves up, and wondering what they were saying; and how hitherto; they had ever managed to speak at all! Most Grammar teachers have a similar affect on students throughout the world, and the Author speaks from experience in this matter, having muddled a good few students herself in her time. Learning the rudiments of grammar, I think, can probably be compared to the fate of either falling into the "Void" of Democritus, or into the "Black Pit" of Nietzsche; and to drowning miserably and painfully in stuttering, verbal inarticulation, within a sea of treacherous participles!

Unlike the Ionian Philosophers however, Protagoras was less interested in things, than in thoughts, i.e. in the process of sensation, perception, understanding, and expression; and as Parmenides of Elea had positively rejected sensation as a guide to Truth, so Protagoras accepted sensation as the **Only** guide to Truth; and he rejected just as positively, any, and every, suprasensual or transcendental, reality. Moreover, in order to make sure that he could never be proven to be wrong, Protagoras stated that there was no such thing as, **Absolute Truth**. Contradictory assertions, he said, could be equally true for different people at different times. (Which seems very logical, and very clever also, and how can anyone find fault with this little philosophy? But naturally, the Athenians managed to!)

"All Truth, Goodness, and Beauty are relative and subjective," said Protagoras. "Man is the measure of all things — of those that are, that they are; and of those that are not, that they are not." All of which is a highly complex and loquacious way of saying, "I don't know what the answer is." The main trouble with the Sophists and the reason why the Athenians got so mad at them, was that by the time they had finished giving you an answer such as "I don't know", (dressed up in all its finery of verbs, and nouns, alliteration, litotes, and hyperbole etc.) the questioner had long forgotten what the original query had been, and in consequence, went home sadly and slowly; shaking his aching head. No sireee! There was no getting away from it — you just couldn't beat those Sophists nohow! said the Athenians, standing disconsolately in the market place, and spitting reflectively in the dirt. They could talk the hind leg off a mule, and then some!

Protagoras symbolized the new spirit of Humanism and Relativism then sweeping Athens, with his terrifying declaration that, "Man is the measure of all things"; and under this onslaught, all the established truths (like the Religious Establishment and the Class Establishment) slowly began to crack. The supernatural forces of Social Order had finally started to break — Individualism had found a voice at last — And logical, reckoning Man, stood up, and took a new, cold, look at his surroundings; and disdainfully surveyed the Myths of the past, which had fettered his legs, and kept him in a prison of old concepts and primitive lies.

But alas! Doom rides swiftly and unfailingly upon the heels of success, and at the home of a Free Thinker of Athens, one Euripides, (not the Dramatist) Protagoras went too far one evening, and read aloud his latest treatise and statement on the Olympic Religious System. "About the Gods," said Protagoras, "I cannot know that they exist, or that they do not exist; the obscurity of these matters and the shortness of human life are impediments to such knowledge."

The Athenian Assembly, horrified at this sacrilegious outrage; (how they found out what was being said behind closed doors is a little bit of a mystery — or was this the first "Leak" in history?) and most of all, they were quite frankly disturbed, at the blatant overtness of the crime — (fancy people daring to say such things in the privacy of their own houses!) immediately banished Protagoras; ordered the confiscation of his writings — and then publicly burned his books in the market place.

Protagoras, it is said, fled to Sicily, in order to escape the Hemlock, and quite possibly it might have been something nastier, **in his case**! — Unlike Socrates, Protagoras had few friends, and almost no circle of influence; as he; like most of the other philosophers, didn't come from Athens. In fact the only two philosophers to be actually born in that city, were Socrates and Plato, both of whom the Athenians probably looked upon as a disgrace to the Athenian merchant tradition. (After all what else could a failed business-man become — but, a philosopher!) On the way to Italy however, the ship in which Protagoras was travelling, sank; (the Captain must have been in the pay of the Athenian Assembly me thinks!) and he drowned. And may the story of Protagoras, and of his life and death, be a lesson to all Humanists, and Relativists everywhere!

Regarding this Hemlock which was dispensed with such regularity in those days, it must be noted that it was really quite a pleasant way to go; (if indeed you had to go at all!) because, after drinking the mixture, (and within a very short period of time) the body began to become paralysed from the feet upwards; and by the time the poison reached the heart; all one's earthly troubles were over! On the whole, it was definitely preferable to cudgeling; and any other little 'transmigration crossings-over' which the Assembly often arranged for 'dissidents'.

Gorgias of Leontini in Sicily was another very well-known Sophist, and supposedly he was the greatest teacher of Rhetoric in Athens, or indeed, in the entire Greek World. He also carried on, or dabbled in, the sceptical revolutionary thought of his day, but; wisely for him, he spent most of his time **outside** Athens, and **never** left himself open to charges of impiety and such like. And I begin to wonder if maybe the real reason most of the scholars dislike the Sophists so much, is because the Sophists **refused to be made into martyrs**; as there is unfortunately, a rather primitive desire in even the best of us, to wash ourselves in the blood of the Lamb and to cater to our sadistic urges to witness suffering and death. Perhaps this reluctance on the part of the Sophists to be sacrificed, is the real reason for their unpopularity in history books. Perhaps this desire to see the good or the innocent crucified for our sake is even some type of suppressed sexuality? Who knows? But, there is most definitely, an unhealthy, and decidedly morbid, desire in most people, to enjoy a really good tragedy! And the sacrifice of Prometheus is possibly the greatest tragedy of all — and possibly that is why it is so popular, and so often repeated in history. And the people **never** attempt to save their Prometheans from the ruthless Zeus authoritarian characters of this world.

But enough on this fascinating subject, and back to Gorgias.

His career was that of a subtle blend, or combination, of philosopher and Statesman, and it must be said that he managed to combine or to blend the two very capably. Born in 483 B.C. in Leontini in Sicily, he studied philosophy and rhetoric with Empedocles (you remember! the one who maintained that he was a God) and he, (Gorgias) became a famous orator in his native Sicily, and then became equally famous as a teacher of oratory, as well —which was an even greater achievement. Despite what Mr. George Bernard Shaw had to say about teachers, it is definitely far harder to get someone to understand a thing — and to get **them** to do it well; than it is, to perform the thing yourself — As that snappy-mouthed gentleman would have known, if he had ever tried teaching anyone how to write! —And most of the Middle-Class swear that it is an **impossible** experience, trying to teach their servants how to mop the floor correctly — so therefore, teaching is quite **obviously, a Talent, all on its own**!

In 427 B.C. Gorgias was sent as the Leontini Ambassador to Athens, and he attended the Olympic Games in 408 where he made a superb speech to the Greeks about uniting all their efforts *(about uniting themselves!)* for Peace — Internal Order — and for External War against the Persians. In this performance Gorgias set the tone for all those other dreary orations which we have to sit through at the commencement of all athletic events, and in which some or other well-known Establishment Personality drones on about the true spirit of Peace, and Co-operation between nations and so on; (and to which no one in the audience pays a blind bit of attention!) The original Olympic Games incidentally, were in reality only an excuse for showing off the best warriors in everyone's army, and for exercising the artillery, (throwing the discus, and slinging the shot etc!) They were the Greek proto-type of the modern military displays which we enjoy today, with row upon row of tanks rumbling past in the streets; soldiers fainting in the sun; little children waving flags; and **everyone** getting their blood-lust up and marching in two-four rhythm around the place. Furthermore for your information, at the original Olympic Games, married women were forbidden to attend, (too much Male pulchritude on display probably!) and so the good ladies had their own athletic events which were held under the auspices of Hera.

But the Olympics were definitely a chance for Gorgias to advertise himself, and therefore, having given his own commercial; or blown his own trumpet, so to speak; he took up travelling from City to City in order to eke out a very respectable living. And everywhere he went, students flocked to him in gay abandon — "Have Rhetoric — Will Travel" was Gorgias' motto.

His book "On Nature" (**another** one, you gasp!) held three startling propositions.

1. Nothing exists.
2. If anything existed it would be unknowable.
3. If anything were knowable, the knowledge of it could not be communicated from one person to another.

Now perhaps you can see why it was wise that Gorgias kept on the move the way he did. The Athenian temper was well known, and it had a very short fuse!

These propositions of his aimed to poke fun at, and, to discredit, the transcendentalism of Parmenides; and they really meant:-

1. Nothing exists beyond the senses.
2. If anything existed beyond the senses then it would be unknowable because all knowledge is acquired through the senses.
3. If anything suprasensual were knowable then the knowledge of it would be incommunicable, since all communication is through the senses.

With these propositions we also have the start of the form of the Syllogism of Logic, as used by Aristotle, among others, in order to prove a point of argument by disproving every other point of argument. Or, (in order to define it scientifically) we have two given premises, which in turn, prove a third — no matter how ridiculous that premise may be.

For example:- Socrates is a man — Major Premise
All men are mortal — Minor Premise
Therefore Socrates is mortal — Conclusion.

And the above Syllogism ("Syl" meaning "to take", and "Logo" meaning "reason" — therefore "to take reason") is an example of Deduction, or of a General Truth leading to a Particular Case. (We can also have Induction; which is proving a point by a Particular Case, leading to a General Truth.) And the Syllogism is a clever little thing, but it is not infallible, and **definitely** not to be trusted, as one can prove all sorts of illogical and irrational rubbish in this way. For example:-

1. Enthusiasm means to have a God inside one — Major Premise (This is quite true, as the actual meaning of the word "en theos" in Greek, is "to have a God inside".)
2. My dog is full of enthusiasm — Minor Premise
3. Therefore my dog is inhabited by a God — Conclusion.

You see, you can do all sorts of crazy things with a syllogism, and the above is also an example of the beginnings of "Sorites", or the Chain-Syllogism, which became very popular with the Sophists. This Chain-Syllogism was the fore-runner to Tertullian and his famous saying "Credo quia absurdum", and that's exactly what the Sophists did with this form of logic. Let us look at another example. The cat is a quadruped, the quadruped is an animal, the animal is a substance; therefore a cat is a substance! Or, another case of illogical logic; a man with only one hair is bald, therefore a man with two, three, four, or ten thousand hairs is bald! This is quite comforting to use as a retort if someone comments on your lack of hair, but apart from that convenience, it is quite meaningless; except of course, to proceed by gradual steps from truth to absurdity. But then, maybe the Truth, like most other things in Life, **is Absurd**! (Unfortunately the Author herself seems to have a bad habit of falling into the sin of Sophistry, and perhaps Sociologists could look into this matter in order to discover whether this disease is actually caused by the profession of teaching, or is due to enduring a long period of living below the Poverty Belt!)

Apart from "On Nature", there are no fragments or remains of Gorgias' work, and we just have to take as "Gospel", the remarks made by other people attesting to his golden mouth. Personally, the Writer wonders if Gorgias and Empedocles, who both hailed from Sicily, had any Celtic blood in their veins, because even in ancient Greece (not to mention Rome) the Celts were looked on as the finest orators in the Ancient World; i.e. from about 500 B.C. onwards. This skill of theirs was due to the fact that their cultural and tribal traditions and education, were handed on orally, as they did not bother to utilize the art of writing until after A.D. 427, about the time of Patrick's visit to Ireland. Consequently the Celts were past masters at spinning a fine tale, and at coaxing a bird out of a bough, and at putting the Land-Lady off the scent; and as Sicily had been affected by Celtic invasions around 400 B.C., one wonders if in fact there wasn't some sort of intermingling of blood and social traditions going on, which helped to produce this upsurge in Sicilian loquacity. But I will leave this point to the dedicated, serious scholars of antiquity to investigate —should there be any who happen to be reading this book — a proposition which I find highly unlikely!

Gorgias though, retired after his long years of service to the ignorant and the unvocal, and after making a (some say sizeable, others only moderate) sum of money from his students, he secluded himself in Thessaly and wisely spent his entire fortune, before death could claim him, (or his bickering relations could stake a share in his worldly wealth.)

He lived to the grand old age of either one hundred and five, or one hundred and eight; and even at the end of his life he was reputed to be as healthy as a boy, and also, to be possessed (so say the historians) of the use of his senses like any hearty youth. I could not discover whether this referred to all his senses equally or not, and neither could I find out to what he attributed his longevity. Possibly he also ate honey in liberal amounts, (that does seem to have been the fashion those days — possibly because there wasn't any sugar), and possibly also, he abstained from beans. I do hope that this book is not going to put some famous canning company out of business!

Another Sophist, Hippias of Elis in Sparta, (and who says that the Spartans were all illiterate bores who did nothing but wage war?) was a complete walking university of his time. He taught the following:- (or at least he offered the courses– rather like some impecunious institutes of our own days who are desperate for business!) Astronomy, Maths, Geometry, Poetry, Music, Oratory and History; and as well he kept busy lecturing on Literature, Morality and Politics. And, in his **spare time**, he compiled a complete list of the victors from all the preceding Olympic Games. (Poor Fellow! He really had to work hard for a living!) When he wasn't teaching, he spent his time protesting against the degenerate artificial city life, and he contrasted Nature with Law, and called Law a tyrant over Mankind. And on top of all this Liberal Social Consciousness activity, he even made his own ,clothes and decorative jewellery! Quite obviously they broke the mould after Hippias was born — they definitely don't make teachers like that nowadays!

Other smart, scornful Sophists of the Age included Antiphon of Athens, who defined Justice as that which is expedient; and Thrasymachus of Chalcedon who is the first person (supposedly) to have identified Right with Might, and to have satirically commented that the overwhelming success of villains in this life, cast doubt upon the existence of the Gods in the next! When the Athenians invaded Melos during a period of the usual Greek internecine strife, and put the entire Male population to death; Thrasymachus (unlike other Liberals, and educated people) was not horrified in the least, but merely yawned and said sagaciously, that the Athenians were simply proving his point, and that they were practising pure relativism in morality! Thucydides the historian, said, that the Sophists said, "In the discussion of human affairs, the question of Justice only enters where there is Equal Power to enforce it — the Powerful exact what they can, and the Weak grant what they must", and to the pleas of Melos' Males the Athenians coldly replied, "If you were as strong as we are, you would do as we do." So the Sophists maintained that they were simply "telling it as it was", and that they were in no way advocating immorality; as **that** had already existed, **long before they had arrived on the scene**!

There was even a Sophist Rhetorician, Alcidamas (a disciple of Gorgias of Sicily) who wandered the streets of Greece preaching against slavery. "God has sent all men into the world free, and Nature has made no man a slave," said Alcidamas, and his words bear a strong resemblance to the thoughts expressed by Rousseau in the turbulant period of the French Revolution. The Athenians of course, turned their collective deaf ear, and went imperturbably on about their business. They fully realised that the System couldn't survive without slavery — at least, **their Standard of Living couldn't survive without it**! And the idea of abolishing it, seemed so ludicrous and unrealistic, that they probably didn't take Alcidamas seriously at all! Doubtless the citizens thought he was demented and suffering from brain-fatigue due to long hours of study, and that is why they overlooked these scandalous declamations of his.

To sum up, the Sophists are those gallant souls responsible for the invention of Grammar and Logic; for having developed the Dialectic; analysed the forms of Argument; and, for having taught men to detect, and to practice, falsehoods in argument (that is, to discern Truth, and to perpetuate Fallacies.) Prose finally became a form of literature in their hands, instead of the customary poetry which was generally used as the conventional form, or vehicle for philosophy; because prior to the Sophists, one had to be a Poet, in order to write Philosophy. Nobody wanted to read it, unless it rhymed!

They analysed everything, and they respected nothing; and no sacred cow was deemed inviolate in their eyes. They absolutely refused to respect traditions that could not be supported by the evidence of the senses, or by the logic of reason; and they began (or rather, continued) a Rationalist Movement among the intellectual and educated classes of Greece, despite the obscurantist ancient faith of Hellas and the Hellenes.

According to Plato they were a disastrous influence, and he said of them, "The common opinion was that the world and all animals and plants and inanimate substances were formed from some spontaneous and unintelligent cause." — Which is generally what we are all agreed on today! But this gentleman in particular, couldn't stand them, as their theories were a slap in the face for the System, the Gods, and the Idealist Philosophers occupied with holding up the System, (like dear old Plato himself!)

The Sophists caused the Greeks, and the Athenians in particular; to discover (albeit unwillingly) their secular origins as people, and to admit the geographical mutability of their morality. That is really what the crime of the Sophists was — Humanist Relativism.

Goethe, the German Dramatist is quoted as saying that "The God to whom a man proves devout, that is his own soul turned inside out." And the "Thinking Shops" which had been set-up in Athens, had made people begin to question exactly who and what their Gods were. This made them all feel a trifle uncomfortable, naturally enough!

The Athenians though were not terribly pleased at the cut and line of their new spiritual apparel, and therefore they decided that a change in fashion was not always a good thing; and that sometimes it is just as beneficial, if not more so, to continue in the garments of yesteryear. But the Sophists had brought them education, and the Athenians had tasted it nonetheless — and now they were choking on it, and wishing to God they could sack the cook! The Scape-Goat, or poisonous Cook, they finally identified in the character of Socrates, and in the next chapter we will discuss this mysterious figure. So the short-lived Summer of Philosophy in Athens was almost drawing to a close, and the death of Socrates would signal the first rains, and the flight of both swallows, and intellectuals, from this Metropolis of Crass-Materialist Merchants. After all, the whole basis of civilization in the Greek World (and it might equally be proposed the foundation of our own 20th century world as well) was resting upon the systematic, and totally accepted social organization of **Slavery**. Slavery in the Ancient World was used as an instrument of expansion; and, as the most important mechanism for accumulating and investing savings in Society. Your average slave was both "moveable Capital" or "collateral" in the Bank, and an immediate solution for any "cash flow" problems which might arise. And here were Sophists like Lycophron questioning the whole structure of Society by making statements such as, "The Superiority of Noble Birth is imaginery, and its prerogatives are based merely upon a word". And even more damaging nationalistically, were the ideas given forth by Antiphon, "as to our natural gifts we are all equal, whether we be Greeks or barbarians". So the Sophists and the Egaliterian Intellectuals and Humanists had to go; and if they had already escaped the wrath of the Plutocrats and the Status Quo lovers; then somebody else would have to be used as the "Whipping Boy". Therefore, Cue — Socrates — on Right of Centre Stage.

CHAPTER 8

WHO IS SOCRATES? WHAT IS HE?

Philosophy comes of age with the martyrdom of Socrates.

And now onto the stage of our drama, steps our Scape-Goat, and premier Philosophic Saint and Martyr — Socrates. And a very mysterious Saint and Martyr of Philosophy he is. In fact one might be forgiven for wondering if indeed he ever existed at all; for, like some other famous characters in the mythology of history; the conditions surrounding him are nebulous, to say the least. But the majority of Scholars assure us that he did exist, and history, as well as philosophy, is neatly ruled off, like an accountant's books, into areas marked, "Before the Birth of Socrates," and, "After the Death of Socrates," and altogether one begins to wonder why they didn't see fit to change the letters B.C. to B.S. (Before Socrates) — and A.D. to A.S. (Anno Socrates), for all the attention paid to this important gentleman. And Philosophy itself is very tidily divided into the Pre-Socratic, and the Post-Socratic periods, although this enigmatical figure, left us not one 'fragment' of his work. It seems however, that he was so busy running around and discussing the 'Soul' with everybody, that he never found the time to sit down and put pen to paper, or stylus to papyrus. But, **everybody** who is **anybody** in Greek History from this period, protests to having bumped into him, at some time of other, and they all appear to be trying to outdo themselves, and each other, in the number of times they actually spoke to him; observed him in a shop; saw him passing in the road; or got drunk at the same table with him. It is indeed truly astounding, how a man of whom so many people knew, and of whom so many talked about; left behind for posterity, **not one single scrap of actual concrete evidence of his existence!**

Socrates of course, is known to us chiefly from the writings of Plato, who is responsible (like an agent for a Star) for having built this philosopher up, and for having presented him to the world as such a saintly and wise person. Practically every second sentence in Plato's Dialogues refers to Socrates; or, is attributed to Socrates. But even Diogenes Laertius said that Socrates accused Plato of inventing things about him. But then — how is one to trust Diogenes Laertius either?

It must be observed that Plato developed (if he didn't invent!) the Socratic Myth; and all the Dialogues include Socrates talking to some other philosopher, and giving his (Socrates' or Plato's — that is the question!) opinions; and, constantly dispproving everyone else's. In the manner of the development of a Philosophic Bible, Plato — like a Saint Peter — establishes the Socratic and True Philosophy in the eternal city of

Athens; and he traces all other philosophical movements to, or from, Socrates, in a similar procedure to that which developed later in the Christian Faith. Not a single philosopher is ever allowed by Plató, to venture into Athens without first calling on the grand Old Master, and then immediately sitting down to have a good old chin-wag with him over a glass of retsina. Parmenides, Protagoras, Zeno, Meno, Gorgias, Timaeus (a later Pythagorean) and Thrasymachus; along with all the men responsible for the invention of Stoicism, Hedonism and Cynicism etc; — *all* — are observed hammering out philosophical issues with Socrates; gaining from his wisdom; and, coming off second best in any and every argument! — Plus there are a host of political, artistic, and other famous people of the day, continually hopping in and out of Socrates' salon every afternoon for tea; and even Aristophanes, the comedist, continually refers to, and derides Socrates in his plays; *but,* the thought has occurred to the Writer of this Guide that possibly the name "Socrates" was really only a symbol, or nickname which was used to describe the average philosopher; or educationist, of that day. This theory of mine seems a little far-fetched it is true! (and it is only a passing thought) but, as we refer to the average middle of the road, citizen of today, as JOE BLOE, I did wonder if that could possibly have been what the name of "Socrates" actually meant! — in other words your general Sophist, or wise man, or educated and cultivated denizen of Athens, during the Age of Pericles. After all there is so **very little proof** of his having ever been alive — except on the sayso of others! But then, perhaps it is the same for all of us. How many people have actually made themselves immortal, except in the thoughts, conversations, or memories of others? And maybe **this**, is the true message of the Socratic Myth.

With his dialogues however, Plato firmly established the character of Socrates in History, as well as establishing a reputation for himself at the same time, (whilst also managing perhaps, to popularize his views and to lend them authority through the mouthpiece of the "Wisest of the Greeks.") To the up and coming Greek Intellectuals, Socrates (under Plato's direction) became as Sacred, as the Oracle of Delphi, had been to their superstitious forebears. And dare I say, that possibly, the figure of Socrates dances puppet-like to the tune of Plato — as Plato's first talent and love, it must be remembered, was Poetry and Drama, long before he became a philosopher. And he (Plato) was a most skilful writer, and his character sketches of Socrates are masterly prose pieces indeed!

By reading other classical writers from this period we get the definite impression that Socrates was continually on the go, and talking in the Assembly; defending truth and morals; standing up in the theatre and identifying himself during libellous ridicule from Aristophanes; picking up pretty boys in the street; (even a saint must have his failings!) and attending the various Games — as well as continually exchanging words with somebody or other's grandfather every fifteen minutes or so. In fact, one is led to conclude that the average greeting in Athens must not have been "Nice day today!", but, "Seen Socrates yet?" All philosophy is seemingly in debt to him in some way or other, and every school arose due to his guidance and thought; and **everyone of importance in Athens**, either brushed up against him in the crowded streets, or, sat next to him, in the Barber Shop. (And if anyone in Ancient Greece seems not to have known this gentleman, or to have been ignorant of his far-reaching influence — then quite obviously that person is either a charlatan or a liar — and **definitely** not worth bothering about!) And in the Socratic Cult which grew up, regardless of whether Socrates met his death because of the Law, or, because of the People; we can conveniently trace an analogy between his character and the personality of Dionysos, and/or Prometheus. Dionysos was a God who was destroyed by the people, or by the bad forces of Life, but who rose again, while Prometheus was the original God of Civilization or *Christ figure,* who sacrificed himself giving that precious factor, *Fire,* to the World. And Socrates gave his life, and died — in order to live on in the works of other philosophers. It appears therefore that the favourite story of all time in the world — is for someone to take the sins of the world on his shoulders — and to pay the price for everyone else and their sinning! The logic behind the Cult of Scape-Goating is obviously that someone must pay; and, that *that someone* should be the most innocent and sinless; and, if not completely sinless — then he should be, the *'wisest and the best'*. This idea seems to be quite crazy; but as it is still persisting even today, I presume therefore that there must be some good reason for it. But exactly why the innocent must pay for the guilty, I personally, have **never** been able to work out!

Socrates' sayings, (like the differing versions of the Christian Bible) are a great source of dispute and contention, and we have accounts of him by Xenophon an Historian, and by Aeschines a Philosopher, and by Plato, his prize pupil. All these reports disagree with each other in some respect or other, and searching for the truth is a little like looking for a piece of the genuine and original Cross of Jerusalem; and it is as equally time-consuming, and unrewarding, an occupation! Aristoxemus of Tarentum who was on the scene about 318 B.C. said, that **his father** said, that Socrates was a philosopher without education, who was "ignorant and debauched"; and so it seems that Socrates obviously didn't please **everybody**. But still and all, he was quite clearly the most 'talked about' man in town, during his epoch, and it is no wonder that the Powers of the time did away with him. Presumably, they also found him extraordinarily tiresome, and very time-consuming as well!

Anyhow, Socrates was the first Philosopher whom Athens managed to actually produce, and together with Plato, he brings the total number of Thinkers of the City, to a grand total of Two; which is not a lot, when one considers the wealth and influence of Athens in Greek history. So, as the Athenians are rather lacking in ethnic academics, it is really only right that Socrates should be afforded so much time and thought; otherwise it might look rather bad for that city, which is the "Cradle of Democracy".

Socrates' father, supposedly, was a sculptor, and he is said to have carved the "Hermes", and the "Three Graces" which used, at one time, to stand near the entrance to the Acropolis in Athens, but which nowadays, may probably be found (thanks to the special and talented acquisitiveness of Lord Elgin and a certain British Ambassador!) in the British Museum in London. And if the Greeks wish to see their own valuable artefacts and historic relics, then they need only travel to Britain (in the manner of countless Egyptians, Africans and others) in order to enjoy the spectacle of a very upright, moral, and civilization-conscious nation, guarding most zealously, and caring most carefully, for *their very own ancient Greek heritage.*

Socrates' mother is said by some, to have been a mid-wife, and this fits in quite nicely with the story which Socrates told somebody or other, that he was merely continuing his mother's work, by carrying on the job of giving birth; but that in his case, he was helping philosophers to give birth to the ideas conceived in their heads. What a great teacher he must have been! The catalyst behind the Athenian Thinking bodies — the force which created mental conception and drew forth the premature 'brain children' of the age — almost a Prime Mover himself — like the râison d'etre of Aristotle's theory.

Yet another tradition describes Socrates as being the son of a slave, which is pretty improbable; as he once served as a "Hoplite", that is, a soldier, in the army; and all citizens were forced to spend a period in national service or defense of the City-State — but slaves, and metics, were generally not allowed; for the simple reason that the Greeks couldn't trust them **not** to work for the enemy, or, not to **betray the Greeks**. Only in times of absolute crisis as for instance during the Persian Wars, did the Greeks allow *barbarians* into their army; and when this sort of thing happened, they generally promised manumission to slaves who would fight and defend their masters. This tradition of not allowing foreigners into the army, still actually persists in some countries even today, but it certainly was a chink in the armour of the Greeks. They were so chauvinistic a people that they just could not admit; nor could they accept; a foreigner — as an equal. Hence the law of 451 B.C regarding the illegality of marriages contracted between Athenian Citizens and foreigners, including other Greeks; and in general, theattitudeof the Greeks to foreigners was that the aliens were not worthy of Hellenic consideration; and that in all dealings with them, there were no moral obligations of any kind whatsoever! The Romans however, learnt quite a lot from the Greeks' mistakes, and they were a bit more canny in their attitude of welding their Empire together. And they allowed the slave, or non-Roman citizen, to move up the ranks, and to fight and to die for the Roman Empire; and, if the foreigners actually managed to survive the war, why then they were suitably honoured — and generally givenCitizenship. There was always more incentive in the Roman System than in the Greek; but the Greeks preferred to fight, rather than to allow one drop of their blood to become adulterated; and they were as chary of sharing their nationality with barbarians as a connoisseur of fine wine is, of dispensing his old cognac with an alcoholic! All foreigners were "Barbarians" — a term which was really meant as an attempted description of the sound of foreigners speaking their own languages; and it is probably derived from the Sanskrit term "barbara", and the Latin "balbus", meaning stammering; and is closely related to the term "babble" in English, and "bearla" in Irish. So it is altogether highly improbable that Socrates was the son of a barbarian or of a slave; especially as slave babies were generally exposed at birth.

This historically puzzling personality Socrates, who left nothing whatever behind (not even a shopping-list) is also supposed to have inherited a house from his father, and to have had seventy minas a month invested for him by a friend called Crito. Both Socrates and Plato were equally fortunate it seems, in acquiring wealthy and compassionate friends who either lent them money, or invested capital for them. Most ordinary people spend an entire life-time searching for just such companions, and seldom, find so much as a trace of one. Some people in fact, never even manage to find a **dispassionate** friend to pass the time of day with, let alone a wealthy one. Definitely; philosophers get all the breaks! But, apart from this house, and the investment, Socrates was not really rich, but only comfortable; although in many people's eyes nowadays, to own your own house is not exactly classified as living below the poverty belt!

He was also supposed to have paid much attention to his physical well-being, and to have participated both frequently and joyfully, in the past-times of dancing, gymnastics, eating, and drinking his fill. Socrates believed that a 'Wet' soul was preferable to a 'Dry' one on every occasion, and he held that souls, like plants, were in need of a little moisture, from time to time. Obviously he was no Puritan — in contrast to his student, Plato.

From all accounts Socrates made quite a name for himself during the Peloponnesian War 431-404 B.C and in fact, for a philosopher, he was rather an active aggressive type of animal, and he pops up (historically speaking) in quite a number of wars, or battles, including Potidaea 432, Delium 424, and Amphipolis 422 B.C.

At Potidaea he saved the life of Alcibiades, a Politician, General, and sometime Lover of his; and at Delium he was the last Athenian to surrender to the Spartans. **Quite** a military achievement! Also at Potidaea, in between saving the life of Alcibiades, and doing whatever else good soldiers did in those days (eviscerating their enemies and so on) he is supposed to have stood without moving for one whole day and one whole night, musing deeply on some philosophical problem. Truly this man was just too perfect for words. One can forgive him a little sexual inversion surely, because how he managed to stand absolutely still for twenty four hours amidst a raging battle, and **not** get his head lopped off, is a real wonder!! In most of the campaigns Socrates withstood cold, hunger, fatigue, and fear — better than any other man — so they say! Although at Amphipolis, there is actually very little reported about him at all. Perhaps in that particular encounter though, he behaved like any ordinary mortal and typical soldier, and simply spent his time grouching about the cooking; making lewd comments about his commanding officers; shaking with cold and fear; and going to sleep in the middle of his watch. Perhaps!

When not at war, Socrates worked sporadically as a stonecutter and maker of statues, and, as we have noted previously, he was a legal bigamist; due to the Marriage Laws of 415. His first wife Xanthippe seems to have been rather put out by her husband's lack of interest in his family, and, with his failure as a breadwinner; but Socrates never appeared to let her nagging get him down — which goes to show how philosophical he really was! Many a strong man has cut his throat; rather than face a shrewish wife — but not Socrates! No matter what abuse Xanthippe hurled at him, he never let it interfere with his biological rhythm and life-style, and he took absolutely **no notice of her whatsoever**.

This acceptance of polygamy was supposed to have been because of the high mortality rate of the Males during wars, and the consequent frustration of the Females in Athens. But as the Greeks (those who actually survived the wars, anyhow!) had this habit of bringing foreign women back with them as part of their share of the booty — there were always too many women running around the place anyway! And even those women who had husbands, were pretty frustated (on account of their old men's preference for young boys!) so one suspects that this piece of legislation was actually devised for economic reasons primarily. Someone had to be found to support these women somehow or other, otherwise how would the Athenian Assembly have managed to have kept them fed and clothed, and out of the way? And the mental vision of scores of hungry women roaming the streets at night was a quite terrifying thought! — no man's life, or property, would ever have been safe!!

There is a bust of Socrates (or, of someone said to be him) in the Museo delle Terme at Rome. He was, despite his physical fitness, possessed of a rather large paunch, which he attempted to exercise away with dancing — but, as he kept adding to this paunch by drinking, his slimming method was not terribly successful. He was happy enough to own only one shabby robe a year, so they say; and to have preferred bare feet, to sandals. Socrates was definitely not a leading light in the Consumer Society, and perhaps that's why the Athenians decided to rid their city of him — He must have been ruining the economics of the new trading system, and disturbing the Market; in more ways than one! He is alleged to have remarked aloud one day, while walking in that great sacrosanct of merchants, the Agora, "Ah! How many things there are that I do not want!" — and that can hardly have won him friends or influenced people. The citizens suffering from this new Greek disease known as "pleonexia" (meaning 'avarice', or the 'love of more and more') and from the even more serious illness of "chrematistike". (meaning 'the pursuit of riches') could not have felt very comfortable when near this man who kept pointing out to them how ill they were; and how much they were in need of philosophical treatment, in order to keep them from completely succumbing to that fatal condition known as Vulgar Materialism!

As we have observed, Socrates was a keen drinker, and he is reputed to have frequently put many of his companions, both to shame, and, to reclining positions on the floor; and as he believed that alcohol "lulled men's grief to sleep", he often enjoyed parties, and was in consequence, a firm favourite of the "Herairai", and of Aspasia, in particular. He gallantly remarked that he had learnt the art of rhetoric from that fair damsel, though we may suppose that he had really learnt it from Gorgias and Protagoras the Sophists. Whatever the truth of the matter, though, Plato described Socrates as, "the most wise, the most just, and the best of all men", that he had ever known.

Whether or not Socrates had learnt the art of Dialectical Discussion from the Sophists, he certainly employed this skill **against** them, and likewise used it to protect himself from cross-examination, by stating sophistically that he **knew all the questions**, but **none of the answers**. However, the Oracle at Delphi named Socrates as the Wisest Man in all Greece; so there we have it. He **must** have been extremely wise — even the gods of Olympus approved of him! — *at the beginning!*

At the start of his career he loved initiating debates with all and sundry, and he is supposed to have risen early each day, just in order to visit the market, the gymnasium, and the workshops; and in order to engage the honest, hard-working, money-grubbing citizens, whom he found there; in spirited conversations about what was — and what was not. His dialectical procedure was to draw the other person, or persons, out, (he didn't mind how many he took on at one time) with questions; urge them to give definitions and opinions; and then ask them more questions, (in order to make them re-define, and to think still more deeply, and to generally confuse them!) And finally he forced them (when they were too hot and bothered to care any more about anything), to come to the conclusion that he had been wanting them to — in the first place!

All in all, Socrates must have been a great old time-waster, and perhaps that's why the Athenians really "did him in"; and perhaps they shouldn't be criticized unduly for this action of theirs — after all, Time is Money!

According to Plato, there were four main points on which Socrates differed from the Sophists; although, according to Aristophanes there was no difference between Socrates and that other crowd of Academic Charlatans. Anyhow, these four points of difference (according to Plato) were:-

1. Socrates despised rhetoric (although he was not above using his own sneaky version of it.)
2. He wished to strengthen morality (don't we all?)
3. He did not teach any actual subject, but simply examined ideas. (Rather like the wandering Spirit of Philosophy in a physical form — and maybe he was a Saint after all!)
4. He refused to take pay for instruction (this must have endeared him to many hearts, but not necessarily to all, for it is a well-known fact that what you do not pay for in this world, you seldom truly appreciate.) If anyone were to be actually foolish enough to walk around handing out diamonds free of charge to people in the street, it would not be long before the market value of even this commodity would begin to decline, as people would begin muttering suspiciously, "What's wrong with them? Why are we getting them for nothing? They can't be any good!" etc. In other words, you are forced to put a price on an item, in order for people to judge it worthwhile, and therefore quite possibly, if Socrates had charged for his knowledge; instead of giving it away free; the Athenians would have thought twice before ordering him to drink the hemlock. Nobody ever disposes carelessly, of an asset!

But, even though he refused pay (or, didn't ask for any) he managed to survive penury as a teacher because he had rich friends, and because on most occasions, he generally left someone else to pick up the tab for dinner. And his ideas and discussions eventually gave birth, directly or, indirectly, to all the Post-Socratic Schools — Platonism, Cynicism, Stoicism, Hedonism, Epicureanism, and Skepticism. One wonders if perhaps his ideas and discussions drove them all so crazy that they went off in self-defense, and in an attempt to find some logic for themselves; and therefore began their own movements! But historically, Socrates is definitely regarded as the Father of Athenian Philosophy, and he is probably the most well-known of all philosophers — Almost a house-hold name in fact — And yet he left no writings whatsoever!

The supposed Socratic Thought (once again, according to Plato) included the following:-

1. Man's main business was to take care of his Soul. This Soul which had evolved from the 'Psyche', or vapour, believed in by the Ancient Homeric, Achaean Greeks, to the "Divine Fire" or, "Logos" of Heracleitus; (plus the idea of the imprisoned God in the Body concept of the Pythagoreans;) led eventually to Socrates' definition of it. And from Socrates, this Soul was then to proceed, through Plato and the Stoics to the Christian Religion version of same.

2. The World was ruled by Good, Intelligent, and Divine Powers, who ordained everything for the best. This was a type of Predestination Theory and had originated from Parmenides of Elea (— or else it was Plato's ideas which he had transferred to Socrates!) And Predestination is naturally a pretty good theory if you happen to be the 'top dog'; but if you're underneath the pile, and scrambling to get up — then it's not such a comforting notion! Also, Predestination always offers an excuse for why some people should be living off the fat of the land, while others are starving; and it is a doctrine to encourage the Status Quo! Socrates was likewise supposed to have encouraged the blind acceptance of Life, and to have advised everyone to leave everything to the God, or the Gods. (It is a little difficult to make out exactly how many deities Socrates actually believed in, but we will come to that later.)

3. Goodness, according to Socrates, equalled the Knowledge of Goodness, and all Virtue equalled Knowledge. In other words, if you knew what virtue was, then you were Virtuous; and if you didn't know what it was, then you probably weren't — Virtuous that is! All wickedness was deemed by Socrates to be involuntary, and simply due to ignorance. A very simplistic explanation, but doubtless a comforting one for some people.

4. All Virtue was One, and could not be taught. The Socratic Dialogues were specifically designed for the purpose of helping people to look within themselves to discover Truth and Knowledge and Virtue; which were all there inside them all the time, and just waiting to be taken out and used. (This idea is rather similar to Heracleitus' 'Inner Depth' or 'Divine Fire', and it also resembles Bergson's concept of the quality of Intuition.)

Most of all, Socrates was interested in the Soul. Look to your Soul he thought, and everything else will look after itself. Caring for the Soul was quite enough. Socrates made no pronouncements (so far as we can ascertain) on such burning issues as Slavery, War, Justice — or the Cost of Living. And like many a Church Leader of today, he considered that the care of the Soul was the complete straight forward absolute, and simple answer to *all* of Life's problems.

In this pre-occupation of Socrates with the Soul, we realise that Philosophy has moved from Physical, (the case with the Ionians), to Metaphysical (The Italian School), and on finally, to the Ethical. Seemingly at this point in time, philosophy had now come to be used, **not** in order to define what the world actually was; or, what life was all about, and what the outcome of Life was; but, at this period in Athens, people had become primarily concerned with **how to live this Life**. Philosophy now constituted the new religion — hence the new morality. And it had also begun to displace the Old Olympic God System. And it is really no wonder therefore that Greece eventually fell into the arms of Rome, and died in that unholy wedlock, when everyone was running around, engaging in futile conversations on all these Metaphysical and Ethical points — instead of actually getting on with living!

Socrates himself paid tribute to the Olympic Gods in public, and did not blaspheme openly, as did the Sophists; but the Establishment suspected that this was only lip service. They therefore became convinced that here they had a case in point and by which they could rid themselves of this annoying philosophical 'gadfly'; (possibly mosquito would have been a better appellative!) who kept biting them when least expected.

According to Plato, Socrates said, "Of the gods, we know nothing"; **and that** closed the issue completely, as far as he was concerned. Also Socrates is supposed to have always agreed with all the religious pronouncements from the Oracle at Delphi. (And why shouldn't he? After all, that weird betel-nut chewing woman, squatting over a volcanic crack in the earth, had informed everyone that Socrates was the Wisest Man in all Greece — You scratch my back, and I'll scratch yours!) And the Oracle had said that everyone should worship, "according to the laws of the country", and seemingly Socrates was in complete agreement with this and did his level best to always appear a good temple-goer and respecter of the Greek religious system. But the Assembly *were not fooled!*

On the whole though, unlike the Sophists, Socrates was not interested in Physical Sciences nor in the facts or origins concerning Life. Instead he preferred to discuss values, ethics, and human affairs; the human character; and the purpose of the Human Life. He was interested in politics, and in Logic also, but only, as a means to an end; and **not**, as an end in itself. He preferred that the State be run as an Aristocracy rather than as a Democracy; and he thought that there should be some type of Philosophical Leadership, or Philosophical Power Syndicate in charge of this State. However we must remember that all of this is, (once again) **according to Plato**, (who may simply have made the whole thing up!) Likewise, according to Plato, Socrates distrusted Poetry and Poets, and extremists in general; (most Artists are extremists!) and Socrates believed in the "Golden Mean"; and he sounds altogether rather plebian in his tastes — to my way of thinking that is!

He thought that the Cynics, (a new philosophy school which had been founded in Athens) were extremists, and, as we have noted, he was disapproving of extremism, and did not really think that the Cynics were going the right way about things at all. In fact, Socrates seems to have been such a model, "silent majority" citizen, that one wonders a little, at the urge on the Establishment's part to remove him so permanently from the Athenian scene! Perhaps they made a mistake, and gave the hemlock to the **wrong philosopher** — and that is why he died! One imagines that the "chrematistike" crowd in Athens were not very clued up on exactly who was who — and which philosophy was which! And maybe, someone made a slight error! After all they were far too busy in the pursuit of riches, and in carrying on the Peloponnesian War, and in planning how to destroy Sparta — to pay all that much close attention to minor details! But the Reader should not take this theory seriously, as the Author is just indulging in a little wild phantasy here.

Before his demise at the age of seventy, in 399 B.C., Socrates inaugerated, or influenced the following Post-Socratic Schools of Thought.
The Cynics — through Antisthenes, supposedly a pupil of Socrates.
The Epicureans — through *Aristippus the Hedonist,* who in turn influenced Epicurus, who later began Epicureanism.
The Sceptics — through Eucleids of Megara.
The Stoics — through Antisthenes of the Cynics — then through Diogenis, who *in turn* influenced Zeno the Founder of Stoicism.
The Hedonists — see above and Aristippus!
The Platonists — through Plato his prize pupil and prime advocate.
The Aristotellians — through Plato to Aristotle.
The Peripatetics — through Plato, to Aristotle, to his students.
And this whole list reads a little like something from the "Old Testament", with Adam begetting Noah, begetting Solomon, begetting David, begetting etc., and it appears that evenPhilosophyhas to have a type of Bible and unifying continuity, in order to get the Movement of Thought actually established into a worthwhile and respectable business!

Anyway, an indictment was brought against Socrates in 399 B.C. in what, one suspects, was a type of "Show Trial". The good citizens of Athens were going to exhibit to the populace at large, that people just could not flaunt the System, and get away with it! This indictment read as follows:-"Socrates is a Public Offender in that he does not recognize the Gods that the State recognizes, but introduces new demoniacal beings; he has also offended by corrupting the Youth." This second charge seems to have been added rather as an after-thought, and *truly,* in a place in which young slave boys were sold as a general practice, to titillate and to satisfy the tired palates of aging men; one wonders that the Athenians dared to accuse *anyone* on that score at all! "Let him who is without sin cast the first stone," was obviously **not** a precept enjoying much popularity in Athens —

and the inhabitants of that City-State clearly did not believe in "do as you would be done by", but — get in first and do it to somebody else — before they do it to you! — And, **loudly** protest your innocence the whole time you're doing it! Socrates might indeed have had his share of young boys; as the pages of philosophical history are strewn with them it is true — but then, seemingly, so, *had everybody else, in Athens!*

The Trial took place before a popular court of five hundred citizens, who were mostly of the less educated class, according to Plato, who was present as always — like your ever-faithful Reporter. At first Socrates insisted on denying the charges, and stated rather unconvincingly that he **did believe** in the State, the Gods, and the Divinity of the Sun and the Moon. But then, when he had gotten tired of the whole farce, he decided to sock it to them, and declared ironically that Athens was like a thoroughbred, but lazy horse, which needed a "gadfly" to sting it into action. And, if likening himself to an insect, was dangerous; it was downright foolish to liken the Citizens of Athens to the hind-quarters of a quadruped! They (the Citizens of Athens) therefore, found him guilty; (naturally enough) and the first time, he was sentenced by a majority of sixty, and a punishment **other** than Death, was proposed. Socrates himself suggested cheerfully that he pay a fine of 300 minas. The Court however thought him extremely parsimonious, and so a second poll was taken, and this time, a majority of one hundred and forty voted in favour of the Death Penalty. Obviously this niggardliness on the part of Socrates helped to sign his own death warrant, and it is a beautiful example of the truth of that old saying regarding the "spoiling the ship for a half-penn'orth worth of tar", and means — in modern jargon — "don't quibble over money when you're in a tight corner!"

For one month between the end of the Trial, and the Date of Execution, Socrates entertained,or kept "open house" in the prison, receiving his ex-lovers, wives, children, and friends; and holding forth dialectically and philosophically to everyone. (One can't help wondering how the other in-mates in other cells viewed all these comings and goings!) Then, when ready, he lay down and took the Hemlock, and since death is after all an inevitable state, to, or through which, we must **all pass** — this lethal cocktail must surely be one of the nicest ways of going! Hemlock works by rapidly paralysing the body, beginning at the lower extremities, and finishing at the brain, (by which time of course, the imbiber is dead!) and supposedly it really is a form of Euthanasia, as that word in Greek really means "eu" good, and "thanasia" death. Socrates might have had an untimely, and an unjust finish — but, he did manage to have a fairly *painless* one.

Of course as was to be expected, once the Athenians had done him in, they got very upset and wished that they hadn't. (Typical of the general

Athenian Behaviour Pattern!) And they accused each other, and they stoned the ones responsible for Socrates' death, so one story goes; or — according to another story, the guilty parties got so ashamed of themselves, that, like Judas — they went and hanged themselves. Whether the 300 minas represent the 30 pieces of silver, I have no idea, but, the story of Socrates is very similar to another *Famous Person's* tale.

What the Athenians were most livid about, was that even though they had located and liquidated their Scape-Goat, they still hadn't solved any of their problems! Which is understandable enough, as people who use Scape-Goats are always operating under the most astounding delusions. (And actually one wonders nowadays why such intelligent people, such as our World Leaders and Politicians; should also bother to go in for such an *illogical activity*!) The Peloponnesian War had cost the Athenians bitterly. They were now bankrupt, and almost friendless in the entire Greek world — due to their conduct in affairs of State with other Cities. They had murdered in cold-blood the entire Male population of Melos — and had savagely crushed Myteline. And neither of these actions was destined to win them friends — or influence. Their olive trees had been destroyed by Sparta, and this in turn had caused them agricultural bankruptcy. The Athenian Navy had been destroyed; and two thirds of the Male Citizen Body were dead. And, the State Treasury, was empty! If ever a time had come when they were in need of philosophy, it was definitely then. But the Athenians had cut its throat (or, more accurately — poisoned it!) and silenced the voice of Truth forever — Or, so they hoped!

The 'Golden Age' of Greece and Athens therefore ended in 399 B.C. with the death of Socrates, and Athens was not only broken economically, (that is financially and agriculturally bankrupt), but she was morally broken as well. The Athenians did try once more to get it together during the period known as the 2nd. Athenian Supremacy, but they never could manage somehow — and things were in a decline, no matter what short spasms of glory there appeared to be from time to time. Athens was dying; but would not lie down. And it was a long time before 'rigor mortis', set in. Or as Toynbee the historian, would have put it, the last "rally" had been attempted, before the final "relapse" into complete disintergration. Athens died in the arms of Rome, or to put it more aptly: she died with Rome's fingers pressing against her wind-pipe. But the actual cause of death was the lack of oxygen caused internally, by an obstruction from *within* her own pharynx! And the name of that obstruction was — 'anti-socialism'. And 'Anti-Social' groups of people never last long, as they tear each other to pieces!

With the conditions which prevailed in Athens at this historic time the divisions in the society grew larger than ever, poverty increased; and in consequence, the number of beggars and itinerants increased also. The

Olympic Gods were dying; the Masses were turning towards the Cults for comfort; and the more educated members of society, were inclining towards the Cynic, or Hedonist philosophies. All of the accompanying miseries of this period shall be identified and detailed in the ensuing chapter, but for now, let it suffice to say — that the entire System of the City-State was under attack from its very *intestinal core*. The problems facing the Athenians were immense, and the Athenians were forced to do something about them. But, unfortunately for them — they didn't know *exactly* what to do! In confusion and fear they sought to quieten the Voice of Reason and Truth, by strangling it. That, however, was **not** the answer. As Hegel the German philosopher said, "The wounds of reason can only be healed by deeper reason." — But even if Hegel had been around in Athens at that time, it is doubtful if the Athenians would ever have taken any notice of *him* either!

Like it or not though, the Athenians had finally managed to become civilized; and being civilized, meant being sensitive, educated, and cultivated; and, in consequence; **weak**. But as everything is indeed its opposite, as Heracleitus said — so therefore this weakness was indeed a strength! This new found strength of the Athenians; this ability to think and to reason, had though a tremendous disadvantage — just as every advantage has — and it was this disadvantage which was worrying the Athenians. They could therefore, elect either to go forward, and to develop more reason — or, to retreat into the darkness again, licking their wounds and wishing that they had never discovered their Souls! The Athenians chose to do the latter. And the execution of Socrates was a symbolic interpretation of this attitude!

The death of Socrates however should not be diagnosed as a cause of the Athenian Fall, but rather as a symptom of the general fatal condition which was then affecting Athens. The Beast in his cage was being shaken; and he didn't like it, not one little bit! and therefore he began to roar, and to lash out — and Socrates, whoever he was, or, whatever he represented, met the full onslaught of the system's rage, and fear, and despair. So, he paid the price of Athenian evolution.

And the Summer came to a finish in a series of violent electric storms, which rocked the earth, shook the leaves from the trees, and scattered the seeds of the flowers and fruits, far and wide. And Plato stood under a gnarled, naked oak, trying desperately, and fruitlessly, to stick the dead leaves back onto the sapless branches once more.

Autumn

Autumn Winds do blow through the streets of the City-State, chilling the bones of the Citizens, and warning them of the misery to come.

CHAPTER 9

STOP THE WORLD — I WANT TO GET OFF
OR
SUICIDES UNLIMITED
The Hedonist and Cynic Movements.

Following the death of Socrates, 4th century Athens was in a complete social and economical mess — and a tremendous philosophical mess as well! The Human Condition sat heavily upon the shoulders of Nature's most evolved Ape, threatening to over-topple the body of Zoological Man — And the triangular conflict concerning Man's Body, or Flesh; his Mind, or Logic; and his Soul, or Psyche; was never more apparent. This, then was the burning issue which had to be resolved; but which was dealt with by the populace in a variety of ways — And hardly any of those methods proved over-whelmingly successful.

There was a head-on clash in the Society — And it was both a Psychological, and a Sociological confrontation. People would have to choose what to do about it — and they would have to choose, whether they liked to, or not.

Some, elected to brazen it out, or, to simply ignore the issue. Others tried to join the progressive forces and to move with the flow. Still others detached themselves, and tried to hide away from the call to battle — but everyone was involved; and a decision **had to be made**. How was Man to live with himself, and how was he to live with his Fellow Man?

Psychologically speaking, we may say that there appear to be three main personality types — the Aggressive, the Passive, and the Detached. There is however the tricky question as to whether there really is such a thing as a Detached personality, because quite possibly, the Detached personality is really none other than a disenchanted, or frustrated, Aggressive — or, Passive person. Even the roles of Aggressive and Passive are often interchangeable, as for instance in the case of the brow-beaten employee who then returns home from work to physically beat his wife —who in turn, takes out all her frustration on the children. And the too-Aggressive Male, combined with the too-Passive Female, often manage to rear between them a totally sexually-detached Homosexual; who cannot accept his Father's Aggressive Male role, and yet also hates his Mother for her female Passivity. So these roles of Passive, Aggressive and Detached have affect on each other, and are interchangeable, and constantly fluid, and as the unhappy and unequally balanced house-hold often produces the psychologically Detached and sexually inverted person, so does the unequally balanced society often produce the sociologically and economically Detached Citizen; and Athens at this period in history; managed to produce a great number of these!

In the world of Biology, we speak of three general states of interrelationship between life forms — Mutualism, Commensalism, and Parasitism. We can likewise apply these symbiotic laws to Human Social Behaviour and note that when the Aggressive Faction in society becomes too extreme, and the social and economic situation is so polarized that only Parasitism flourishes; then the Balance and Harmony of Life is lacking, and the Society is in deep trouble. The Aggressive forces of this society are too strong, and they cannot be compromised with, changed, or, adapted to, by the weaker members. The Aggressive forces, like the immovable object, refuse to budge. They will not tolerate a change — they will not allow Nature, or Evolution, to fulfil its function, and to carry out its work. The Passive (naturally) find the pressure on them to be quite unbearable, but they are in a quandry on how to deal with it. They feel that they cannot accept it, and yet cannot fight it either — nor can they flee from it physically. They are unable to deal with it in any way whatsoever. All they can do is to 'switch off' — that is — to Detach.

Some of the weaker and more sensitive members of the Aggressive Faction cannot accept their group role either, so they also 'switch off'. The Detached Sector grows. People begin to detach themselves mentally in diverse ways, in religion, art, alcohol, drugs, science — and even madness. They detach themselves physically from a society as well, as emigrants, or beggars; gypsies; or itinerants of various types. Naturally there are both Creative means of Detachment, and Destructive methods as well. The overall compulsion of the people though, is to move — and seemingly at this point in time, there is no place for these diverse atoms to go in the void —but to split from both the Positive Aggressive and Active elements —and equally, to break from the Passive, Negative and Re-active elements — and to leap out into space as free, detached atoms, or 'Drop-Outs'! So there comes a period of social restlessness before the actual Revolution and overt change, and there is a manifest social detachment, a building-up of the 'Out-siders', or Third Parties, who will break; align; break again; and then re-align, until some balance is restored. This movement is in fact the **real Revolution**. What comes after, is only the messy cleaning-up process — just as the fever which attacks our body is only the outward sign of the inner disease which had already taken root inside us, and which began to poison our systems — a long time before we first became aware of it.

Athens in the 4th century was in a situation akin to this, and the fever which gripped her was only the outer symptom of the illness from which she had long been suffering. There had been of course previous occasions in history when this had happened, and there would be times in the future when it would happen again — as indeed this social confrontation is still, (and is continually) happening everywhere in the world to-day. And one of the most potent examples of this tremendous Social Unrest in societies, and which illustrates this point, is the act of Suicide — and the frequency of this act, and, the irregularity — depending on the conditions of the society.

Suicide we may notice, is rare in times of overt warfare; but in times of covert social warfare, it is rife. Whenever Man has a chance to kill his brother, or, whenever he is desperately trying to save himself from **being killed** by his brother, then self-slaughter is at its lowest ebb. But in times of peace, due to the aggression between people in societies, and the pressure which the Weak, Sensitive, or Passive members have to bear — there is an upsurge in suicide as a form of Detachment; or as an escape from the Social, Psychological and Economical pressure. Of course Suicide can occur for a number of other reasons also — such as, temporary madness or personal grief. But an act of Suicide, in general, calls attention to the fact that all is not well in the Society, at large. That something is dreadfully wrong with the laws and the living-conditions of a group of people, when some members prefer to leave the group permantly — and, to choose, to leave **the World permanently**, at the same time. Suicide we may say, is the ultimate form of Detachment — it is seemingly, the last escape hatch; and no living organisms choose to use it until the 'elán vîtal' or survival instinct has been completely destroyed in them. Or, has in fact, their survival instinct itself actually led them to Suicide? Is Suicide, in fact, the **only way** for them to survive!

As with all living organisms, people are continually searching for the chance to move, and when this movement is denied them, and the pressures of the Social group are so immense that they cannot manoeuvre either up or down; perhaps they then detach from the main body and disperse laterally, instead of vertically — And perhaps this is what Suicide in the Society really means. Whatever the reader feels about this subject, he may decide for himself, but the fact remains that in 4th century Athens the conditions of the Society were such that the Act of Suicide became completely commonplace and almost fashionable — and this then is the background to the Cynic and Hedonist Schools of Philosophy — and may be the reason why they actually arose!

By the time of the Cynics the early Pre-Socratic Philosophers had propounded vague cosmologies; the Sophists had doubted everything but the power of rhetoric; and Socrates (whoever he was) had asked a million questions and answered none of them. The whole situation was very disturbing; and **very uncomfortable**. Physical, Metaphysical, Ethical, and Political speculation sprouted everywhere now in Athens, a city, which although too poor (or not sufficiently interested) to maintain a State Medical Scheme, suddenly became the intellectual centre of the Greek

World, with the opening of the first private universities, already to formulate the future Civic Leaders of the Greek City-State.

Having weakened the old religion of the State, and the Olympian God Systems; the philosophers (or rather, one should say the Establishment) now struggled to find within Nature and Reason, some substitute for this religion, in order to keep afloat the sinking ship of State Morality. That is to say, the State Establishment had now to provide a new guide for the people on how to actually **live** Life. If philosophy was going to replace the Religion, then the Philosophy would have to become a Religion itself! But the real motivation behind the inauguration of these private schools (which actually concerns our next chapter) was the staggering onslaught of new semi-religious and anti-establishment philosophical movements, which were springing up at this time.

Due to the conditions of the Age, and the influence of the Sophists (as the re-action to the action) there arose this natural philosophical phenomena which was most frightening to the City Fathers, and the army of Detachment grew daily and multiplied alarmingly. The Establishment muttered fretfully in its beard, hid momentarily behind its ever shrinking sacks of coinage in its counting houses, and then, decided to push philosophy forward — in order to use it to form a bond of civic loyalty — and to make it a natural ethic and substitute for the divine commands of the deities which were not now believed in, adhered to, *or even* respected! What the 'Establishment' saw happening in Athens and Corinth was so frightening to them, that they chose to try to re-direct the people and their energies into safer and more circumscribed channels — in order to stop themselves being drowned in this flood which was bursting the banks of society.

Their initial answer to this problem was to establish a school of classical philosophy (with the emphasis on Rhetoric) for the sons of Colonial Greeks. And this school was run by one Isocrates (436-338) a Passive — who had managed to join the ranks of the Aggressives — (in other words a poor boy made good!) who had studied under the Sophist Gorgias; but, who had made both his name, and his social position, *by criticizing the Sophists.* This school of Rhetoric by Isocrates would take care of the Sophists, and those hungering for Sophism; imagined the Establishment. Then some years later Plato began his Academy for the sons of Gentlefolk; the Upper Class, or Aristocrats, (even though some of them were down-at heel — their blood was still the same true-blue colour!) And Plato's school would stop any of these young dandies from getting any funny ideas about insubordination or about, "logic", being everything! And because Nature certainly does hate a vacuum, even later on in this story, Aristotle would appear on the scene with his Lyceum for the intellectually minded heirs of the middle-class, and, in time, he would help to create the atmosphere appropriate for his own intellectually minded

Upper Middle-Class — in order for it to rise to power and fame, during Alexander's Timocracy.

But, the underground, or anti-establishment philosophical movements, which erupted spontaneously at the time of Socrates' teaching and subsequent execution; these were the new Mental Cults — philosophical analogies to the Mystic Religious Resurrection Cults. And these were the Forces which really galvanised the Establishment into action and caused them to establish philosophy schools. And as we saw in the previous chapter, all these new Post-Socratic Schools could all be traced back to the Grand Master Socrates (in one way or another!) — and truly, the ingenuity of scholars is marvellous!

Firstly there was Antisthenes, a student of Socrates', who began the Cynic Movement, which later burst into full flower under the influence of the eccentric, Diogenes of Corinth. Aristippus, another student of Socrates' then began Hedonism, and his student Epicurus began Epicureanism. Then Epicurus joined forces with Eucleides of Megara, (who was also an ex-student of Socrates', whose student Stilpo became a Cynic, and who in turn taught Zeno, who began Stoicism!) — and this Eucleides was also responsible for the later development of Skeptism — helped along by the intellectual collaboration of Pyrrho and Carneades. And of course there was Plato (the most beloved disciple of Socrates, and who perhaps we should liken to Saint John, rather than to Saint Peter!) who began the Academy, and who begot Aristotle, who began the Lyceum, who begot etc. Yes, indeed! Everything neatly ties back to Socrates. Truly an admirable effort!

In this chapter however we shall mainly consider these strange; diametrically opposed; and yet very similar movements — Hedonism, the philosophy concerning the love of Pleasure; and Cynicism, the philosophy concerning the acceptance, or, love of Poverty, (and possibly also of Pain!) Both these philosophies were created, or formed as raiment for the clothing of the Detached; for those seeking something other than the materialistic life of the average city merchant and vulgar materialist. And one of the many points in common which they shared, was their cheery and willing, acquiescent attitude towards Suicide — which is why this chapter is entitled "Stop the World — I want to get off!"

But exactly why did these movements arise? And what were the specific conditions which led to them? Everything in Life has a reason, and the rise of a philosophy which eventually becomes popular, is basically due to some need in the people. It is true that the Leader of the Philosophy Movement may be a trail-blazer, or pioneer; an individualist who is ahead of his time; and who is needed to initiate a new evolutionay step-forward, but — who is never appreciated in his life-time; and who at best — can only expect to be included in some type of collective statue which will be erected long after his death — (And which will prove to be a suitable resting facility and public convenience for weary pigeons, and, a useful still-life object for bored and mindless camera-clicking tourists!) But he would *never* attract disciples to his creed, or students to his movement in the first place (or in any place at all!) UNLESS his philosophy answered some burning question within them — or, UNLESS it was a tune which drew aresponsefrom within some breasts. It is the same with all fashions and all cults and movements; and after all, it was girls with pretty legs; just dying to exhibit them; who were the first to adopt the Mini Skirt of the 1960's. And if the entire universe had been composed of females with crooked, mis-shapen and bulbous legs and thighs, it is highly unlikely that, **that** particular fashion, would ever have gotten off the ground! In order for some idea to succeed, there has to be some type of demand or need; and in order for a product to sell, there must be ready and waiting customers. You can only send coals to Newcastle, if their own stocks of that mineral material have already been depleted, and, if there is a **real need** for this carbonized vegetable matter.

At this period in Greek history there was such utter confusion, spiritual panic, and moral disorder in Athens, as the Olympian Gods began to die, and as the mass of people turned to the Cults to satisfy themselves; but the Merchant Bourgeois however, had nothing to turn to, (the Cults were for the poor!) and even their money was beginning to dwindle away rather alarmingly before their eyes. With the disposal of the State Religious Faith, the individual had been completely freed from all restraint — civic, personal, national and private; and all the old ethics and mores now failed to function; and life for the Bourgeois became increasingly difficult. The Sophists and their Intellectual Nihilism, plus War, and the consequent economic problems, had led to the utter Cynicism of the Hedonists and the Cynics — for Hedonism, the love of pleasure; was REALLY just another form of Cynicism — and *both* of them were philosophies for the Detached.

In 4th century Athens the son had become completely freed from the moral obligations to his parents; and the male from the duty of marriage. Also the women now felt relieved of the onerous duty of child-birth for the welfare and good of the State. And the average citizen felt no urge whatsoever towards any type of political responsibility. Sexual morality declined even more than before, and marriages became rare; while free intercourse with Courtesans became both commonplace and increasingly popular. The Family System broke down completely (and it is important to remember that the Family System is the backbone, or foundation of the State) and men took to courting only the famous whores of the time ; and the philosophers were no exception in this. Phryne, Lais, Nicarete, and Metaneira were household names and famous in the art of seduction during the 4th century, and they were extremely closely connected with the philosophy movement in general. Lais of Corinth in particular (reputedly the most beautiful woman of her time and who eventually was the proud owner of the largest tomb stone in Corinth!) is on record for having happily and willingly given herself to Diogenes the Cynic, while refusing to bestow her pleasures on well-known artists of the day. Obviously philosophers were thought to be endowed with more sexual "joie de vivre" than artists! Both Danae and Leontium taught Epicurus the philosophy of pleasure, or, so they said! And even the Hetaira Archeanassa amused Plato — though how much, is not recorded. However as fascinating as the subject of Greek Courtesans is, and as much as they can be said to have influenced the Philosophical Movement, we must get on with thephilosophersthemselves first, and return to their women 'fancy' (or otherwise) later.

With all this attention paid to the 'easy' women of Athens I have in fact been endeavouring to show the moralbreakdown in Athens, or, the **overt** moral breakdown. Just as we earlier discussed the **overt social conflict**, or open social warfare, and its ever pre-existing, antecedent **covert social conflict of class dissatisfaction**, and the growth ofDetachment;so, the morality in Athens had never ever been anything to write home about! But the decline had previously been a covert one, and now, the society was *openly immoral.* The sickness was reaching the stage of blatantly showing itself, and the fever, in consequence, was rising. Athens had always had whores there before, and it had always had State-Run Prostitution, but now Prostitution had become so fashionable, that co-habitation had **replaced marriage** — and therefore the fundamental production of new progeny necessary for fighting battles for the State, was being affected. Babies were needed in Athens, and yet women had begun to practice contraception and abortion on an increasingly alarming scale. And infanticide had also became fashionable, with girls very high up on the list for exposure as girl babies are generally considered a bit of a waste of time in any society! The old Eupatrid Families began to die out in consequence, and the Lower Classes began to multiply with horrifying rapidity. In 431 B.C. the Citizen Class in Attica equalled 43,000; but in 400 B.C. it had fallen to 22,000; and by 313 B.C. it totalled only 21,000. And the few citizens there were, didn't wish to go to war and to fight either — at least not for their own group the Greeks. Many people actually deserted Greece in order to take up arms in the armies of others (principally the Persians) and by the time of Alexander the Great, the Greek armies were able to converse easily, and almost effortlessly, with their enemies — even to recognize many faces, and to give messages from home — before stabbing each other in the gizzards! So the Greeks were forced to begin bringing in the Celts, to act as mercinaries for them — and this proved to be a very dangerous thing to have done, and Athens in particular, became filled with Slaves — 'poor citizens' who had sold themselves into slavery in order to feed their families and to pay their debts; bankrupt and totally ruined farmers — dispossessed citizens fallen from grace, and from the money table; wandering semi-religious philosophical groups — and nomad teachers and preachers. The more interesting of the two largest philosophical groups, historically speaking, very similar to the 13th century religious movement in the Christian Church (notably the Franciscans) was the Cynic School. But, perversely, (as is Human Nature!) we shall deal first with the other — the Hedonist Movement.

Aristippus was the Founder of the Hedonist Philosophy, and as we have seen, he was an ex-student of Socrates'. His motto was, "I possess, but am not possessed", and this sounds fairly logical if you care to ruminate on it for long enough — but then most things seem wise or logical if you spend enough time and thought on them. Even the words of a prize fool may absorb (or develop) import, after enough pensive study and recollection. But Aristippus is also reported to have said, "I had rather be a beggar than a dunce; the beggar has no money, but the dunce has no humanity;" — so there we have it really. These new philosophical movements were composed of educated beggars, who were living on their wits and words, rather than on their skill in looking pitiful; and in fact, a whole new Socio-Economic Class had arisen in Athens due to the aftermath of the Peloponnesian Wars.

Aristippus however decided not to hang around poverty-stricken Athena too long, but to hop off to his native Cyrene, which was a Greek colony on the coast of Africa. Here in this small, rich trading-centre which had largely escaped the worst of the wars which had torn the Greek world to pieces; a new wealthy, colonial Upper-Class had arisen, with pleasure-loving habits; semi-oriental in overtones. And Aristippus thought that his home town was now ready for him, and that he could supply a philosophy, which would be completely in tune with its new Life-Style. This only goes to prove that the American author Thomas Wolfe, who said that "You can't go home again" was probably referring to "home" in the evolutionary sense. Cyrene, had progressed, and moved on evolutionarily, and was now rich enough, to afford philosophy; and so in consequence, Aristippus went home; and, with moderate success, he *even* managed to stay there!

On the way to Cyrene however, Aristippus was ship-wrecked off the coast of Rhodes, and in order to prove how optimistic a person he really was — and, what a lover of logic and intellect — we are informed that he attempted to encourage and uplift the spirits of his downcast friend and companion by telling him not to be pessimistic. "But how can we be optimistic?" his companion asked, "Here we are in the middle of nowhere, (there was not a greatly developed Swedish Tourist Trade in Rhodes in those days!) with not a drachma between us." But Aristippus pointed down at the beach on which they stood, and drew his companion's attention to some geometrical figures drawn in the sand. "Cheer up," said the bold Aristippus, "I see traces of Men." And this must surely be one of the most remarklable statements and observations in all history, and it is very impressive to see that mathematical signs can have such a heartening effect on a person. How different is the attitude of the average school-child nowadays!

Anyhow, once in Rhodes City, Aristippus wandered into the nearest gymnasium, discoursed loftily with the students; (thereby earning his bread and olives; and a sufficientquantityof retsina to bide him over;) and after a while, he even managed to get someone or other, to pay for his boat ticket on to Cyrene. Later in life, when asked about the subject of parental duties towards their offspring, he recalled his time in Rhodes, and replied, that parents should always arm their children with such wealth, that, even after a shipwreck, it should (the wealth!) be able to swim to land with its owner — No he wasn't referring to filling their mouths with gold teeth either! He was advocating the filling of a child's head with education and the knowledge of some skill, and, **even more importantly**, he was advocating the filling of their souls, or spirits, with sufficient confidence, and faith in their own abilities; and in their personal cause. What a wise educationist was Aristippus!

Again, on the subject of education, Aristippus was once asked to define exactly in which way Educated people were superior to the untutored, and the great Hedonist replied, "as broken horses are to the unbroken!"

Personally, however, I don't particularly care for this answer of his, and much prefer his alternative reply to this seemingly obsessional Classical World moot point, which he gave at a later date to another earnest enquirer, and when he stated that, "If the student devives no other good *(good, here meaning Education)* he will not, when he attends the theatre, be one stone upon another." (I like to think that this later definition of the use of Education must have been composed on a suitably pleasant, hedonistic, and pleasurably sensual day, whereas the former must have been arrived at on a singularly trying occasion after the attempted mastery of a metaphorically, if not literally, unbridled member of the equine species.)

Having finally arrived in Cyrene, Aristippus, (who agreed with Socrates' idea that Happiness is the greatest Good) resolved at once to market this new commodity of Hedonism; which then began to prove immensely popular with the Cyrenaics; just as the Mini-Skirt in the 20th century became the vogue with the girls who had pretty legs — (and even with some who hadn't!)

Hedonism, taught that whatever we do, is done through either hope of pleasure, or, fear of pain; therefore pleasure is the ultimate good; and everything; including philosophy and virtue; must be judged according to its capacity of bringing us pleasure. Our knowledge of things, the Hedonist maintains, is uncertain, and only our feelings can be trusted to be true; and wisdom lies not in the pursuit of abstract truth, but in aspiring to enjoy pleasurable sensations. The keenest pleasure is neither intellectual nor moral — but it is physical and sensual; and the Hedonist believes in living only for the Present, as the Present is all that matters. Pluck pleasures as they appear, says the Hedonist, and as I drink my morning coffee, I personally am inclined to agree with him, and feel that there must be a little Hedonism in all of us, and that possibly it is not a bad thing! And I can see how and why this philosophy became so popular in Cyrene; and how Aristippus, (possibly tongue-in-cheek) managed to earn himself a living with it! Hedonism stressed that it was wise to obtain and to seek more and more pleasure continually — and this thought in itself should have been a comfort to the rich and to the fortunate, who must have smiled, and dropped a drachma or two, in the direction of Aristippus — in gratitude for supplying them with this moral compensation!

Furthermore, Aristippus proclaimed, a wise man will show discriminating respect for public opinion (very prudent advice!) but he will seek as far as possible, "to be neither the master, not the slave of any man." And these words of counsel he attempted to put into action in his own life by playing up to the rich, in order to survive; and by never, **ever**, giving lessons, **without receiving payment**. Aristippus, to my mind, was an impoverished teacher, valiantly trying to up-hold his end, and to stay alive in a world of Cyrenaic commerce; and when he did have money, (because it seems that Hedonism in itself does not promise money — only how to enjoy it!) he spent lavishly on women, wine, fine food, and good clothing. Hedonism for Aristippus, may have been in fact the only possible philosophy for the damned; and an heroic attempt to distil some joy from the bitter draught of social and economic injustice, and inequality.

Aristippus must have spent his time walking the razor's edge, so to speak, in his pursuit and flattery of the affluent; in order to carry out his occupation; as his profession forced him (as it does the private tutor or governess in the homes of the rich) to learn, that being courteous, (as well as being the very soul of cajolery one's self) does not always cause one to be inviolate from the slings and arrows of the *outrageous plutocrat*. On one occasion, Aristippus had to endure the insults of Dionysos I of Syracuse, who, in order to round off the conversation, and to press home his point as it were; spat copiously, and vociferously, into the philosopher's face. Aristippus took it all with a good grace — probably he could not afford to do otherwise — and when asked by some supercillious person with a sneering expression, why it was that he, a wise philosopher, knelt before an idiot like Dionysos I; the sage explained tolerantly and painstakingly, that it was unfortunately necessary; and really no fault of his; but, that the King Dionysos it seemed, (like so many rich and powerful people) had his ears located in his feet. An interesting speciman for medical examination and the progress of science was Dionysos! Some people say however, that nowadays, most of the wealthy and powerful members of society have their ears positioned in their cheque books. Still, maybe the ancient Greeks were different from us — not only mentally, but also physically!

Aristippus himself though, was not above a little spitting or spatting of his own, because one day when a rich Phrygian named Simus, was being a perfect bore; showing the philosopher over his new luxurious house; and droning on about the cost of everything, and how exclusive it all was etc., Aristippus surprised the proud owner in mid-sentence by casting a well-aimed globule of philosophical mucous in his face.

"Why?" asked the astounded and irate Simus, "did you do that?" "Well, sir," answered Aristippus, rolling his eyes wildly, "Well, what with all this marble and fine gold and all, I just couldn't find another suitable place in which to spit!" And how many people would love to be able to emulate the philosopher's actions, when being treated to a heavy session of boring boastfulness on the part of a member of the New Rich Class? Unfortunately (or perhaps fortunately) few people have Aristippus' courage — or foolhardiness!

The same sneering fellow who had asked Aristippus why he knelt at Dionysos' feet, also enquired one day, why it was that philosophers frequented the houses of the rich; but that the rich did not frequent the houses of philosophers! (This sneerer was quite possibly a student who had received a low mark in his Hedonism study course!) But even this sort of obnoxious and aggressive question did not phase Aristippus, who at all times managed to keep his "cool" — philosophers, by trade, are made of hearty stuff, and have learnt in the hard school of knocks how to deal with just such examples of insinuating sarcasm. He replied imperturbably, "Because the first (meaning the philosophers) know what they want; but the second, (meaning the rich) do not!" And that closed that issue Q.E.D.

Some other colleague, or acquaintance (everyone seems to have wanted to 'have a go' at poor old Aristippus) thought to ruffle his feathers by asking him why he lived with a Courtesan who conferred her favours on so many. But the ever calm pleasure-lover replied that he personally had no objection to either living in a house, or sailing in a ship that other men had used before him, so why should he feel any differently about a woman! And when a mistress of his told him that he was responsible for her interesting and lively condition he answered her blandly, "You can no more tell that it was I, than you could tell, after going through a thicket, which thorn had scratched you." And that, put paid to that paternity suit at the start. Incidentally, Aristippus the Hedonist, like Diogenes the Cynic, had at one time shared the favours of the exotic Lais of Corinth, or so the accademic gossips say, and it seems that *that* particular woman must have take a course in just about every type of Greek Philosophy there was available. Definitely, Lais was a most intellectual wench, and obviously deserving of the enormous tomb which the Corinthians erected in memory of her having been the greatest conqueror of men, of all time — and even greater in her appeal and affect on affairs of State, than Alexander the Great!

Before his death in 356 B.C. Aristippus bequeathed his philosophical legacy to his daughter Arete, and his entire estate was contained in these few words of wisdom, which he hoped she had effectually learnt and committed to heart — "to set a value on *nothing* that she could do without." So, with no money — but with a great deal of intellectual sapience — Arete succeeded her old man as the head of the Cyrenaic School of Hedonism, and carried on the family business of making a living out of the wealthy Upper Classes — in much the same way as the small crocodile-bird earns his daily bread by playing dentist to that dangerous reptile. Picking the teeth of a crocodile, or pandering to the whims of a potentate, seems a rather capricious, and even dangerous way of securing one's staff of life, but then Nature develops a use for everything, and life is wonderfully varied and interesting; and futhermore, we **all have to make a living don't we**? Incidentally, Aristippus lives on today in the American Constitution, in which it is stated that it is the right of every citizen to avail himself of Life, Liberty, and the Pursuit of Happiness. On which ever Astral Plane, Aristippus happens to be located nowadays, it is hoped that he is sufficiently contented; even perhaps, pleased; to see his ideas enshrined in such an outstanding and famous a doctrine!

The Hedonists may only have been an insignificant sect by the 3rd century B.C. but their doctrine of maintaining Human well-being in the sum of individual happiness (and especially, physical pleasure!) in the hands of one Hegesias (a disciple of Aristippus) degenerated, or, progressed — (depending entirely on your individual viewpoint!) into a sort of religion of pessimistic quietism. And under the influence and rhetoric of this Hegesias, the movement began to extend a powerful incentive and direction towards suicide; and a wave of such deaths spread throughout Cyrene, and later still, through Alexandria. In fact everywhere that Hegesias went, people started dropping like flies, and when Ptolemy II came on the throne 285 B.C. he expelled this suicide advocator from Egypt, in order that he should be able to manage to keep **any sort of population** in his kingdom at all! After all, how could he collect taxes if people kept getting the better of him, and escaping the System, by dying! Possibly the same reasoning motivates all State Legislature against suicide, even nowadays. It is ironic to note that it is both legal, and commendable, to kill a person, during martial combat, but it is illegal, and very reprehensible, to take one's own life, at *any* time! One's life does not in fact belong to oneself it seems! And people who disapprove most vehmently of suicide, generally do so because they themselves fear death, *so much so,* that itseemsto them, to be an impertinence on the suicidee's part, *this leaping across the void, so carelessly, and so willingly.* There is possibly also a tinge of guilt attached — because a case of suicide is, in final analysis — a case of social murder, as we pointed out at the beginning of this chapter. The person who detaches from life so drastically, generally does so because he has been forced into such a situation that he has no choice (or thinks he has no choice!) or has completely lost his élan vitâl, or survival instinct, due to the tremendous pressure on him. Therefore suicide is a very controversial subject and people tend to regard it according to the degree of acceptance and mental comfort which they feel towards the condition of Death, itself. Hegesias however, definitely felt no ambiguity about it, and although he started out more optimistically in life, and rather like Epicurus of Samos (the Founder of Epicureanism) he slowly began to conclude, that life had so much more in the way of **pain** to offer; than in the way of **pleasure**; that the only logical outcome of this naturalistic philosophy was to down the hemlock; or — to cut the throat. The Ptolemy in Egypt would possibly have been wiser, not to have banished Hegesias (thereby making suicide a forbidden sweet, and extremely desirable) but to have followed the sagacious example of the Assembly of Miletus in Ionia a few years earlier, when they had been facing a similar problem. As the number of Ionian females despatching themselves so summarily from this world, had grown so alarmingly disproportionate, those prudent gentlemen of the Council, decreed that any woman who died as a result of her own hand, was to have her body ceremoniously paraded through the market place, *stark naked.* The idea that the great mass of Milesians would thereby see them without their lip rouge, and minus their corsets (which kept their various lumps and abundancies of flesh in more aesthetic folds) deterred practically the entire female community from committing any such actions from then on. So the story goes according to Plutarch anyway — unless he was just making the whole thing up in order to give history students a little amusement!

Anyhow, the Hedonist Movement tended to completely get out of hand after the death of Aristippus, and Theodorus of Cyrene, another disciple, commenced preaching direct and unmoralistic atheism, so openly in Athens, that the Assembly there immediately had him indicted for impiety. Epicurus, who had been studying the Cyrenaic Hedonism, also observed what was happening to most of the leading lights of this movement, and probably noted to himself that no good could come from unambiguously denouncing the State — or from being too obviously 'different'! Or perhaps he was simply a rather bad student, who couldn't comprehend the full and true meaning of Hedonism. Anyway, he 'dropped out' of his Hedonism studies and went on to found Epicureanism — but we shall discuss that philosophical school in a later chapter. The Hedonists themselves gradually faded out of history, as the conditions of life began to improve with the periods of colonial expansion and consequent economic growth during the Alexandrian and Roman epochs. Or perhaps, they really disappeared because their philosophical faction was not a self perpetuating organization, due to the frequency with which the members killed themselves. Or maybe even, there was so little actual pleasure to be found and enjoyed, that Hedonism as such was unable to be followed satifactorily, and therefore ceased to function. Some of the Hedonists did manage to merge later with a number of moderate members of the Cynic movement however, and together they formed a type of safe 'silently suffering majority' religion — But it is the least moderate, and the more extreme members of the Cynic movement which we shall consider now.

The actual Founder of the Cynic School was a gentleman by the name of Antisthenes, although the better known, and most popular figure of this clique, was his disciple Diogenes. But first let us examine Antisthenes, who was born the son of an Athenian Citizen, and a Thracian Slave (a very inflammable genetic mixture!) in the year 444 B.C.; and who died in 365 B.C. He is reputed to have fought bravely at the Battle of Tanagra in 426, so it seems that in his case (as in that of Socrates) being a warrior, in no way inhibited the cause of philosophy! Perhaps of course, it was the sight of all that blood-shed which caused him to decide that there had to be some higher way to the acquisition of peace and tranquillity other than that which was to be found at the tip of a sword.

He studied with Gorgias the Orator Sophist, and with Prodicus, the Humanist Sophist, and then he began his own school in Piraeus; a notable water-side, red-light area, and hot-bed of corruption in those days; and filled with poor, enslaved, foreign, and generally confused people.

But like many another philosopher (or so they say!) Antisthenes heard Socrates talking one day, and was so impressed, that he collected all his students and went over to attend the Grand Master's lectures. From then on, and until Socrates partook of the fatal cup, Antisthenes closed the doors of his own school, and walked from Piraeus to Athens and back, every single day. No mean undertaking indeed! None of the historians whom I consulted seem to know exactly how he lived during this period — in fact they dont't appear to have bothered over much, or to have dwelt upon this subject for any great length of time at all. To we practical working people concerned with putting a roof over our heads, and margarine, or even a little jam, on our bread, however, this does constitute a bit of a mystery. If he took all his students to Socrates, then how did he manage to earn any money? But then possibly, as the early philosophers were such lofty men, they were able to make do on very little — and maybe in this respect they were physically akin to the Olympian Gods, who lived; (so we are faithfully informed) on nectar, ambrosia, and air!

The essence of this new Cynic philosophy, or doctrine, was to reduce the things of the flesh to bare necessities; in order that the soul might be as free as possible. The Motto of the Hedonists had been, "I possess, but am not possessed", but the Motto of the Cynics was, "I do not possess, in order *not* to be possessed."

This was probably quite alright for Antisthenes and his disciples, because it appears that the majority of them were so poor that they didn't have anything to possess in the first place! And therefore they did not have to arise, go sell what they had, and to give it to the poor; in order to follow their way, and as Christ was later to urge the people to do in Palestine. Oh, dear no! It seems that the Cynics didn't own a single video or dish-washer between them — not to mention an electric iron! The question however which is really interesting here, I think, is whether people actually **give up** the world — or whether the world **gives them up**, instead? Or —whether it is a combination of both? The Cynics were all poor and dispossessed people already, or so it seems, and Property-less Antisthenes must not have been classified a Citizen of Athens because the Citizens or 'Demos', and the respectable men of the Assembly, were *all* property owners. How Antisthenes and his disciples managed to escape being sent to the Laurium silver mines, is what puzzles me! I imagine the Assembly must have been just dying to get rid of these dirty, ragged, barefoot intellectual beggars who were parading up and down the streets and preaching sedition. To tell people that the object of life was not the consuming of more and more goods, was of course, the greatest sedition imaginable in Athens of those days. Why the economy, and the whole System itself, was very likely to tumble down, if people in large enough numbers, actually began to believe that!

Antisthenes however, did not go as far as Proudhon did in the 19th century A.D. in proclaiming that "all property is theft"; but he did come uncomfortably close. And the ragged cloak, with which he draped his skinny limbs, was enough to strike real terror into the hearts of the well-fed, and the richly attired. Even Socrates is reputed to have pulled his leg, by announcing one day, "I can see your vanity, Antisthenes, through the holes of your cloak!" But Antisthenes, like Saint Francis of Assisi, had no vanity whatsoever, and only a disinterested contempt for the things of this world. In fact the only weakness of character which the poor man ever exhibited, was in his love of writing books, and I personally find it rather difficult to criticize him on this point! (A case of the pot calling the kettle black!) And he left ten volumes behind him when he died, including a history of philosophy.

After Socrates had been sacrificed on the altar of the State, in the interests of Law and Order — (how convenient it was for the rulers that Socrates had had such an almighty admiration for the "Law" itself, and had decided that he should **not be ABOVE it** — regardless of how idiotic and corrupt that Law was!) Antisthenes resumed teaching in his own school once more. It still worries me as to how he managed to support himself during his long Sabbatical, as, unlike the Wise Men of our own times, he did not receive a grant from some beneficent government, in order to pleasantly while away his hours behind some ivy-covered walls. Anyhow, this truly humble and self-effacing man (who would never have survived at all, if he had lived in the 20th century) chose as his lecture centre, the gymnasium, or school, "Cynosarges" (meaning Dogfish, in ancient Greek) and which place was maintained for people of lowly or foreign birth — obviously lowly was thought synonymous with foreign! The Greeks were in fact, in deadly earnest regarding their doctrines of the superiority of Race and Mentality, and they were equally earnest in holding to the idea of regarding *all* barbarians as intrinsically base. There must be a message here for all of us I think, and I also think, and I ponder upon, and I question — the true meaning of that famous saying (by that equally famous English poet Shelley) "We are all Greeks!" Was he perchance referring to the beauty, and culture, and learning of the Greeks? Or, to their heroic and dogged persistence in not surrendering to the Turkish invaders in their lands? Or, was he endorsing their ancient doctrine of ethnic elitism, and racial superiority? After all, in the eyes of the Classical Greek, this very same poet was a Barbarian; and if he had been alive at the time of Antisthenes, he would have found himself down in Cynosarges with the rest of his ilk. Or perhaps various people in the northern hemisphere like to imagine that the TRUE GREEK (whoever or whatever that creature may be) moved upward at the time of the Asian invasions, and that within their northern veins, there runs the blood of a finer stock of people? It is wondrous and passing strange, how the Human Animal always likes to pursue these quaint illusions of high pedigree, and to prove his lawful descendency from the High and the Mighty; the Kings of Yore; and the Powerful of Old.

Anyway, Cynosarges was maintained by the State as a place of education for the poor and illegitimate students of Athens, and any reader who wishes to more fully understand the type of environment in which Antisthenes worked, need only venture into the slums and ghettos surrounding his own native city; and to take a look at the children, and at the living conditions, of the migrant workers in his homeland - in order to get a general picture of what Cynosarges must have been like.

Gradually, the word, or the name, "Cynic", meaning the "dog", became attached to this school, and to its new philosophical creed. There is however another explanation concerning the choice of nomenclature and that states that the word "Cynic", (meaning dog) referred to these philosophical gentlemen themselves (Diogenes in particular!) because they tended to behave like the canine species, when in public. As dogs do not have the same puritanical, repressed, and inhibited personalities which Human Beings possess, so do they tend, it is true, to be rather direct in dealing with, and attending to, their natural desires regarding food, sex, and the excretion of inner pollution! It is said that the Cynics behaved in the streets of Athens, in the same way as did the dogs! And that, that — is how, and why, they earned their nickname! So there are the two official versions, and the Reader may believe whichever one he cares to. Personally I have another theory, and that is, that possibly the name grew from the concept that it is after all "Il Mondo Carne" — "A dog's Life", and that the Poor and the Dispossessed social outsiders were treated like dogs in Athens in those days, and that they chose this name for themselves, in order to illustrate their social station in life. Surely if the Athenian Assembly had seriously wanted to stop these outrageous displays of attention to bodily functions which were being carried out in their public thoroughfares; then they could simply have built some dormitories, eating rooms (cafeterias, refectories etc.) and public toilets — for the convenience of the Cynics. That they did not do so, damns them completely in my eyes, and I feel therefore that they deserved whatever trouble and hygene hazard, the Cynics presented them with. One imagines also that the Cynics weren't the only people running around the streets and behaving in this fashion, and many a country nowadays also needs to look to the problem of creating enough facilities and rest-rooms for its inhabitants — so it behoves us not to laugh too loudly at the Cynics!

But, whatever their practices, and no matter how bizarre or extreme they may have been, the Cynics certainly made Athens an extremely interesting place to live in; and possibly the Tourist Bureau of those days thoroughly understood and appreciated the treasure in their midst. And we have all enjoyed slightly less extreme, and more moderate versions, of the modern Cynic; encamped on our pavements in the 20th century; who likewise, add an exotic flavour to our hum-drum cities and centres of commerce.

Due to the number of out-of-work, bewildered, and property-less people roaming the streets of Athens following the Peloponnesian Wars, this new philosophical sect attracted many followers. Interestingly enough, they condemned slavery (not loudly enough, or threateningly enough to upset the Establishment however; or else quite obviously they would have "done them in" — as they had "done in" Socrates) but they *did* condemn it! The system of Slavery though, was as indispensable then, as it is today, and the only difference between then, and now, being that today, the slaves are given a "Vote". But, our Members of Parliament (the modern form of the Athenian Assembly) are all men of property, just as they were two thousand years ago; and the slaves of our Laurium silver mines are nowadays paid a wage — although they certainly do not choose their occupation now, any more than they did then. Necessity makes the

Miner — not Desire! The exploitation of Man by Man continues always — in some form or other — Not, because of any essential economic system, or Natural Law — but simply because Greed begets Need. And the Greedy Men of this world must needs create the Needy — in order for the Greedy to fattern off the carcasses of the Needy. In order to create a feast for some — Man must needs create a famine for others! This is an ironic truth, but hardly a comforting one, for those who are hungry.

Antisthenes' school for the *Poor* in Athens, rose in great influence among them; and although he took no fees for instructions, he and his students canvassed the streets and hovels of their area like dedicated social workers, and they accepted alms, in order for their movement to survive. And so this Sect developed into a type of Monastic Body; albeit a rather a sexy one. But we shall come to that later. Ah! you say. Yes, yes! I say. We must imbibe some knowledge before passing onto passages which titivate our fancy. Work before pleasure is the rule!

One day, one of the priests of the Olympian God System approached Antisthenes and began rambling on about the wonders of Heaven, and how good it would be in the Next Life; and how it didn't matter about this one; as in the Elysian Fields, Antisthenes and company would get as much "tiropetta" (Greek Cheese Pie in the sky!) as they liked. Antisthenes regarded the priest cynically for a moment and then asked quietly, "If it is all so good, then why do you not die now?" Whereupon the Priest suddenly discovered that he was very late for a sacrifice, and scurried off to the temple in speechless embarrassment— unable to debate the question.

Antisthenes though a patient man, was not above using a club on some occasions, when the words of wisdom failed to penetrate thick heads (all teachers and students please note! Corporal Punishment was in vogue in Athens!) and he layed around him quite vehemently when deciding tricky and particularly difficult cases of marital cacophony and strife. And eventually, the Cynics added to their civic and social duties by becoming the arbitrators of the Poor — a type of mobile Citizen's Advice Bureau, dispensing counsel to all in need.

At first however, the great man refused to take on the eccentric Diogenes, as a student, but Diogenes tenaciously persisted in his endeavour to become attached to this sect, and not only **joined** the Cynic movement, but almost **took it over**. Diogenes originally, was a bankrupt Banker from Sinope, (a colony of Ionia) so the story goes; and he arrived in Athens as did so many others, looking for some way in which to make his living; for a place to put his head; and a way to put some food into his belly. Was he really a Banker we may ask? Or only a down-trodden clerk in a bank which had gone bankrupt? This is definitely a very sticky point of etiquette as most people who work in banks as clerical slaves love introducing themselves to other people — as Bankers! "I'm in Banking," they say pompously, and immediately visions of wall-safes and expensive dinners, bottles of claret, and mellow cigars; fly before the inner eye of their companion. It is as difficult today, to find a person confessing to merely being a **clerk** in a Bank, as it used to be in Britain to find a person (before the Comprehensive School Education Scheme was introduced) confessing to being an ex-pupil of a Secondary School — and not a respected Old Boy or Girl from a Grammar. Just about the whole world seeks to claim membership of the Middle, or Upper Middle Class if possible! And with everyone protesting that they are members of the Inner Circle as it were, sometimes one wonders whether there actually is a Lower Class or outer circle, after all!

Anyhow, Diogenes who was born in 412 B.C. and who died in 323 B.C. (strangely enough on the same day that Alexander the Great passed away) appeared in this 'Neoplutoi' (New Rich, and Old Poor!) Athens; adopted the beggar's garb of wallet and staff; and made a home in an empty tub, or wine cask, in the courtyard of the Temple of Cybele in the City centre. Very probably he slept in a tub, simply because he didn't have anywhere else to sleep; and although too poor to own a bed, he managed to attract countless famous Hetairai (including the famous Lais) and invited them to tête a tête with him in his empty cask. One finds it rather hard to imagine the glamourous Lais conducting her affairs in public in this way, but then who knows? Maybe she was publicizing herself and her wares, and drumming up a bit of trade for herself, in this rather drastic and overtly exhibitionistic manner.

Diogenes drank from his hands, without the benefit of a cup — as he had observed children do; slept on the ground (— when he wanted a change from his tub) ate whatever he found lying around the place; (— including raw meat) and followed not only the teachings of Antisthenes, but adapted certain doctrines from the Mystic Cult of Orphism as well as incorporating various ideas from Pythagoras. And he traipsed the streets of Athens in the daylight hours, bearing a candle, or lamp, in his hands, and proclaiming to all and sundry that he was in search of an Honest Man. This is not really as funny as it sounds, considering how few Honest Men (or Women, for that matter!) can be found in abundance in the world nowadays. In the ancient times there was a similar scarcity of Righteous People, and the way things were going in Athens at that time, Sodom and Gomorrah could be considered to have been only small potatoes in the vice and corruption business!

Diogenes was the perfect example of the Detached personality. He injured no one; but he completely refused to recognise any of the Laws of the society, as he realised that they were all corrupt. (Perhaps he had been a real Banker after all, and that's why he realised how hypocritical the system was, as it takes a thief to know a thief, so they say!) And long before the Stoics came on the Athenian scene, he announced that he was a "Cosmopolites" or, "Citizen of the World" (from the Greek, 'cosmos' meaning world, and 'polites' meaning city.) and like Chekhov's character seeking to be a **'World Soul'** in "The Seagull", the narrow confines of nationality were far too limiting for him — and besides which — belonging to any particular City or State quite obviously wasn't getting him anywhere — so what was the use of rigid nationalism!

Like most philosophers in general (and Dionysos, the God of Wine in particular) Diogenes liked travelling; and he spent some time in exploring Syracuse; and on one occasion was captured while hitch-hiking around the Mediterranean, and sold into slavery to a gentleman named Xeniades, in Corinth. So Diogenes the most radical of philosophers, shared the dubious honour and pleasure of experiencing the joys of active participation in the slave market, from first hand experience; (a sort of 'inside view' of things!) with that most conservative of thinkers — Plato. It is strange indeed that two such diametrically opposed philosophers should have had such a thing in common. One feels that possibly even in these circumstances, Plato must have had a more humane time as a slave, and that more than likely he was able to bring more 'savoir faire' to his role of bondsman — than was Diogenes.

When Xeniades asked Diogenes what exactly he could do (possibly Diogenes had not exactly proved a good investment in either the kitchens, or in the stables) the philosopher answered modestly, "Govern Men". So the befuddled slave-owner put his new acquisition to work, tutoring his sons. Incidentally it is from this time in history that we derive the expression "worth his salt", as slaves were actually exchanged for that precious commodity in those days, and as Xeniades soon discovered that Diogenes was just not worth his particular allocation of this essential condiment; he let the trouble-maker go!

The eccentric Diogenes made the entire Cynic Movement famous and historically memorable, with his coarse good humour and scandalously free speech; and almost proved to be a complete one-man publicity department for the others of his band. There are many fabled and noteworthy quotations attributed to Diogenes but we must only mention a few; or else we will never manage to bring on our stage, the other philosophers who are still waiting impatiently in the wings. Once, when he saw the son of a famous Courtesan throwing stones at a crowd of people, he warned him sharply and succinctly, "Take care lest you hit your own father." And on another occasion when he was visited by Alexander the Great, while he was sitting in his tub and meditating, the powerful king (supposed to have been powerful anyway, although it might have been Aristotle who was the real power behind the throne!) asked him what he the philosopher, wanted, and Diogenes replied tersely that all he wanted, was for him (Alexander) to get out of his sun! This remark may have been motivated by a need for warmth, as Athens in Winter, with all that marble, can be an extremely chilly place; or maybe Diogenes was a fanatical sun-bather, and even more keen than a modern-day Australian on securing a healthy sun-tan. Whatever the reason behind this rather discourteous retort however, Alexander is reputed to have then said, "If I were not Alexander, I would wish to be Diogenes." And Diogenes is then said to have returned the compliment; which must surely give all of us food for thought!

Diogenes was a contemporary of both Alexander and Aristotle, and he died, as the Historians insist on telling us, on the same day as the Macedonian King. Alexander however was in his early thirties, while Diogenes was aged ninety and some years; and the philosopher is supposed to have finished himself off, by the simple procedure of holding his breath, until he finally expired. Suicide was a legitimate way of Life (or should one say, Death?) for the Cynics.

After his death, the people of Corinth (who must have been considerably saddened by the loss of such a colourful and cheery figure to their city) raised a large marble statue of a dog upon his tomb; and although I did not find it on record, doubtless, his funeral abounded in scores of weeping women, as Diogenes had been a singularly sexually exciting character in his time. (It must also be noted that the life-cycle of this philosopher was strangely similar to that of Dionysos the Wine God, and etymologically speaking, even their names are alike, as "Dionysos" in Greek, means "the son of Zeus", or "the son of God" — while "Diogenes", means the "one derived, or, coming from a God". But I shall leave this interesting piece of trivial information, for the Reader to ponder merrily at his own leisure!)

This philosophy of Cynicism actually equalled more in the nature of a sect than a philosophy school, because the members were not particularly interested in logic, or in ideas; unlike Plato and the other classical philosophers. Their philosophy was really a Way of Life —especially, for the poor. Metaphysics, to their way of thinking was a complete waste of time, or simply "Typhos", which was a term of contempt, meaning a mist, wind, or illusions or — the dire consequences of a bellyful of beans! The Cynics were only interested in finding a way to actually live, or, to endure this dreadful life, in as moral and as sensible a way, as possible; and they pursued not the Physical, nor the Metaphysical questions of Life, but only the Ethical issues. They believed that all Wisdom came from Nature, and that the only real philosophy was Ethics; and that the aim of life was happiness. And, they put this philosophy into practice in daily life; instead of merely theorizing on it, and putting students to sleep, in a classroom!

The way to achieve happiness said the Cynics, was to lead a good life, and not to pursue only the external aids to pleasure, but instead, to follow a simple, and natural Life-style. Pleasure was alright in itself, if it came from one's own labour and efforts, and, if it didn't bring remorse. (How many pleasures are there, which are not attended by the Bitch Goddess Remorse, one may cynically ask!) But Wealth ate away the soul, they declared, just as rust destroyed steel objects. Slavery was certainly and totally unjust, said the Cynics, but it was really rather unimportant; as Man in general, was a slave to so many things. (How true!) There were many different kinds of slavery, the Cynics contended, and only the Internal Freedom really mattered, and therefore external liberty was just a side issue. (It is obviously this attitude which convinced the "Establishment" that it was safe to leave the Cynics alone; otherwise they would probably have bought Hemlock in bulk, and poured it liberally into the drinking-water of Cynosarges!) Only Virtue itself was really important to the Cynics, and Virtue meant eating, possessing, and desiring as little as possible! In point of fact the Athenian and Corinthian Establishments must have smiled with pleasure on hearing these words. The Cynics were actually making the Poor **happy with their Lot** in life, and the Revolution was still light years away! "Thank the gods, and Thank Philosophy as well!" the Rich must have muttered.

Sexual desire was okey though, said most of the Cynics, (there was some division in the ranks on this issue however!) and indeed Diogenes and some other extremists wanted to incorporate a policy of free love and community wives. But then most of the philosophers of the Post-Socratic period felt exactly the same way on this subject, and many other progressive gentlemen heralding in various epoch making movements in history have come up with an identical solution to this problem of sexual ownership. It is strange to relate however, that **women** never get carried away with such megalomania; and progressive females are **never** heard demanding community husbands, and sexual serfs. Quite obviously sex is much more important to men than to women; and possessing a sex object, or having one available for possession, at the drop of a hat; is very important to them also. Therefore, it behoves women, I think, to start looking at the world with fresh eyes — maybe we should start sharing out our menfolk (on our own terms of course) in order to bring peace and security to the world!

But conversely, Antisthenes, the Founder of Cynicism, had advised that Masturbation was superior to actual Sexual Intercourse, and that this pleasure was to be encouraged in place of the other; and that Sexual feelings were to be **completely eliminated**, if possible. He also attempted to give up the art and the pleasure of eating, as well as surrendering the fleshy indulgences of the libido. And he is supposed by and large, to have found it easier to discipline the appetite of his stomach, than to quench his sexual desire! However, like Heracleitus, Antisthenes only drank water, and this probably helped to keep him in a state of grace, and free from too much temptation in this area. The Cynics avoided marriage, like the Plague; and those who could not manage celibacy, only patronised the prostitutes. But it seems, that on the whole, they were tremendously attractive to both the Hetairai, and to the Women of Virtue in Athens, who all pursued the philosophers unashamedly. Could this possibly have been because these Athenian Ladies had the perverse desire to drag down these men of pure detachment? And could it have been some type of challenge and thrill, to degrade these ascetics? Or, could it possibly have been that the Cynics were the **only** red-blooded men around the place; and the only men who **weren't practising sexual inversion**? Or, were all the Athenians over-sexed anyway, due to the lack of entertainment facilities (e.g. Television) which we enjoy today? I leave it to the Reader to decide for himself! The Cynics stated (and quite logically and coolly) that the hunger for sex was the same as the hunger for food; and that therefore if we encouraged the satisfaction of the food drive; by eating in public — why then shouldn't we satisfy the sex drive; by answering that call in public also! In both life and death, Man should be independent and choose the time and the place for everything, they said; and Diogenes certainly proved this point; over; and over; and over again!

On the whole, the Cynics thought that the best society was one that was completely without aritifices and laws.- By Nature, Men were **not** civilized animals, they argued; and Men only lived in societies for fear of solitude and danger (and we could probably give the same reasons for the institution of Marriage!) and Man should peel off this dishonest superficial veneer of civilization. The Stoics, and Rousseau are therefore, the direct descendents of the Cynics (as are various strict religious orders of Christianity) and after the death of Diogenes, the Cynics became even more like a Religious Order; but-like an Order, which was minus a religion. They had a rule of poverty; lived only on the alms which they collected; existed in a state of either **extreme** celibacy, or **extreme** promiscuity (both states probably amounting to one and the same thing!) opened free schools for the Poor, everywhere; and continued sleeping in the streets, and entrusting themselves to Fate.

Cynic ascetism maintained that great training ('ascesis' in Greek means "training") and toil, were necessary for life; and some Cynics, in a similar manner to the Hedonists, said that Man should be the Master of his pleasures and become completely detached, so that he would not be dependent on them. They cut loose from the whole system of City-life and vigorously attacked all forms of convention, and the normal standards which had been laid down by the Establishment. The true Cynic felt it his mission (a Divine Mission in fact!) to wander through the world, as a doctor of souls, dispelling all Man's illusions, and teaching truth and virtue — by ferocious criticism of the false and the wrong.

The Cynics indulged in great freedom of speech, and deliberate immodesty, in order to strike hardest against all the City-State hypocrisy which they saw around them. Their partly comic, and partly serious preaching and writing, later also had an effect on classical literature and thought, and the style of the Sceptics was particularly influenced by them. They believed in complete individualism in both their Life-style and in their teaching, which is why it is very difficult in consequence, to actually pin down a standard behaviour or thought pattern for all Cynics. They all regarded themselves as Citizens of the Universe however, (complete Cosmopolitans) and not as members of the rigid City-State; and like those other great cosmopolitans — the Gypsies — were nomadic wanderers, possessed of an insatiable need to travel and to teach. This though immediately causes us to bring into question the old truism regarding Gypsies; and to ask ourselves if the Gypsy is a person who sincerely **likes** to travel? Or is it simply that as he was once dispossessed and without a permanent home, he was therefore forced to live in this untidy way, until gradually he began to accept it as the 'norm' — or, biologically speaking; to become so adapted to it, that he specialized in it, as his own way of both survival — and of defence? I often wonder myself, if all the people who publicly deplore the wandering habits of the Romany or the Tinker, were actually given the chance to have these free souls living permanently next-door to them on an Estate — if, they then wouldn't suddently decide that it was much better for the Gypsy to be a 'travelling man' after all! But, just as the Writer, who for some reason or other finds himself ostracised from society, and forced to take up the pen in solitude — only to begin to like that way of life after a awhile —like it so much in fact that wild horses, or promises of garden parties couldn't tear him from his stationary hermitage and lonely exile — so the Gypsy, when all is said and done; looks over the modern plumbing, and listens to people tell of the delights of working in the system; sniffs delicately at the pollution smog cloud hovering over the city, and says to himself, "By God, maybe they didn't want me to begin with, but I don't think I'm all that keen on wanting them now, either!" And he hurries on his way to green fields and pastures new, and knows within his heart (and is quite sure about the matter) that it is better to travel hopefully — than to arrive! And perhaps, there was something of the nature of this attitude to life, in the Cynics of Ancient Greece also!

On the whole, though, the Cynics played the game of life with the cards they had been dealt; and they were optimistic pessimists; doing what they could, with **what** they had. Like the first fish thrown up on land, they knew that they could choose to remain melancholy marine animals out-of water; or, to begin the evolutionary leap towards becoming Men. The Cynics chose to Detach themselves from both the squalor and the hypocrisy of the City-State and the power struggle, and were well-known amongst the other dispossessed folk, for their wisdom and their realism in facing life.

Besides Diogenes the Dog, however, there were other famous personalities in this interesting Movement, as for example, Crates, a cheerful hunchback who worked among the poor most strenuously; and the magnificent Stilpo, another Cynic, who, when questioned on how much, (and of what value) property, he had lost during an invasion of his city, answered sagaciously, "They were not able to carry off the one thing I value most — my education." And besides one's education, one's memories and experiences are likewise inviolate; and extremely valuable commodities — also completely invulnerable to attack, me thinks!

Crates (who was around the ancient world in approximately 328 B.C.) taught Zeno the Cypriot, who eventually founded Stoicism; and he (Crates) was a Theban, who like the gentleman in the New Testament, had turned over his fortune of 300 talents to his fellow citizens, before beginning his career of preaching in the slums and of giving practical help to the needy. Unlike Diogenes, he denounced Sexual Activities of any kind however, and criticized the people for their sexual looseness; counselling hunger as the cure for all sexual desire. (His reasoning probably being that the cravings for the satisfaction of one appetite would occupy the mental processes of the sufferer so entirely, that all thoughts regarding the other desire would therefore be banished utterly from his mind!) His rich pupil Hipparchia however, fell in love with him and threatened to kill herself, unless her parents gave her to him. Crates though, was as shocked and disgusted at this idea, as were Hipparchia's respectable parents, and he threw his empty beggar's wallet at her feet, in order to dissuade her from this reckless step. But she would have her way, and she married him against all opposition — and it is recorded that she not only married him, but, that she consumated the marriage in public as well! Definitely, the Cynics were an interesting bunch of communistic ascetics!

Some Cynics, as we have seen, indulged the appetites of the Flesh, while others did not; but they were all wandering mendicant teachers; owning a single rough garment; who went bare-foot all year round; and who generally existed on a coarse diet of lentils and cold water. Doubtless it was this diet of lentils, cooked without the benefit of cummin powder, which was responsible for much of their philosophical pessimism, and for the stress which they laid on the "typhos" of life.

In the Christian world we have had examples of a type of Cynicism with the Italian, Saint Francis of Assisi, and before him there were the 4th century Saints Basil and Gregory, who also advocated a monastic way of life completely stripped of all excess goods and emotions. There was also that fascinating social and religious phenomenon, the "Pillar Hermit" of early Christian Egypt, who sat upon his lofty dais for years, refusing to come down or to mix in a sinful world. This movement spread throughout the Christian world and one gentleman, by name of Daniel, sat on a pillar outside Constantinople for over thirty-three years — continually being covered by snow and ice, and suffering horribly from the elements — but steadfastly refusing to decend. Then there was the craze for monasticism in Ireland during the period when that country was the land of 'Saints and Scholars' and people tore off willy-nilly to mountain tops and secluded cells. And these are just some examples of Monasticism, and Monasticism itself is actually an example of a severely polarised community in which a large number of people are forced to "opt out" — whether they do it for philosophical reasons, or not. Christian or non-Christian, the monastic movement provides a home, and an aim in life for the Dispossessed and the Disenchanted. While it is rather difficult to judge how much the early pagan philosophy movements of monasticism were influenced by sects in India (such as the "Gymnosophists) or by ideas from further East — we can say with certainty that they were to some extent, a reaction to the society and to its lack of logic, and justice, and harmony. And so long as we have societies, we will probably always have monastics, or spiritual 'Drop-Outs'.

The Cynics were the direct antithesis to the classical philosophy movement of Socrates, Plato and Aristotle, and they were only concerned with the well-being of Man — which aim was to be attained by the rule of right and of reason, and by the innner knowledge of truth. The Classicists on the other hand, favoured long hard work, patient study, and scientific thinking. But then the classicists were actually from the Establishment itself — secure Middle, or Upper Class 'Insiders'.

But the "Outsiders" of society, the Cynics, arose from a different class of people, a class composed of both old and new Dispossessed. They were mentally, perhaps also physically; and definitely — *intellectually*-dispossed. And this class multiplied increasingly, due to the wars between the States; and more especially, due to the wars between the citizens of each City-State — i.e. the war, between the 'Haves' and the 'Have Nots'. The actual movements of Cynicism as such, disappeared from the social scene by the end of the 3rd century, but as we have pointed out, it simply popped up later in another guise in the Christian world, and it is still with us in some form or other, somewhere in the world today. And Cynicism, and the later sequels to it, were all derived from that questioning of the Role of Society which had begun with the Sophist Hippias — "I believe all of you are kinsmen, friends, and fellow-citizens, not by law, but by Nature; for by Nature, like is akin to like, but Law is the Tyrant of Mankind, and often makes us do many things which are against Nature." Of course Hippias is not really the first to have criticized the 'System', but he is one of the first few whom we have on record for doing so.

Athens which gave birth to Cynicism, was not an expanding society anymore, but instead it had become a continually contracting one — and the dance of Athenian supremacy was finally coming to an end under the dictates of progress and evolution. To quote the words of the late American Author Flannery O'Connor, "Everything that rises must converge"; and the Athenians were converging — but *very* reluctantly! They wanted things to continue just as they had been, with no difference, no change — in a very static and Parmenidian world. They could not, (or they refused to) come to terms with the flow and flux of life, and insisted on back-pedalling furiously — their heads resolutely stuck down under the sand.

The Hedonist and Cynic Movements signalled the coming of the end of an era, and of the end of the Greek City-State, and of Individualism as a creed. Once more, this time under Alexander, the Greeks would be given the chance to work together and to make something of themselves, but — they would muff it. The Greeks, unfortunately for them, had become their own worst enemies. They would fall, lose their lands, and their influence, simply because they seemingly loved to fight each other, **more** than they loved to fight anyone else! The keyword to describe the Greek character was Jealousy. Jealousy had been both to their advantage and to their disadvantage. Jealousy had caused them to expand in the first place, to go to other lands, to learn, to invent, to trade, and to compete; and by this very competition; to improve the standard of their life. But now, Jealousy would cause them to lose everything which they had ever gained. Jealousy and rampant Individualism, would be their eventual undoing.

The Cynic Movement in particular stressed the good of others, rather than the cultivation of this vicious selfishness and narrowness of outlook. And inevitably it led the way, in some degree, to the more universal doctrine of Christianity — which originally was based upon the need for a philosophy of broad influence which would appeal to the masses; and which would unite them to a certain extent — which is what the Romans deemed most necessary, anyway!

This was a peiod of great upheaval in the Classical World; and the way of life, and the mode, or, business of slavery in particular; was beginning to destroy the very system which it had built. There were just too many slaves, and too many poor. Too much misery, and too little justice. Too much unhappiness — and, as always, **far too many wars!**

In order to round off this chapter (and as promised earlier) something more must be said on the subject of the "Women of Pleasure" in Ancient Greece, and of those in Athens, in particular. They might of course, be referred to as 'Women of Easy Virtue', or whatever other euphemism people like to use, in order to describe their function, and the Trade of Prostitution itself. As so many prostitutes were involved with the Philosophers, and in the philosophy movement also, they must have had some effect on the flowering of Intellectualism in Greece at that time, and so a few words about them, should not go amiss.

Firstly there were the "Porni" who were obviously mostly girls of foreign origin who were working in the low-class brothels of the town, and who were particularly in demand in Piraeus, where the Merchant Fleetwas stationed. These "Porni" did not however, have a great effect on the philosophers because they dealt mainly with the ordinary worker, or sailor, and as is the case nowadays in large cities, these girls were members of the Dispossessed Class — girls from families in which the father had been killed or enslaved, and the family split apart, so that the girl had no Protector. Nowadays the average whore does not come from a family in which the father is enslaved (at least not generally) but usually she has lost her Male Protector at an early age due to some reason or other, and thus is forced onto the streets. Orphan girls in ancient times like those in modern times, were always more open to exploitation. In fact that is really all that prostitution has ever been about — it is the open and easy exploitation of certain defenceless females by some Male Patriarch or Patron; in order to make money out of other Males who are in need (i.e. sexually frustrated.) There are various romantic pictures presented of prostitutes in literature, but hardly one of them is true to life. Most prostitutes are unhappy, poor, down-trodden souls; very few retain any wealth — or achieve any status; and most of them would not be in that position if they'd ever been able to get a man to provide for them legally (i.e. in the institution of Marriage) or — if they'd ever received some education, or learnt some skill which they could have used in order to earn a living. Solon, (640 — 558 B.C.) the wise Law-Giver of ancient Greece, decreed that all fathers had to have their sons taught a skill, or educated in some way, so that they could support themselves. He did not consider the girls of the family however. If he had done so then he would have received my undying admiration. But like most men, he only saw the story from his own Male angle and in fact he institutionalized prostitution in Athens in order to stop the 'Respectable Women' being troubled. So the whore pays for the Lady, and contributes to keeping her a Lady; and the Lady (nine times out of ten) has only harsh words for her less fortunate sister. What it boils down to is that the girl from a poor family who has not received any training for a trade, or position, has no hope of making a decent living (no pun intended I assure you) and therefore must sell herself, in order to survive. If Society seriously wanted to banish prostitution from the streets, or anywhere else, (and it quite obviously doesn't) then it would start gigantic re-training, or work-planning schemes, for girls such as these, and then they could learn some accomplishments in order to put the margarine on their bread, and possibly even a little jam as well. And thus speaks the moralist — So, Zarathustra look out!

The amusing and amazing thing about the Athenian and Corinthian experiments in prostitution is that a large number of the Hetairai (how large a number is not disclosed) were educated and skilled women — far more educated than the Ladies of Virtue residing behind their husband's walls. But even that may be a romantic picture drawn by Male Scholars, who after all are understandably a little touchy on the subject of the exploitation of women, and who would probably not like to consider the idea that their great Male Thinkers and Statesmen were carousing and demeaning themselves in a low, vulgar fashion with illiterate women!

If it is true though that the Hetairai were interested in Rhetoric, Philosophy, and Logic etc. then it is an even greater indictment of the men of Ancient Greece that they should have presumed to buy, sell, and use these intellectual women like so much horse-flesh (incidentally, the Author does not condone the exploitation of horse-flesh either! No exploitation anywhere is her motto!) and it is strange but understandable, (and like all the paradoxes of life), that great men who thought great thoughts, should have been able to descend to great depths in their attitude to, and treatment of, women. This is all just part of the Male/Female Hatred Syndrome. What is remarkable is that these women with their cultivated minds could have borne to have earned their living in this way. But then, "Necessity moves Everything" as the atomists said, and as there were no official jobs for women at that time, they had to do what they could, as they had to eat — and that was that!

The Philosophers themselves thoughwerea rather strange breed, because apart from Alcidamas, no one really raised his voice loudly on the Slavery Issue; and the exploitation of women in prostitution is just another form of slavery — even now! But then they didn't raise their voices against the exploitation of young male prostitutes who were used by older men, either! Truly the immoral morality, and the comfortable rationalization of Man, is astounding — and never fails to impress.

It is also astounding that Lais of Corinth was reputedly able to bring to the game, or skill of love, something fresh and amusing on each occasion that she indulged. At least this is what the Scholars say! No doubt Lais must have had a more cultured and cultivated clientele than the average Call-Girl nowadays, or else she would not have been able to manage this. Living by the flesh is a little like living by the sword, and probably — spiritually speaking — much more dangerous. It would be most interesting, sociologically speaking, to read an account of what Lais herself had to say on the subject, and not to have to rely solely upon some rosy, romantic accounts from her male customers. Unfortunately there is nothing on record to tell us exactly how the Hetairai went about their job, and how they felt about their occupation. Were they very liberated women who slept with the men they fancied? Or were they working girls doing what they had to? Whatever the answer is the Hetairai were constantly on the go, and in and out of the philosophy movement continually,and obviously a source of inspiration, and comfort to the philosophers of the day. Therefore they mustbe considered as contributors to the general cultural scene in Greece at that time; no matter how scandalous was their profession. One thing is sure though, and that is, that the male scholars who write of this period can no more do justice to describing the situation from the woman's angle, than they can fly auto-propelled to the moon! And the lovers of history, obviously need some female Historian to delve deeply into this subject to bring forth some more information.

CHAPTER 10

PHILOSOPHY GOES CLASSICAL AND BECOMES ESTABLISHED.

PLATO-The Philosopher in search of a King — and a Solution.

As previously shown in Chapter 9, following the death of Socrates in 399 B.C. Athens started falling apart at the seams. It was now "down-hill" all the way in Greece, and the City-State was a dying institution. Democracy just did not work — or at least the Athenians just could not seem to make it do so.

At the end of the Peloponnesian War, the Naval supremacy of Greece had passed into the hands of the Spartans; however, as they refused to deviate — not even to the slightest degree — from their old system of Feudalism; which entailed a closed economy, and a perpetually rigid social system, based upon a programme of total asphyxiation of the individual — they did not bother to exploit this opportunity. The Spartans had the ships, and the control of the seas; but they did not know how, (or, did not desire) to develop a commercial empire. So, once again, Athens raised her bloodied head, and attempted for a second time to become the greatest power in the Mediterranean. This she actually achieved by 370 B.C. and once again found herself ruling a co-alition of Greek States. But in having won the battle, Athens had lost the war, and her second supremacy period cost her dear. By 355 B.C. she was once more without funds, friends, allies, or, confidence in her role — and she was in a state of dangerous isolation.

Both commerce and industry flourished during this period of supremacy, but the development of this industry and commerce caused bad blood between the Athenians and the other Greeks, and even between the Athenians themselves. Most of the Greek States moved uneasily under the yoke of the Athenian control, and in consequence were continually and sporadically revolting. While in Athens itself (to quote Plato) there was created "One City of the Rich, and the other, a City of the Poor." —Needless to state, both these cities were at war with one another.

The Athenian Spartan conflict, and the Peloponnesian War; like the Persian war (like every war anywhere, at any time) had shuffled the sociological deck of cards; and in the game of life, some people drew a lucky card and became very rich (richer in fact than they had ever dreamed possible) while others were not so lucky;and they became destitute and dispossessed, and joined the ranks of the Poor down in the streets. Isocrates the Historian, described the situation in Athens in 366 B.C. in these words "The rich have become so unsocial that those who own property had rather throw their possessions into the sea than lend aid to the needy." So, as the Greedy became even more avaricious, the Needy became even more desperate, and they swelled in numbers — causing untold problems for the Greedy.

Due to the terrible inflation which occurred as a result of the sudden boom in the city economy during the 2nd Athenian Supremacy period, as people moved from the devastated land into the city centre, and wealth became a moveable asset rather than an immoveable one — so Banking, like other City activities and businesses, suffered in consequence; and when eventually the air went out of the balloon, so the Banks were forced to close, and the Middle Classes were hard hit and began to fall to the level of the Lower Classes. And with this falling of the Middle Classes, the poor began to rise even more threateningly. It is after all the Middle Class who acts as a guard dog to keep the poor man away from the rich man's throat. Destroy this guard dog, and the social system is left unprotected and wide open to attack, revolt, and anarchy. Societies in which there is a large and comfortable Middle Class are therefore generally the most stable; as they provide a not impossible goal for the Lower Class to aim for, and as generally this Middle Class is a most productive group which can also supply the much needed Liberals and Artists of a community. One cannot create Middle Class morality on a Lower Class income unfortunately, so if the Upper Classes are to rest safely in their beds, and to enjoy a good night's sleep it is absolutely essential for their own good that they incorporate a strong Middle-Class as overseers for them.

But at this period in history the Intellectuals of Athens, more and more, began to direct their sympathies, and to give their support to the Poor — (after all the teachers and philosophers were almost as poor as the street people by now.) The Rich, tried to keep their wealth intact, and to beat off any overtures or entreaties on the part of others; and the Middle Class, (what was left of them) began to mutter darkly to each other in the Market Place — And during this gigantic change-over to a new and completely mercantile economy, everyone began to hate, and to fear, everyone else.

There was no point in trying to return to the Land, it was still suffering from the ravages of war, (the Spartans had burnt large areas) and the olive tree (a staple crop for the Greeks) takes an extremely long time to grow — (16 years to bring forth fruit and 40 years to reach perfection) and the fig trees were not in a much better condition either. Farmers gave up on this impossible struggle and set off for the town, dragging their families behind them. The Greek World, and Athens in particular, stood poised on the brink of an economic abyss, similar in catastrophic results to that which occurred in the U.S.A. in the 1930's A.D. (In the U.S.A. the crash on the Stock Market, due to inflation, was also accompanied by a problem of land erosion in the South; and the destitute farming communities had to forsake the land and to head for the city. In the U.S.A. there were Bank failures at this time, and growing numbers of poor in the streets; crime waves became a common feature also, and the only factor which really prevented the situation from becoming worse, was the economic boom and industrial production stimulated by the 2nd World War.)

In Athens, the more intelligent members of the community also realised that there was need of a war; a war to supply them with reparations payments, booty, and large amounts of land on which to expand; and more importantly, land for them to send their poor to, as colonizers and settlers. In fact, the Athenians had precisely the same problem as the British have always had, and that is, that their land area was far too small to satisfy their population growth. The Athenians (the British were later to follow their example) had found out, quite early on in life, that the only way for them to survive, and to deal with the ever sticky problem of social discontent and class warfare, was to build-up trading posts and colonies, and to send their poor and discontented to these colonies, so that they in turn could become rich — without having to take a single drachma off the rich ruling classes of Athens! But the problem facing the Athenians in 366 B.C., was that they had made so many enemies in the Mediterranean, that they couldn't follow through with this old and much used plan of theirs for getting rid of troublesome people and dissident citizens. So therefore colonization as a form of pacification of the social problem in Athens, was out! War was still a good bet for eradicating the unproductive rabble and easing the social pressure, but there was one very large obstacle in the way of a war; and that was that — **Nobody** actually wanted to go to war, or to fight for anyone else! Nobody thought it a good idea for **him** to risk his neck; although he thought it a good idea for everyone else to do so. The people of Athens had become cynical in the extreme; and the war which was needed, in order to create new prosperity for them, would eventually be waged by the naive Macedonians under Alexander. The Athenians would be very happy to partake in the spoils of a military campaign, but they had no intention of actually participating in it. But Alexander, and the expansion of the Hellenic Empire, really concern our next chapter, as the Philosopher Aristotle was one of the master minds of that neat piece of economic engineering. For now we must deal with Aristotle's teacher, Plato, and observe how he believed the dangerous situation in Athens should have been resolved.

Plato, and some other intellectuals of the day, decided to detach themselves from both the leaders, and the led; and observing the situation quite coolly came to the conclusion, that the only possible solution to alleviate the political mayhem surrounding them, lay in the establishment of a type of Elitist Communism — with the State being ruled by a Philosophical King, or Group of Academics, who would keep all the classes in their correct place — that is, in a type of rigid Parmenidian immobility — which would never allow any dangerous Heracleitian flux, flow, or change!

Life, however, equals change and development — and Life always will. That is what Life is all about — Change! So, the philosopher was chasing an illusion — and he was destined to end up empty handed. Plato also wanted one part of Greece to be dominant over the other City-States, as he thought, that if the Greeks were more unified, less individualistic, and considerably less free; then there would be more order and harmony in their lives. And so he commenced his search for a strong philosophical dictator to rule his Utopia, and this quest of his would involve a life-time; a great deal of effort; and not a little despair!

Unlike his student Aristotle, Plato knew absolutely nothing about Biology, and this was a great shame, because he never did manage to understand what the life forces really were, and in consequence he spent a lot of time searching for an ideal world, which could **never** become reality. Plato had been interested in poetry before becoming enamoured with philosophy; and poetry (at least considered so in those days) was an idealistic occupation concerned with idealistic people and events and places. When Plato turned from poetry to science, he turned not to earthy Biology, nor to commonsensical Physics; but to abstract Geometry, and to the safe realm of numbers; and far away from men, and their concrete problems. He then attempted to fit messy, untidy, mortals into his pure, idealistic academic plans, and he was fated to fail — right from the start. Plato had no faith in evolution, and in the eventual rise of man to a more thoughtful animal — more able to create a better world for all. Therefore, the only solution as he, Plato, saw it, was to find a stong tyrant who would carry out Plato's plans, for the good of the whole. He therefore commenced looking around the Greek World, in order to find such a man. Athens, he considered, was a dead loss! They were in such a confounded disorder, that the philosopher held no hope for them in his heart. But we shall now consider the two States far from Athens, which could have provided the answer to the unification problem of the Greeks; one of them in fact was chosen to fulfil the dreams of Plato; and the other; to carry out the plans of Aristotle.

Although Athens and the older areas of affluence and influence in the Greek World, were going through this traumatic and weary period of progress into a mercantile economy and form of primitive industrialization (with all the accompanying and agonizing growing pains) there were two areas, which until now, had not been of much importance; but which had been quietly building themselves up; and readying themselves, for the challenge to leadership, in the Mediterranean. One of these areas, was Macedonia; from which Alexander would soon emerge; and thence proceed to conquer more land, than any Greek had ever dreamed possible. The other area which could possibly have taken the leadership away from Athens, but which didn't, was Syracuse. And it is Syracuse which we shall examine now. It was on the Kingdom of Syracuse that Plato laid his money

— and he lost. We might almost say that Plato even lost his shirt on this race, so badly did he gamble! And it is most surprising, as the Greeks are generally renowned for their skill in such enterprizes. It seems however, that Greek Philosophers are an exception to the rule; and perhaps all outstanding individuals are actually quite different from the rest of their particular race; and that the law of National Characteristics does not apply to them. Or perhaps philosophyitself is detrimental to the gambling instinct, and therefore, those of you perusing these words, and who fancy a game of cards from time to time; should give up reading this book right now! I leave this matter entirely up to your own discretion however, and whatever the outcome, the story of Syracuse will begin right now, with no more circumlocutions, unnecessary asides, or meaningless observations.

In Syracuse Sicily, in the Italian colonies (Magna Graecia) Dionysos I and his family had been quietly enjoying a long period of stable and prosperous sovreignty; free from the troubles which had been afflicting the rest of the Greek World. By building strong defences, and by paying his soldiers well, he had established himself for thirty-eight continuous years, in a completely unopposed and secure, dictatorship. Dionysos built up a huge navy (an armada of two hundred ships) organised a very large cavalry; and even began the manufacture of weapons in Syracuse itself. The Catapult was invented as the most modern death machine of its time, and all over Syracuse, soldiers practised in deadly earnest; readying themselves for the big day. The plan of the King, was to expell the Carthaginians from Sicily completely — after all they had been a thorn in the Greek flesh since their first coming in 558 B.C. — and then he intented to take over all Sicily himself!

Dionysos, incidentally, is the King who condemned Phythias, a Pythagorean, to death; whose friend Damon took his place in the prison cell so that Phythias could go away on some business which he had to complete before the execution. As Phythias was late in arriving back, and as Damon was nearly executed in his buddy's place, this story has been told throughout the ages in order to teach the qualities of loyalty, friendship, and trust. Dionysos himself was so impressed with these two, that he pardoned Pythias, and even became a little interested in Philosophy himself; which is principally why he was to invite Plato into his court later on in life.

But Dionysos did not let philosophy stand in the way of his war plans, and he took on Carthage, and fought Hannibal's descendents as ferociously as if he had been a barbarian himself. But no matter what atrocities each side committed, and no matter how long they fought, the Carthaginians remained in Sicily, and so Dionysos decided to turn his attention elsewhere. What he couldn't manage against the barbarians, he felt sure he would easily manage against his fellow Greeks, so he commenced subjugating all the Greeks colonies of Sicily, beneath his Syracusian heel — and then he went north, and resolutely trampled all over the City-states of South Western Italy. In this process accordingly, he built up the wealth of Syracuse in war booty, and firmly established his tyranny; and in his leisure time, he also quite often indulged in a little verse writing. Dionysos was a rather cultured despot it is true, but this poetry must have been pretty bad, because the Greek Poet Philoxenus preferred to be sent to the quarries as a slave, rather than to be forced to endure it! Of course Philoxenus was a man of high taste and discrimination — and perhaps that is why he took such a drastic stance.

But it is true, that Dionysos does not appear to have enjoyed very much success with very many intellectuals; and even Plato; whom he first met when the philosopher was travelling abroad; had words with him; (and not kind ones!) and this disagreement stung Dionysos so badly, that he sold Plato into slavery, in order to teach him a lesson. More than likely he did not send Plato to the quarries, (as had been the case with the poor unfortunate Philoxenus) because the Overseer there was probably complaining about what bad workmen, poets and philosophers in general, made; and therefore Plato got off with rather lighter punishment.

Plato however did not let a little thing like being sold into slavery, disturb him. He obviously figured to himself that this war-like state of Syracuse, might provide him with a chance to prove his theories on politics, and to create his perfect state — What a dreamer he was! Poor Plato wanted so badly to establish a philosophical dictatorship, that he probably would have shaken hands with the Devil himself, in order to do so. However, Plato is not alone in this foolish attitude, as there are many intellectuals used for evil purposes in the world, solely because they had this terrible craving to see their plans, or hypotheses, put into action — and perhaps ambition, is the worst sin of all!

On the death of Dionysos I, his son Dionysos II immediately ascended the throne, but the real power in the Kingdom, rested with Dion, an uncle of Dionysos II; and a member of Plato's Academy in Athens. Dion, with the aid of Philistius, an historian living in the Syracuse Court, really ruled the place; and he, Dion, thought to establish Plato and his theories firmly in Syracuse. Plato of course had been looking for a king to control, and here was his golden opportunity. And both Dion and Plato, probably decided, that Dionysos II, would not be half as hard a nut to crack; as had been his old man. Dion, who had been supplying Plato with money in order to keep his Academy in Athens solvent, then decided that Plato should tutor Dionysos II, and should particularly give him a lot of attention in the subject of philosophy, so that eventually they could establish their Utopia (or, perhaps it should clearly be designated as Plato's Utopia — as Dion probably just followed the teaching of Plato on this issue) in Syracuse; and then unite all Sicily under them. They probably even had ideas of taking over the whole Greek World eventually, but the grave mistake they made, was in omitting from their calculations — **the human factor** — and this humanfactor proved to be the veritable spanner in the works. Dionysos II (the 'spanner') became very bored with Plato, and with Geometry, and Virtue, (and who could blame him, after all? Plato could not have been an easy person to live with either — Puritans seldom are!) and warned by others in his Court, that the Athenians, (through Plato and Dion) would take over Syracuse; expelled Dion and Plato — who then both went to Athens. This was therefore, the second time that Plato had been ignominiously thrown out of Syracuse; the first time he had been sold into slavery by Dionysos I, and now he was being exiled by Dionysos II — but, still he did not give up! One wonders really if the man had any sense at all? Quite obviously he had no pride! To be thrown out of a country on two separate occasions, and to still desire to come back, is beyond understanding. Plato must have been absolutely desperate to see his theories put into action; and seemingly, would have stood anything — just to be able to do so!

Only six years later, Plato again visited Syracuse (completely unasked!) and tried (completely unsuccessfully), to have Dionysos II reinstate his uncle Dion. Probably Plato and Dion had lost hopes of actually managing anything only through the offices of Dionysos; whom, I am sure; they looked on as a rather stupid, and ignorant — and very troublesome, boy! But this troublesome boy had sense enough not to allow Dion, his uncle, to return; and Plato left again for Athens, the sound of a slamming-door, resounding loudly in his ears. Truly, this philosopher and his exploits, puts one in mind of a Door-to-Door Salesman; and one can understand his bitterness, and the misanthropic inclinations in his old age — a most natural development, surely!

Plato now however, completely gave up on the Syracuse experiment; apart from hatching plots in the Academy in order to help Dion to gain power, and to take over control in Syracuse. There was though, an attempted coup d'etat by Dion, which failed miserably, and during which, Dion was killed; and the Academy of Plato, burnt their papers and letters; and finally settled down to accepting the inevitablity of 'never seeing their Philosopher King ruling their Utopia! (At least not in Syracuse!) Dionysos was eventually dethroned by other powers however, and Syracuse came under the direct rule of its mother city, Corinth and the stubborn young maths-hating king ended his days, by begging for his bread, and teaching school. (Hence the need to beg his bread! As we all know, that apart from a few Sophists, most teachers are so badly paid, that they are forced into mendicancy anyway!) And doubtless in his later life, Dionysos wished that he had paid more attention to Plato, and that he had learnt a bit more Geometry as well! The moral of this story must surely be that it is never amiss to learn something, as one never knows when it will come in handy — and **even Geometry** can be useful!

Now, what about this philosopher, and very strange personality, Plato — who was trying (so unphilosophically) to take power illegally in Syracuse, in order to build an Intellectual Dictatorship of a State, with the life and manners of the Spartans — and, it must also be conjectured, with the idea perhaps, of taking over the whole of Greece under its domination. Plato is definitely a paradoxical character, and a little information on his background and writings is necessary therefore, in order to understand him.

Plato the philosopher, was born in 427 B.C. and he died in 348 B.C. A true blue-blood Eupatrid, he came from a most aristocratic family which traced its lineage back to the early kings of Greece; and his original, and true name, at birth, was 'Aristocles', which means, 'the best'. However, due to his muscular frame, and his fame in wrestling at the Isthmian Games in his youth, he officially adopted the nickname 'Plato', meaning 'the broad'.

Besides wrestling, writing poetry, and running after both young girls and young boys (and being run after by them in turn!) — he spent his misbegotten youth hanging on the words of Socrates, during his discourses in the market place; and developing philosophical ideas — and developing in particular, his memory — in order to faultlessly reproduce all the words of wisdom of his old teacher, some twenty or so, years later. Plato had a phenomenal memory — or possibly, a very vivid imagination!

It is interesting to note that like all the other philosophers in this chronicle, Plato began his actual philosophizing rather late in life; and, after much experience, thought, study, and travel. Obviously Philosophy is one skill which improves with age, and all those undergoing, or suffering, the "mid-life crisis", concurrent with reading this book (probably a very small percentage!) should bear this in mind. When you are too old to enjoy a discotheque, and when your body starts re-acting badly to rich foods, then don't despair; but take up philosophy instead. Philosophy is just the thing to fill the Autumn and Winter of your life with deep contentment — at least that is what it seems to have done for the Greeks.

But enough of this moralizing and back to Plato.

When Plato was in his early twenties, in 404 B.C. at the end of the Peloponnesian War, the old Aristocratic Class of Athens (an Oligarchic Group to which he was related) seized power for a short period in a desperate attempt to rid Athens of Democracy, entirely. There came about in consequence thereof, a period of fierce reprisals, counter-reprisals, and vendettas in Athens; but Socrates the unflappable, sat through it all, scarcely losing his cool — let alone his head. And as we noted, previously, the Aristocrats running this short-lived Junta, were all relatives of Plato.

Then the Democrats came into power again (you have not forgotten what is really meant by the word Democrat in Athens, I trust!) and they then decided that Socrates was responsible for all the troubles which had been caused them by the arch-conservative, 'best', or, 'first' families. This was not at all logical, but then few political actions are based on anything resembling logic, and naturally the Democrats knew that there were other people really to blame, but as they couldn't catch them (or didn't want to disgrace the System too much by executing someone from a family related to Poseidon the God of the Sea!) they chose the 'sitting-duck' Socrates — who was too slow, and too stupid to get out of their way. They reasoned that with this public execution they could purge the State of all that was harmful and incorrect. And so they charged Socrates with every crime that they thought would possibly stick — and then, they threw the book at him!

Plato was deeply mortified about the whole business so the story goes, and after the traumatic death of Socrates, he left Athens and travelled to Megara to visit Eucleides, a Cynic; and then he went on to Cyrene, to visit Aristippus the Hedonist. Still deeply troubled, he later made his way to Egypt, to study Maths in that country — and as was the fashion with rich young Greek gentlemen of his day.

In 395 B.C. Plato interrupted his journeys and studies long enough to return to Athens to join in the Battle at Corinth in 394, but by 387 B.C. he was off again, and this time to study the Pythagorean Philosophy, under the tutelage of various Italian Mystics. Then came the fatal meeting with Dionysos I of Syracuse, and in no time at all, Plato had formed a life-long friendship with Dion — run the gauntlet with Dionysos — and been sold into slavery.

He was (very happily for him) redeemed, or ransomed from his unhappy condition by friends who paid for his release and brought him back to Athens in 386 B.C. These same friends then kindly and most considerately bought for him, a piece of real estate in one of the Athenian suburbs named after the God Academus. So Plato began his Academy, eight years after Isocrates had started his school of rhetoric. And the Academy, although the second university of its type in Athens, and the third in the Greek World (if we consider Pythagoras and his school in Crotona as the first) was to prove to be the greatest, and most prominent intellectual centre in Athens, in the years to come.

Apart from trips to and from Syracuse, where he was still trying to set up his perfect State, Plato obviously considered that his travelling days were over, and therefore he hung up his spurs, (or whatever it was that travelling Greeks did in those days) donned a cap and gown, and entered the classroom. This donning of caps and gowns actually began with Plato, as in his Academy all the students had to wear this new and rather strange apparel and created much inspirational material for the satirists and comediens of the day.

Over the portals of this institute was engraved a dreadful warning, in the inscription — "Let no one without Geometry enter here." Plato might just as well have written (for the likes of people like myself anyway) "Aband—on Hope, all ye who enter here!" But Plato had unfortunately become a 'Maths-Mad' gentleman — an affliction which had been caused by too much close contact with the Pythagoreans in Italy. And he now began an obsessive attempt to reduce everything in life to a geometrical line, and as the years went on, this love of tidy Mathematics caused the development in him of a most passionate hatred for untidy Humans. The "oklos", the "mob" — which Socrates is reputed to have had so little feeling for, had also engendered a strong emotion of revulsion in Plato. Or perhaps, it was Plato who had always disliked the 'Mob' so much, and maybe he only put those contemptuous words into Socrates' mouth in order to suit himself. How can we know for sure? Most of what we do know about Socrates is only through Plato, so therefore nothing is really certain on this subject.

This Academy of Plato's was a type of religious fraternity, or so it was said, and the school was dedicated to the Muses — those violet-tressed lovelies who had originally inspired all the Arts in Greece. There was Calliope the Muse of Epic Poetry; Clio for History; Erato for Love Poetry; Polyhymnia for Songs of the Gods; Melpomene for Tragedy; Urania for Astronomy; Euterpe for Lyric Poetry; Terpsichore for Dance; and Thalia for Comedy. One doesn't imagine that Thalia the Muse of Comedy ever got much of a look in, in that austere place though, as Plato (like Pythagoras) frowned on unseemly mirth, and probably even frowned on *seemly* mirth as well!

This newest centre of higher learning in Athens, charged no fees to students at all; but it had no trouble maintaining its cash-flow, as there were continual 'donations' made to it by the wealthy of the Greek World —including Dionysos in Syracuse, (before the attempted 'coup', naturally!) And the students (including a few females as well as the customary males) came from the Upper Classes; from good, respectable, 'born in the purple' Eupatrid Families, who had no problems financially, and who were only too eager to keep this establishment going. In fact it must have been a great comfort to them all, to know that Plato was there, to instruct their off-spring in healthy reactionary views, and to keep their progeny away from the dangerous notions of the Cynics and the Hedonists — as well as from any other "off colour" groups. Most people of their class and bank account would have paid anything at all that was asked of them, and would probably have thought that the service they received for it, was worth such a trifling sum. Bringing-up revolutionary teen-agers is, after all, not a joke!

Plato therefore was taking care of the minds of the up and coming generation of the Upper Class; and making sure that they didn't pick up any nasty habits like 'Democracy', or, 'pity for the poor', or, 'burning revulsion against injustice'. And as well as carefully controlling the mental processes of these future leaders, he was running an 'operation centre' for the envisaged take-over bid in Syracuse. Ostensibly the Academy taught Maths, Arithmetic, Advanced Geometry, Music, Astronomy, Law, Philosophy; and Moral and Political Philosophy. But in principal it was a factory, just as Oxford, Cambridge, Yale and Harvard are factories today, and dedicated to turning out the neat sausage-type rulers of the State — and of **every** State. It was a place where people were trained to act and to think, and to work legislature in a certain way (a necessary way!) in order to have a harmonic balance in the System. It was the cradle of Philosopher Kings — or so Plato wanted it to be. Sometimes of course he made the mistake of allowing certain students in — like Aristotle for example — who was later to refute a great deal of his master's teaching. But Plato worked long and hard on his Assembly-line of intellectuals, and turned out many promising products of Élitism, in consequence. This then, was the answer to the problem — (or part of the answer at any rate) — the production of Philosopher Kings, or Guardians, of a wild, unruly world. And while outside the gates of the Academy, Athens churned and burned, in social unrest and flagrant political injustice; inside the Academy, Plato sat dreaming, and writing his momentous political and philosophical treatises on how to control this unruly mob; and on how to turn it into a logical, industrious, mathematically precise society — and a society moreover, which would be **completely emotionless**. In Plato's eyes, "emotionalism" was the worst sin of all!

Let us now examine some of Plato's writings.

Basically, Plato's writings consist chiefly of a series of Dialogues repudiating all the other philosophic works available (excepting those with which he happens to be in agreement!) and as an ex-playwright, Plato very cleverly managed to put the criticism for all the other philosphers' doctrines, into the mouth of Socrates, the Saint of Philosophy — and thereby managing very neatly, to achieve the substantiation, and sanctification, of his **own pet theories**. In all these philosophical conversations, Socrates loquaciously, and unendingly, discusses with other philosophers and personalities of his time (or even from *before* his time), various aspects of various philosophical problems. These other people simply supply the "feed" lines, like second string comediens; while all the best lines, naturally, belong to Socrates. In fact everybody, besides Socrates, seems to be a complete fool, and almost too stupid to be even able to tie up his own shoe laces. It is of course all very satisfactory for Plato, and obviously very, very, convenient, also. Socrates his star, is dead, and is therefore quite unable to dispute any of the points given as his. And all the philosophical ideas in which Plato believes can then be neatly trotted out, and proved infallibly and pontifically — and none can dare to challenge!

From even a brief perusal of his writings, we can see that Plato has a strong admiration for the doctrines of Parmenides and Pythagoras above all — but he also manages to adapt, and to twist the theories of Anaxagoras, Democritus, and Heracleitus, to suit himself. His whole output of philosophy, in fact, is a concatenation of all previous philosophies to that date; a thorough castigation of all dangerous humanist doctrines, such as those pursued by the Sophists; and an increasingly rigid and fascistic formation of a programme, for a most **uncomfortable**, but very **tidy**, and monolithic State. In a word, Plato is a 'Monic' Philosopher. **Only one way** is correct, according to him. There is only one truth, one leadership, one class of people to rule, one System of Gods, and of course, only one correct philosophy! Plato had the most terrible emotional bloc' towards change, and Change of *any kind,* was bad news to him. A complete unexpurgated conservative, Plato wanted the perfection of the Athenian Supremacy in the Mediterranean to remain forever, static and stagnant, and with no shift in the Balance of Power in *anyway* whatsoever. Conservatism is of course, an incurable illness of the Establishment, and it is a fatal one as well. The Conservative naturally has something to conserve or preserve — unlike the Poor who are dispossessed and have nothing to save — and the Conservative generally goes very unwillingly to his death — frequently kicking and screaming all the way! If life is good, then why should one leave it? he reasons. But willingly or not, die he must; just as everything else, in turn, fades away, or, rises and falls. Life is a continual flux and flow; and nothing abides forever. But Plato could not accept this. If he could have, it would have meant his being forced to read the writing which was on the wall there for his entire social class — as well as for himself. Instead though, he turned reactionary; and chose to ignore the facts of Nature which were visible for all to see —and therefore he remained forever, *evolutionarily illiterate!*

Plato was also very influenced by the static Eastern thought of Egypt, and he believed that the Caste System of the priests there, was a very good idea. Change of any kind in his eyes led inevitably to decay, not to re-growth and progress. And he saw it as his duty to uphold the Greek City-State in all its tarnished glory, and by establishing an Oligarchical Leadership, to help resist all movement towards a broader electorate. He was also a supremely confident elitist and like the Feudal Kings of Europe he believed in a Divine Right, not of mere Kings, alone, but of Philosopher Kings, or Guardians of the State — and in order to achieve his ends, he thought that all means were permissible, and, or, expedient!

Plato wrote on the Physical aspects of Philosophy, and the Metaphysical; and on the Ethical and Political aspects as well. In fact there was almost no stone unturned when he got through denouncing and expostulating on every important issue of his day — and his work incorporated a number of myths and parables, skilfully paraphrased in order to prove his point — and which originated from the Ancient Greek myths concerning the cosmogeny and cosmology.

His work, which was prolific indeed, includes Socratic dialogues with Protagoras, Gorgias, Parmenides and others, but his major works detailing the structure of his "Utopia" are, the "Republic", "The Statesman", and "Laws".

As Plato grew older and more bitter, and saw that his plans for the heedless and inattentive Kingdom of Syracuse were coming to nought, so too did his writing become more repressive in tone, if a fraction more resigned in pitch. He also wrote voluminously on the trial and death of Socrates (that is his version of the proceedings!) in his works "The Apology", "The Crito", and "The Phaedo". And again, using Socrates as his vehicle, he also delivered his ideas on his principle doctrines of Forms, Virtue, and the Soul. So, before launching into the summarizing of his major political works, let us first look at what Plato had to say on these three important subjects.

Most of his ideas on Form, Virtue, and the Soul, are in this humble writer's opinion simply a mixture of Pythagorean and Parmenidian mumbo-jumbo, plus a dash of Democritus and Empedocles, (in very diluted form) with a few brick bats at Anaxagoras, Heracleitus, and the Sophists, thrown in for good measure. Of course, if Plato sounds appealing to you, then you may wish to read him for yourself and write your own indignant book, refuting me. But whatever you think of this philosopher it is quite certain that you wouldn't have survived for very long in his perfect State — even Plato himself would probably have been termed a political dissident in it — and doubtless he would also have been executed — the very first week!

To Plato, the External Senses and Realities were not really important, as he believed that there were Eternal, Internally Knowable, Forms, or Ideas, which were the Supreme Reality. If you are still following this torturous doctrine, what it boils down to is that there is only one True Form of Beauty, Order, Justice and Truth — and that these forms are ideal forms, which never change according to circumstances or experiences, and which can *never* be anything else. Incidentally, Plato's ideas on Justice are a little hazy at the best of time, as in his eyes, Justice equals Inequality, in *his* State! But we shall come to that a little later.

The Soul, according to Plato, was the main moral and intellectual responsibility of Man. If we got our Souls right then the World could look after itself. Of course he could be right at that, but it does smack a little of the "Look after the pennies and the pounds will look after themselves" saying; which inflation has proved to be completely erroneous, and absolutely unworkable, as an economic doctrine. This Soul, he said, was immortal; and he believed (as did the Pythagoreans) in the pre-existence of it; and he even developed an interesting theory known at the Doctrine of Recollection, or "Anamnesis" (that is the opposite of "amnesia" meaning "forgetting" in Greek), and which may be regarded as a stab at establishing a Hereditary Memory — except that Plato was never scientific enough to have tried to do that. He believed that the Soul, which was imprisoned in the Human Body, had lived in the Past, and would escape to live again, at Death. It, (the Soul) was immortal and self-moving, and self-generated —and the Christian Church eventually found a lot of material in Plato's work which could be most happily and instructively used by them for a more worthy cause later.

The Soul, said Plato, was composed of three parts:-

1. Reason, the Ruler of the whole body, and the Intellect itself, which was found in the Head.
2. The Higher Emotions (i.e. Love of Fame and Just Anger) which were located in the Breast.
3. The Lower Carnal Desires (e.g. Lust) and which were positioned, appropriately enough, in the Belly.

So these three sections, (rather resembling Freud's ideas on the composition of the Psychological Personality of the Id, Ego and Super-Ego) made up the Human Soul; and it was up to Man to balance these three, and to keep the Head **above** the Breast and the Belly. (Metaphorically speaking of course, as physically, it seems rather impossible for there ever to be any re-location of these parts.) Plato neatly illustrated this theory of his with a word picture of a Charioteer and two horses. The Charioteer, or Driver, symbolized Reason, and he battled with the aid of the good horse (which symbolized the Higher Emotions) to control the bad horse (which symbolized the base Belly Desires and Drives, or Animal Instincts) and if he battled sufficiently well, the base Belly Desires, and bad horse, were both subdued.

One definitely has to hand it to Plato; it is all very neat, and it is also possibly the first psychological example of the Personality Conflict in Man. And quite obviously this little analogy must have influenced the young student Freud — unless he just stumbled on the idea of the human inner-conflict, all by himself! Exactly how much the Thinkers of the Nineteenth and Twentieth Centuries really owe to the Greeks, will probably never be truly known. But then, who knows how much the Greeks themselves owed to the Civilizations and the Thinkers further East of them!

Anyway, in Plato's theory, the Belly, as always, lets Man down! And it is true, it must be admitted, that Mankind's *collective* Belly is generally the main cause of all his woe. If we didn't need to eat then maybe we'd become pure spirits and good, gentle people. But I have a sneaking suspicion that if we didn't fight each other for food, then we'd fight simply for territory, or, for something else. It just seems to be in the Monkey Nature of Mankind to be aggressive over everything, and anything. Still and all, the quadruped world would probably apppreciate it, if we stopped eating meat!

Anyhow, these Souls of ours were formed by an old Craftsman — and once again Plato employs parables and myths to put his ideas across. This Craftsman (representing God to the Christian Platonists who came later) formed these Souls out of pre-existing materials while contemplating the World of Perfect Forms; and this Craftsman represented to Plato, the Moving Cause of Life, which Anaxagoras had named "Nous", and which later on, Aristotle would call the Prime Mover — only, in Aristotle's case, he had to mix and confuse the whole issue so much, that he finally decided that there were more Prime Movers than only one! Most people of course would much prefer to have only one; as most people are *monic* both by nature and desire; and furthermore, the monic myth is always so much more tidy and easy to understand — and to accept!

The materials with which the Craftsman worked, were Chaos and Space (we have a good bit of Democritus here with his Atoms in the Void, plus a rather large helping of the Creation Mythology.) And at first there was disorderly movement in the Universe (which represented Democritus' theories on Necessity, which Plato was neatly tidying away) and the Craftsman dealt with all this disorder or brutal Chance, and constructed the body of the Universe into regular geometrical solids of Fire, Earth and Water. — And with this little piece we have the Milesians and their theories tidied away as a well! Plato was a very neat thinker, and must have been an agony to live with — a place for everything, and everything in its place etc. The brutal or blind chance which he so smartly accounted for here, obviously represented all the savagery, and disharmony — and any other things going on in the world, which Plato did not particularly care for!

As far as Plato was concerned there was only one Universe (the Monic theory again!) and it was everlasting; and on top of that, there were absolutely no other galaxies! Life was an eternal circle; a 'rehearsal for death'; a beautiful, perfect world; with only brutal chance to cause disorder in this perfectly balanced, harmonic and mathematical pattern of life. — And Plato was going to deal with this brutal chance and non-mathematical movement, as sternly as possible, — and with anyone else who had ideas regarding the free movement of life at all! And as Plato grew older he became an even fussier 'old woman' in his thinking, and obviously believed, as did the Council of Europe meeting at Vienna in 1815, that it was his 'divine duty', to keep the 'Balance of Power' in the World, just as it was. While I have always suspected that those gentlemen in Vienna were really more motivated by their individual greedy empires, than by any philanthropic desires, I must confess that the same idea has also occurred to me, regarding Plato himself. If Plato had attended the Concert of Europe (a fittingly harmonic and Pythagorean name surely!) I'm certain he would have found himself in complete agreement with Castlereagh, Canning and Tallyrande. Everything in its place, actually equalled — *everything in our own pockets* — to those Statesmen; and Plato also wanted to make sure that the world spun under **his** direction; and around the wills, and whims, of **his own social class**. All virtue to Plato's way of thinking consisted in other people fitting in with **his plans, and ideas**, (but then sure, we're all a little selfish in this life, so maybe I shouldn't be too hard on the old Puritan!)

As we remarked, Justice (or Plato's conception of it) involved inequality; as he had decided that the demarcation lines of the Classes should be drawn so securely, that there would be no stepping out of line in his perfect society. And he has an explanation of this Social Containment Policy in his writings, which is based upon the original Creation Myth of the Ancient Greeks, in which the first men on Earth are formed by the Gods from the metals of Gold, Silver, and Bronze — or Copper and Iron.

The Men of Gold are naturally superior to the Silver, and likewise, to the Bronze Men. And the Gold Men in the Creation Myth represent the past Heroes of the Heroic, or Homeric Age, at the birth of the Greek States. In Plato's version of the story however, the Society is to be based on the Men of Gold acting as the Leaders; with the Silver Men delegated to a lower position than the Leaders — (but of course higher than the workers, in fact a type of Administrative Class). And the Bronze Men are the lowest of the low and definitely must keep to their Worker Class. And there must be absolutely **no mingling of blood**, (or metal) between these three stratas. And in order that the people will acquiesce to this policy of discrimination, there must be perpetuated a "Noble Lie of Blood and Soil", which will convince the populace that it is infinitely better to have this discriminating policy for separate development, and that people are much happier staying well within their own social barriers — and are much better off when doing what is expected of them. In the Twentieth Century we ourselves have a stirring example of the Platonic Social Class Programme at work quite openly in the "Apartheid" system in Africa. But it is equally to be observed covertly in action, anywhere in Europe, wherever the old class barriers are still intact; and, wherever the worker is only too happy to doff his cap in the morning, and to make obeisance to his master — on the condition of course that he himself can feel superior to all those outlandish and illiterate non-Europeans and others, *socially lower* than himself!

The Platonic System of course, is not fool-proof, as there is always someone trying to move in or out of his or her grading, and discontent is rampant — as people just **will not accept** their 'proper place' in the scheme of things. Also the Biological Instinct for Non-Random Selection causes people to want to mate, or to mix their metals; and that primitive desire and emotion, can prove *really* fatal to the whole scheme!

But Plato was prepared for some small upsets to occur, and in consequence he had worked out a Policy of Eugenics in order to keep his rigid social and racial programme in operation — and this form of controlled Birth, and Good Breeding, must have been a source of inspiration to many a fascistic government in our more enlightened age. And there is an interesting phantasy by Shakespearian Scholar Edwin A. Abbot A.D 1838-1926, with his story 'Flatland' based on the Platonic Myth of the 'Noble Lie', and the perfectly structured society. And, appropriately enough — in this imaginery country, *all* the classes have a suitably Platonic, or Pythagorean, geometrical shape. So that the lowest figures are Straight Linesor Isosceles, and progress in mathematical precision through Triangles — up to the Priests and Rulers who are Hexagons and Circles. Naturally the Women, as the lowest class of all, never develop beyond Straight Lines! But then as Plato stressed; Justice, equals inequality!

The acceptance of the Class System Plato believes, will make everyone happy with his lot in life, and all people must be taught Temperance, and Satisfaction with their position on the Social Ladder. This is best for all, as people are definitely not born equal, to Plato's way of thinking, and they cannot make themselves equal either; as God has put into the Men of Gold a special Divine Right, and a Talent, for Ruling etc. — and the Men of baser metals should just accept this fact. Plato sees the rise in Democritization as something just too dangerous and anti-natural for words. "The City shall perish when it is guarded by Iron and Copper," he specified most soberly; and as I think of my Copper and Iron ancestry I ponder whether he could possibly be right. It is quite certain, that if Plato were around today, he would be very confused on how to deal with the phenomena of the U.S.A., for the whole place is run by people who originated from Copper and Iron; and they all look perfectly happy; and seem quite comfortable with their way of life. Plato might be hard pressed to account for such tremendous productivity also, and for the high degree of cultivation possessed by them. And maybe it's just as well that we cannot come back to Life after Death — the shock of disillusionment with our pet theories would only kill us, *all over again!*

All Plato's works are full of convoluted myths from the ancients, but there is one in particular which bears looking at rather closely, as this myth really does contain some words of wisdom, and this is The Myth of the Cave.

In this story, Plato likens the gathering or garnishing of Wisdom, to being a very painful process (which we would probably all agree is definitely true!) and he draws an analogy between a group of prisoners who are bound hand and foot in a cave; sat to stare at the interior cave wall; while prohibited from looking at the sun (and therefore only able to view the moving shadows on the walls in front of them) — to dull-witted Man, before the attainment of Knowledge, or Wisdom. Man in his ignorance, sits bound in his dark mental cave; never seeing the Light of Truth and in consequence only discerning the hurryings and scurryings of the real world outside, by the moving shadows of illusion in front of him. But, says Plato, if one of these prisoners however, should actually manage to escape; or to be brought forth into the light of the sun; then at first, he would be so blinded by the brilliance of the experience, and it would be so painful —that he would immediately wish to return to his dark captivity. And so it is with Man, and with the first stirrings of Wisdom and Knowledge in his soul, says the Philosopher, and Man feels uncomfortable, and wishes to return to the ignorance and sloth of the cave, because he feels so overwhelmed by the bright Light of Truth. But, should the prisoner from the cave be forced to stay outside in the daylight; and should he be made to continue to walk up a hill towards the very light itself; then, he would finally become so very enamoured of the beauty of the sun as an object in itself; that he would **never** wish to stumble back into black ignorance again. And so it is with people, in the pursuit of Wisdom and Truth, and they finally begin to fall in love with the object of their search, as an *entity in itself.* But should the former prisoner however, venture back, to try to free his earstwhile companions, and to tell them of the beauty of the great world outside, and of the wonder of the sun,they would only refuse to believe him, and, indeed, would spurn all his entreaties to leave the cave — as Wisdom and Knowledge come to men solely from their own efforts and experiences — and nobody can truly teach another, or, lead him forward to a better life. The way to Truth and Excellence is a long and difficult path, and the journey must be undertaken in solitude.

A more modern adaptation of this myth and almost as compelling (if not perhaps also more explicable) is the short story, "The Country of the Blind" by H.G. Wells, in which a man who *can see,* lands unexpectedly in a country of *blind* people — tries to convince them that there is such a thing as *sight;* and is in consequence, rewarded by the inhabitants with abuse, suspicion, and pitiless beatings. (A Prophet knows no glory in *any* country it seems; and Plato also must obviously have found the whole teaching business to be a singularly thankless task!)

In his account of the Trial and Death of Socrates, Plato has Socrates declaiming that he is some type of divine missionary insect sent down to stimulate the world. What he actually says of course is that he, (Socrates) is a 'gadfly' whose purpose is to sting, nip, and generally worry, a large, pedigreed, but rather lazy horse, which represents the City-State of Athens. If Socrates actually thought of himself as a stinging, and rather annoying, and worrisome fly, then Plato must have visualised his own role as that of a slightly more vehement and virulent wasp; whose duty it was, to sting into awareness (or subjection) all the rather idiotic people he found himself surrounded by.

In his "Republic", which is a voluminous work consisting of ten books, he begins to lay the foundations for his perfect State — again using Socrates as his mouthpiece — or a Socrates in conversation (dialectical conversation naturally!) with others; and a very convenient brain-child this Socrates is — convenient for Plato that is — almost like a literary device, or a philosophical "deus ex machina".

But in order to give Plato his lawful due, here is a summary of the "Republic" (which must surely be a misnomer considering how Plato really felt about politics in general!) so that the Reader can make up his, or her, own mind about this philosopher.

The first principle is that Justice equals Inequality, and therefore the State is divided rigidly into various classes — the Myth of Blood and Soil once more!

This State is to be ruled by Philosophical Guardians, and there are to be a number of Auxiliaries (Soldiers) in order to keep the Status Quo, and, (more importantly) to keep the Workers, in their proper states and places.

There will be controlled breeding under a very scientific Doctrine of Eugenics, with marriages arranged by a State Lottery (which will be **fixed** — like many modern State Lotteries!) in order to only breed 'desirable' children from correct genetical mixtures. And besides this rigid breeding programme there will also be a very severely controlled and specifically formulated Education Policy, with great emphasis on Mathematics, as Plato deems this subject essential for the creation of *discipline* in people. (Perhaps that is why there was so much emphasis on this dreadful subject when I was a child! I never did learn how to add or subtract, but I did indeed develop a healthy respect for my teacher, who wielded the cane so vigorously!) And the Philosopher Guardians of the State will have an especially rigorous training in additional extra-curricular Gymnastics, in order to thoroughly form their personalities, and to make them suitable for Leadership. (I defy **any** Reader to tell me that they would sincerely like to live in such a State!)

There will be extremely strict censorship of Art and Literature; as Plato felt that emotional novels, or plays, or even poetry; were not conducive to the public good. (Mind you the Novel had not been invented as a literary form in those days, but if it had been around, it is for sure that Plato would **not** have liked it!) Naturally, Plato believed that more attention should be paid to strict discipline in study, rather than to allowing sloppy emotionalism to dominate; and even music itself, fell beneath his severe and stony gaze, and he was very particular in his statements regarding the playing of different types of harmonic counter-point. He therefore decided, after due thought, that Dorian (rather martial music and very Spartan in taste — or should one say tone!) could be tolerated, and even encouraged, for the good of the collective Soul of the State — and that it would appeal to the highest Patriotic Instincts in the Citizens, and inspire them to fight for the honour, and the glory, of their City. But Lydian music was far too plaintive and tender for his tastes, and he ascribed all weakness and sentimentality; effeminate luxury; and gross immorality; to the performances of this type of music. And Phrygian music was deemed the worst offender of all, as it was in a Minor Key (which is generally more haunting and hypnotic to the ear) and was at the same time orgiastically passionate and wild — and far too tempestuous to ever be allowed in **his perfect State**. The Arts, Plato felt, were very important for training the mind, and he thought therefore that they had to be controlled; in order to train the mind the *correct Platonic way.* And so all instrumental performances would have been banned in Plato's ideal State and only music accompanying suitable mind-forming verses would have been allowed. It is quite sobering for this particular Writer to note also, that she herself would most probably have been imprisoned (or executed) for the verbal flippancy which she has so wilfully displayed in the pages of this book — and her emotional attacks on the injustice of slavery would have been especially frowned upon.

In Plato's eyes, Liberty equalled Anarchy, and his Republic was to be administered by a group of Communist Aristocrats, or, by an Aristocratic and Communistic Élite; who would own no property; but who would have all the Power in the State. Private property was to be very carefully supervised, and the actual Leaders were to have none at all (in case **they too** became corrupt!) And most people would agree that the love of private property is the root of all evil in our societies — but how could one possibly, ever manage, to convince a Leader to surrender (without a fight!) his fair, or even unfair, share of it? Plato was **such** a romantic!

But let us examine in more depth this perfect System of his.

In Plato's Utopia we will get rid of everyone except the young, (a callous idea, true, — but speaking as a teacher — it does have its points!) and remember that Heracleitus advised the same solution for Ephesus also. Then, with these youth, (and for both sexes) twenty years education (or, maybe one should call it training), will be given. This education will necessarily include the teaching of Myths — in order to win from the young, subjection and obedience to their parents, and, to the State. (In fact, we do the same sort of thing ourselves nowadays, with our religious and civic instruction in schools; so maybe Plato was not quite as crazy as we might like to think!) At the age of twenty these youth will then be given physical, mental and moral tests. The failures of this 20 + System (the British you may recall used to have an 11 + System — perhaps, they were a little more advanced than Plato!) will become the Economic Classes of the State — the Businessmen, Farmers, Workingmen et al., who will have limited private property, and differing degrees of wealth. Meanwhile the survivors of this first test will continue their training for another ten years, at the end of which, they will again be tested; and those who fail, will then become Soldiers, who will possess no private property whatsoever, and who will have no rights to engage in business either! These Soldiers will then be forced to live together in a type of military communism, in order to keep their idealism strong and lively, and, in order to be always as prepared, as the Spartan military machine was. (One wonders exactly what point Plato was actually making here with his series of tests. Was it that Soldiers were smarter than Businessmen, because they managed to stay the academic field longer? Or was he proving that they were dumber, or more malleable, or what? Whatever the point was, it can't have been nice, and probably all Soldiers and Businessmen would heartily and instantly form an immediate dislike for Plato, on ever coming across him in life!)

Now, we get down to the real nitty-gritty. Those who pass this Thirty Year Test, will then study 'Divine Philosophy' for five years, and their course will include Maths, Logic, Politics and Law. And at the age of thirty five, these hardy few, this intellectual band of brothers, will then be flung out into the wide (but never wild or wicked — not in Plato's Utopia) world; and forced to earn themselves a place; a position in life; and most importantly — **a living**. Doing exactly what, you may ask? You may ask this question sceptically and patiently, and until you are quite blue in the face; but please don't expect an answer — Plato doesn't give us one!

At the age of fifty — those who have survived this really fearful and traumatic experience — of being discourteously and abruptly tossed out from the protective scholastic womb into the real world — the hustle and bustle of tooth and claw life in the jungle of survival! (And how many university professors one may ask would survive even three weeks on an assembly-line, away from their ivory towers and ivy covered walls?) Anyhow, those who have survived this dreadful experience, will immediately become (and without election either!) members of the Guardian, or, Ruling Class. Some people might of course wonder why Plato didn't stay with his Poetry, and spare us all this rubbish, but then again it *is* a system for leadership, and it definitely *is* unique — whether or not it would actually work, is another matter entirely!

So, these Philosopher-Kings will have all the Power, but have none of the Possessions; as ownership brings on a bad attack of Belly Desires of a

Carnal Nature. There will be no laws of the land, but these Solomon like (or should one say Solon like, for he was reputed to have been the Wisest Lawmaker in Ancient Greece) individuals, will have enough wisdom to decide each individual case, entirely on its own merits. These saints of sagacity (rather resembling the Supreme Court Judges who sit on the Bench in the U.S.A.) will have no money, no property, no families and **no permanent wives** (the accent being on the word permanent) to distract them from their duties; while the ordinary people — the Businessmen and the Workers etc. — will control the country economically; and the Soldiers will administrate it militarily, and therefore, make sure that everything progresses smoothly. This State, is in fact, not unlike Sparta, in some aspects; although in Sparta, they never paid that much attention to Maths, Logic or Politics — but they did believe in a "place for everything, and everything in its place"; which is probably why the Helots were always so miserable, and continually revolting!

Marriage will be a Eugenic Sacrament. "The best of either sex should be united with the best as often as possible, and the inferior with the inferior; and they are to rear the offspring of one sort of union, but not of the other; for this is the only way of keeping the flock in prime condition." And those words of Plato's should be a warning to everyone, and should show them that he was **not** joking about specialized breeding.

All children will be brought up by the State, and will be given equal opportunity. Social classes will not be hereditary (thank God for that small mercy at least, you may say!) Girls shall have equal opportunities with boys — not because Plato really believed that women were equal with men; his other writings have shown us that he did not hold with that strange creed at all; but, he did not want Sex, to rear its ugly head in his perfect community, nor, emotional and time-consuming Love, either. And consequently, he thought that by having a more equal society — superficially at any rate —he should be better able to control this corrosive drive, and pernicious influence of life!

So, in this Utopia (which appellation may sound strange to our ears) we do have provisions for individualism, to a very slight degree — in order to keep the Merchants and the Artisans happy; as even in the countries of the East Bloc', nowadays, individualism in agriculture is encouraged on a small scale in order to give incentive to the workers. And the communistic principles of Plato's programme in fact, are already actually in force in some parts of our globe — while the plan for Eugenics, has been carried out in various countries, at various time in history — and is probably still being covertly adhered to, in *some* places. The policy of Feminism which he advocated, is also part of the current fashion in our world, but solely for economic reasons; and it creates no freedom, or any real equality for women. And finally, the idea of a Philosopher-King is as always, very rampant in our System. Either, with the use of Kings, and the continuation of our Monarchies; or, with the election of learned gentlemen with strings of degrees after their names; who generally convince us of their overwhelmingly lofty intellects — while tying us up into even greater economic entanglements than we had ever suffered before! Therefore it can be said with some validity, that Plato's theories did not in fact die, and that they are still in healthy circulation two thousand years and more, after his death. We may laugh at Plato, but the joke is really on us, for surely, if we look around carefully enough, we will see, part, (if not all) of his schemes, in action *somewhere* on our planet.

But even with this major plan for Human Social and Political Balance and Containment (one hesitates to use the phrase, for 'Human Happiness'!) Plato still could not manage to put it into action in his life-time — all for want of a young dictator, or King, in order to start the programme off. The heirs of Plato were born too late in the day for him to make much use of them — unfortunately both for him; and for us! So, although Dionysos of Syracuse could not be made to co-operate, Plato kept on writing about, and defining, 'Politics' (and its use in controlling the "oklos", or rabble) and therefore we have his very informative "Statesman", in which he specifies the functions of a State.

In the "Statesman" he tells us that the Ruler is much more important than the actual laws themselves (which sounds suspiciously like the birth of the Personality Cult in politics) and he defines Statesmanship as the Art of all Arts; and a Statesman as a King; and Statesmanship as Kingship — so beware whom you call a Statesman nowadays, in case they are developing ideas above their station! He also decided that a State which was a mixed Monarchy (rather like Britain today) was the ideal one; and that the quality of Leadership itself was a natural talent; as in life there was always the survival of the fittest. But who exactly is the fittest, one may ask? And as the Writer of this book casts her pensive gaze around the world at many of its Leaders, she cannot help but mutter to herself, in paraphrase of the Sophists, "If these are the fittest, then one cannot be sure that being fit is really a healthy state at all!" Plato however went on to liken the Leader of the State, to the Shepherd with the Sheep (who naturally symbolized the Led) —an analogy to be much used later on in the Christian mythology.

States themselves, said Plato, were divided into three main kinds.

1. Monarchy — the Rule of One. A Tyrant, or Constitutional Monarch.
2. Aristocracy or Oligarchy. — The Rule by Wealth and Power.
3. Democracy — the Rule extended to all those *not* slaves, women, or foreigners.

And the Citizens of the State were divided into the following categories:-

1. Those who produced basic essentials.
2. The preservers of produce.
3. The producers of supportive things needed in basic essential manufacture.
4. The defenders from the cold and from enemies (the army, weavers, builders.)
5. The providers of diversions — poets and musicians.
6. The producers of secondary materials e.g. lumbermen.
7. The food producers.

Plus the Slaves, Merchants, Civil Servants and Priests; all obviously necessary, but **not** warmly regarded in Plato's heart, and not deemed worthy of a separate mention.

But due to this ill-fated, and unsuccessful enterprise of his, in trying to find a Philosopher-King, Plato lost a lot of his original enthusiasm and idealism; (although he lost none of his contempt for the masses) and in his later years he came up with a type of compromise solution to the problem of founding, and preserving the Perfect State. And "Laws" is just such a pattern of compromise, and, is on the whole, similar to the "Republic", with a few notable exceptions.

In "Laws" Plato had decided that the best form of government was a combination of both Democracy and Monarchy — and how very convenient for most of us — as that is exactly the type of government a great many European countries enjoy today! He decided also, that the failure and decline of Persia had been brought about due to the servitude of its people — the Greeks always despised the King-worshipping Easterners —and he came to the conclusion that the decline in Athens, had come about due to excesses in Music — Musicians everywhere, beware! (Incidentally the early Christian Church was in perfect agreement with Plato on this point it seems and they banned the use of the Ionian and Aeolian Modes — which correspond to our modern Major and Minor scales — on the strength that it was Modus Lascivus — or, Wanton Music!)

Plato decreed then that the King in his State must have a good memory; be quick at learning; and as well—he had to be courageous, noble, and temperate. It is indeed comforting to know that Alexander, under Aristotle's tutorship, qualified for all of the above, with the possible exception of the last! And possibly some people reading this book might care to run a mental check over their characters, and to discover whether they too, possess these qualities, or virtues, in great abundance, and

Theatre at Segesta in Sicily.

ABOVE: *Polychrome terra-cotta antefix, head of Silenus, Gela (Sicily), before 450.* RIGHT: *A Spartan girl running.* BOTTOM: *Athenian girls with lyres.*

LEFT: *Attic Geometric grave vase.*
BOTTOM: *Mycenae, Lion Gate.*

TOP: *Metrical epigrams on marble cenotaph, Athens, soon after 490.*
BOTTOM: *Literary papyrus, early third century A.D.*

ABOVE: *The Dying Gaul in the Museum of the Capitol at Rome. A Roman marble copy of a bronze original, the original forming an element of a group raised by Attalos of Pergamum commemorating his victory over the Galatians.* LEFT: *Head of a Celtic Warrior. (Sculpture about 240 B.C.).*

West front (restored), Great Altar of Pergamum, About 180.

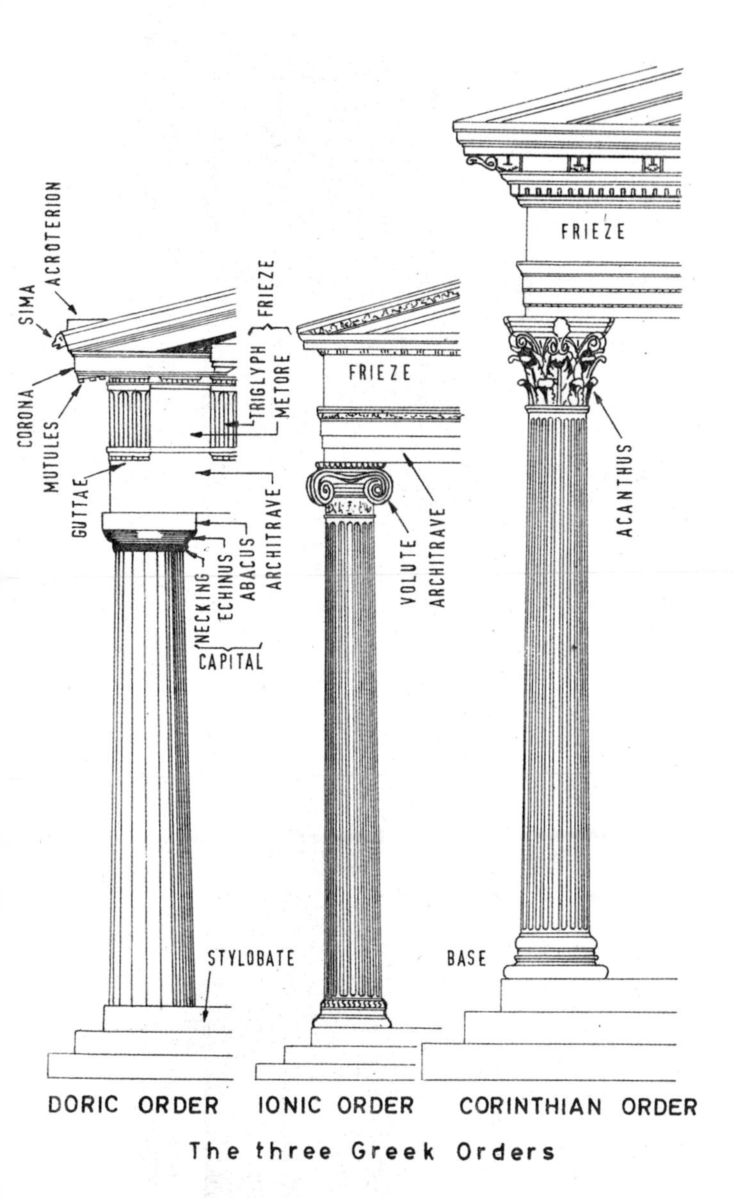

The three Greek Orders

LEFT: *Socrates.* CENTER: *Thucydides.* RIGHT: *Herodotus.*

therefore in consequence ought to be Kings! Unfortunately the matter will have to be taken up with their particular governments, as reading (like Hedonism) may bring us pleasure; but it cannot solve **all our** problems!

The people of the State were to honour the Gods; or, be purged! — a dire warning that. And this does seem passing strange; as according to all accounts, both Plato and Socrates thought that all badness or evil in the world was simply a result of ignorance; so then why should we execute people — simply for being too ignorant to honour the Gods?

Also, in "Laws", Plato had decided that the City-State was to be a small one only (more on that later!), with only community property; and with nobody either wealthy, or, poor. (But what about the slaves?) Education was perhaps the most crucial issue, and there had to be stability in the Laws, and in the Literature; as the Youth tended to be very impressed, and even indoctrinated, by what they saw on the Stage (— as they are by T.V. nowadays!) There was to be complete prevention of, and prohibition of, **promiscuity** in any shape, form, or size. And Plato defined the various types of Love under the headings of 1. Love of Body, 2. Love of Soul, and 3. A Mixture of numbers 1. and 2.

In order to keep things on an even and Platonic keel in his State, Plato completely forbade the first, and the third types of Love. And he also wanted to enforce TABOOS, and Fears of Impiety, in people — in order to regulate their morality, and to direct their Mating Instincts. Hard work, he thought, would get rid of passion; and passions were the curse of Man; and drove him to act entirely without reason. And a man who acted without reason, was little better than a slave (the highest of condemnations in Greek eyes!) — and the Slave was capable of all the vilest actions anyway — And NEVER to be trusted at any time; as he could always committ the worst crimes imaginable. And if anyone in the State chose to challenge these laws, and, (Heaven forbid!) rob a temple in Utopia; then he would receive the Death Penalty immediately, without any recourse to mercy; or appearances before Higher Courts; or second thoughts — or anything! The populace had indeed better take care of their Souls in this Utopia also, because the Gods were infallibly proven, and the Souls of Men were proven; and this had all been proven by Plato's own theory on motion, and the source of Life i.e. the source of all motion!

Now the geographical position of this City-State, also much occupied the mind of Plato in his waning years, and he came to the conclusion that it should be far away from ports, and from foreigners, and from all corrupting influences in general. And therefore, it was to be located inland, with the number of Free Citizens fixed at 5,040; plus their families and their slaves. These numerically fixed and static Citizens were to elect 360 Guardians, who in turn were to be divided into groups of 30 each (the Pythagorean obsession with numbers was definitely undermining Plato's faculties, one thinks!) Each group was to administer the State for one month at a time. (Good Lord! the mess of continual beaurocratic change-over would have been immense! — Truly Plato must have been going senile when he figured this theory out!) Then the 360 Guardians, would in turn choose a Nocturnal Council of 26, who, naturally enough, would meet at night, (probably this was the statistic which he had worked out would be the ratio of insomniacs for the total figure of 360) and these night-owls would then legislate on all vital issues. The Councillors would also allot the land in equal, indivisible, and inalienable plots, among the citizen families, and would keep up constant supervision on the drainage of this land, and the erosion of the soil. Trade would be kept to a bare minimum, and no gold, or silver, held by the people; and there would be no usury, and no lending of money for interest. (And possibly, no lending, even WITHOUT interest — as nobody **had any money**!) Everyone was to be encouraged to live as an active farmer on the land; and people who had acquired more land than they needed, were to surrender it to the State; and limits were to be placed on personal private bequests. The whole plan was so simple, and so hopelessly unworkable. Maybe in fact, Plato is really studied nowadays in our universities, in order to stop people trying to emulate him; or, to discourage them from coming up with their own hopelessly unworkable theories, and Idealistic and Utopian ideas! But wait! There is still more! Women were to have equal opportunity for work with men; and men were to marry by decree, between the ages of thirty and thirty five; or, to pay heavy annual fines. And everyone once married, was to beget children for ten solid years! And drinking, and other public amusements, were to be strictly regulated. (More than likely the beer would have been turned off in all pubs, from a main pipe-line at 8 p.m. every evening! — Although, on consideration of the enormous problem faced in the world today with alcoholism, and all its accompanying evils, perhaps we may say that *that* wouldn't have been such a bad idea, after all! But then, people really only drink because of their sorrows; or, out of boredom; so Plato still hadn't put something positive in place of this addictive grief!)

There would (naturally), be complete State control of all Education, all Printing, and Publication; and all other means of forming the Public Opinion, and the *individual character*. — Ah! but "one can't make an omelette, without first breaking the eggs!" I hear die-hard Platonists say! And even the Author must admit that, to a certain degree, most modern States nowadays, have just such a system of censorship in operation, anyway!

The Highest Official in the State would be the Minister of Education Plato decided, and all intelligence in, and the personality development of, ALL children would be *controlled* (some might even say that we also do this nowadays, but that we don't generally mouth off about it!) and Literature, the Sciences and the Arts would all be under heavy censorship as well, with no utterances, or expressions, of any ideas, which could be HARMFUL to Public Morals and Piety. The State would dogmatically determine which and what Gods were to be worshipped (I don't really think any facetious comment of mine needs to be added to this, the facts (nowadays) speak for themselves!) And any person questioning the State Religion would be summarily imprisoned; and if they foolhardily persisted in questioning the Religious Ideals of the Community; then they would inevitably be rewarded with Death. We can indeed observe from this last law, that the curious Intellectual is in fact, not always well repaid; and indeed History is crammed to excess with examples showing us the folly of actually being a Dedicated Thinker; and the Philosophical Enquirer would quite obviously meet his doom in such as place as Plato's perfect State — and in a very short time as well!

But, Requiescat in Pace, Plato — a good deal of your fascist ourpourings in the Winter cycle of your life we will simply put down to disappointment, and to overstrain from teaching. Old teachers are by the very nature of their occupations turned into arch-conservatives, despots and reactionaries. And it is really not their fault; but, as the Sheriff of the Wild West used to say, "It goes with the territory." Teachers equal the students' *policemen* in Society, and policemen are generally rather unhappy, and possibly, even a little morally confused, at the end of their working lives. "One cannot touch pitch and not be soiled," was an old, but true saying, and I imagine one cannot spend one's life dealing with so much ignorance, without also being a little affected in one's turn. Of course the same thing can probably be applied to the doctor also, and perhaps he even ends up catching the diseases, (or worse still, the hypochondria, and fear of the diseases) of his patients! Alas poor, unhappy Plato — what noble mind was here o'erthrown! His Philosopher-King he could not find, in order for him to put his dream world into action; but his student Aristotle, could, and did find someone, who was both a King, and philosophically inclined — and he shaped him for his own ends — just as Plato would have done if he had had the chance. Alexander, being a half-wild Macedonian, and therefore not a pure Greek; would possibly not have been a suitable choice in Plato's eyes, but, he certainly did the trick for Aristotle. And probably also, Plato's Athenian pride would have been a little hurt, to see this 'almost' Barbarian, managing to achieve such feats of glory for the Hellenic people, which no other 'pure' born Greek had ever managed. But Plato should have known from all his years of study, that the threat to power lies very close unto the centre; and that the point of stress and likely breakage, is very near the axle of the wheel; or, in the words of the great American historian Will Durant, "Around every Rome there lurks a Gaul, and around every Athens, a Macedon." And Athens by its very nature, was destined to be conquered by Alexander, just as Plato, by his, was destined to be surpassed by his student Aristotle.

Perhaps though a post-script needs to be added to these words of admonishment which I have so arrogantly delivered to Philosophy's most famous and popular son.— Plato most certainly greatly affected the thinking of Western Civilization, and especially that of the Christian Church — and possibly, (as a sceptic and agnostic) I do not appreciate him enough. He also deeply effected literature, and we frequently find Platonic references in many writers' works. Indeed Shakespeare was jammed with Platonic inferences and thoughts; consider only Hamlet, and the advice given by one of the characters to his son. And the statement which this old hypocrit makes, is (among other pieces of wisdom) "Be true to thyself and then thou canst not then be false to any man", and surely this direction is the Shakespearian equivalent of the Platonic Socratic instructions regarding the care of the Soul — look after your soul above all other things, and every thing else will follow!

So Shakespeare was obviously deeply influenced (or his audiences of that day were influenced) by the Platonist Theories and Doctrines. And again in "Hamlet", that great and despairing *Thinker* himself is forced to utter the following great revelation — "There is a divinity which shapes our souls, rough-hew then how we will" — and this is surely a paraphrase (a most elegant Shakespearian paraphrase — but a paraphrase nonetheless) of the Platonic myth about the old "Craftsman" who forms the World and the Souls of Men. So quite obviously, Plato's ideas have lived on in the work of dramatists and writers who could the more appreciate his imagery, even if less artistic people (like the Author) couldn't!

But whether his writings have been a source of inspiration to other artists or not, basically I dislike Plato because he is a 'MONIC' philosopher, and this monism spells a rigidity which I personally feel (and most Sceptics would feel the same way) brings the breath of death to life — His, is a rigid doctrine which allows no change, and which believes that once a harmony or balance has been established then it must be adhered to, at all costs. But the balance and harmony of life exists in continually changing patterns —*nothing does abide forever* — and it seems more sensible to accept this principle and to learn to live and work with it. Therefore Plato symobilizes all the sterile, and barren, death-loving and negative forces of life, and I totally reject him.

In final analysis Plato really represents the Autumn of the Greek City-State life, and the cold wind of change blowing through Athens, in particular. The Decline and Fall of an Empire — a life-style, or, a person —is as inevitable as the Change in Seasons. And all the crying over spilt milk will *not* put it back in the cup! Instead, one must go forward hopefully into Winter, and meet its challenge — and see what wonderful new experience can be gained from it!

An Indian Summer Interlude

Aristotle and Alexander

attempt to 'patch-up' the broken down Greek Empire.

CHAPTER 11

THE INDIAN SUMMER OF THE GREEK WORLD.
ARISTOTLE — The Philosopher who found both a King and a Solution– And the Short-lived Hellenic Empire.

The rise of Aristotle the great Biologist and Philosopher, is interconnected with the rise of his student, Alexander the Great; and with the formation of the New Hellenic Empire. And both these events were themselves associated with, and dependent upon, the rise of Macedonia in the Greek World. And so we shall turn first to an examination of that interesting country and its inhabitants.

Macedonia in the north of Greece, might be said to have been an area of 'Noble Savages', to use the words of the intrepid French Explorer when he first set eyes on the Aborigines of Tasmania. These Macedonians (fortunately for them, neither sighted by the French, nor invaded and genocided by the British) were a mixture of Thracians and Illyrians, and for all we know, they may even have been Celts; because it is extraordinary to remark how different they were to the Greeks of the South, and how peculiarly similar their life-style was to that of the ancient Scottish and Irish, whose clan systems were to appear in Northern Europe at a later date in history.

These noble savages totally scorned life in the cities, and, despising trade and business, stayed happily upon their feudal estates, hunting, and drinking, and itching to go forth into battle. Their Kingdom in Macedonia was a type of Communist trust among these country Barons and Squires, with the King, a figurehead, and mere necessity for a type of over-all feudal unification; but with every aristocrat on his individual large estate, considering himself the equal, or perhaps even the superior, to his Liege. Their system of alliances was similar indeed to that later followed by the Normand Knights, and by the Nobles of Poland in the time of the "Liberum Veto"; and this Macedonian free leadership system had all the inherent weaknesses of those other two ill-fated and evolutionarily temporary forms of government. Undisciplined, freedom-loving, impetuous, and passionate people; honourable and cheerful slaughterers in war; the Macedonians — like the Heroic Men of the Homeric Age–practised a type of Noblesse Oblige completely unfathomable to the average tricky Greek city-dweller of Athens. They were the perfect material for an experiment in founding a unified Greek World under the leadership of a Philosopher King. And if a philosopher could not be accounted for, then a King would be found, who would take guidance, and who would be suitably malleable material in the hands of a philosophical Master Craftsman. So Aristotle, sitting and listening in Plato's classes for twenty years must have dreamt and thought. And he must also have reckoned, that what his teacher hadn't achieved in the construction of a perfect State ruled by an Aristocratic Elite; he, Aristotle, would manage to bring about, by constructiong a perfect and unified Greek World under such a young and flexible sovreign. And that he, Aristotle, would furnish the perfect Greek Super-State, in which a Timocracy would flourish in place of either an Aristocracy, or a Democracy; or indeed in place of any other imperfect system.

This new word Timocracy will be explained a little later in the Chapter, so the Reader need not worry.

But, we must ask ourselves, was Aristotle in fact, only one of a group of people; a group who set about unifying Greece under Macedonian leadership, in an attempt to cure Greece's social ills-by building a large empire into which the Poor, and the continually increasing Dispossessed, could be scattered, in order to build colonies; to increase the Mother Land's wealth; and most of all — to get out of everyone's hair! The only way that the Greeks could ever survive their economic ills (without actually cutting their own throats!) was by colonization and expansion (or so it must have seemed to their leaders). They were such competitive people and so anti-social towards each other, that they could not even manage to live together any more; but had to move on, and out. There were just too many big fish in their small pond; and every small fish was just as anxious to become as big as the big fish, who were as anxious, (if not more so) to become even bigger! There was no myth of 'Blood and Soil' at Work in Athens; and absolutely no one was contented with his lot in life.

The type of Democracy which had existed in Athens up to this historic period, had always led inexorably to recurring bouts of Oligarchy, Revolt, Repression, and continual Social Conflict; and Plato had thought that this Greek Devilment, could only be exorcised by the establishment of an Aristocracy of Spiritual Elite, or, by the imposition of a Philosopher King; or, by a special Intellectual Monarchy. Aristotle however, coming from the educated Upper-Middle Class (his father had after all been a doctor, and not a member of the old landed-Gentry like Plato's) saw that the solution lay in establishing a Philosopher King, or a Monarchy, which would function or, supposedly rule; but, **under** the guidance of a group of educated specialists; and that the real system which would be in operation therefore, would be that of a Timocracy. Timocracy, incidentally, is derived from the Greek prefix 'time', meaning a 'value', or 'price', and the suffix 'cracy' meaning to rule. Therefore in this new system of Aristotle's, the people of value (obviously the educated Upper-Middle Classes, and bearing a strong resemblance to the group in favour in France during Napoleon's time, and to the men of 'go ahead' ability in the Rome of Julius Caesar) would be able to rise; and they would have a considerable say in the running of a type of Mixed Constitutional Monarchy, i.e. a Democracy with a Monarchy, but one directed by the men of substance — intellectually speaking that is!

The Macedonians, Aristotle thought, were obviously the right people to put these theories of his into practice. Ignorant, and mainly illiterate; pure and courageous; they would become the 'dogs of war' — and be used —to build the new Greek World. Alexander was simply the innocent; the child used by a group of adults; and the pawn in the hands of a team of Chess Grandmasters — which pawn could be moved around on a board; in order to win a game for them. Alexander had the fame and the name; but the power rested elsewhere.

The actual connection between Aristotle and the Macedonian Monarchy, went back a great number of years. Philip, the father of Alexander, came on the throne of Macedonia in 359 B.C. and his father, Amyntas II, had previously employed Aristotle's father as the Court Physician; therefore Aristotle and his family, from Stageirus, Chalcidici, in the North of Greece, were well known in the Macedonian Kingdom.

At the particular point in time when Philip ascended the throne; Macedonia had until then, been completely untroubled, and unspoilt by any worrisome considerations of such abstracts as Art, Literature, or Philosophy; but it was then decided however, to send Philip to study a little, in Egypt — as even the Macedonians had begun to feel that it was high time they got some sort of education. The young Macedonian Prince, was however, far too sensible a fellow to allow himself to get too carried away, or, to destroy himself in the wilful pursuit of pure intellectualism; and he deemed to be of much greater importance, the military ideas, and strategies, which he picked up, while in Thebes.

Soon after this experiment in Higher Education, Philip married a wild Molossian Princess from Epiru; who bore a striking resemblance (personality-wise) to Medea, (only in Olympia's case, she didn't murder her progeny, but her husband!) and he then set about creating a strong Macedonia. His idea was to build a Macedonia which would rule Greece, and which would eventually expand into the East, and thereby create an enormous empire–in order to feed all those dissident, and quarrelsome, Greek Children.

Philip of Macedonia was the bravest of the brave; and he left part of himself on every battle field, in order to prove it! His eyes, ears, legs and other parts of his anatomy were all willingly surrendered in the cause of a good fight; and by the end of his life, he rather resembled the neighbourhood's roving 'Tom' — battered, and bruised, but still going strong! The only battlefield however in which he fared ignominiously, was his own marital one; as Olympias insisted on taking snakes to bed with her. She was a fervent follower of the Dionysos Cult, and she drunkenly asserted, time and again, that Philip had not in fact been responsible for the seed of Alexander being implanted in her womb; but that a God had impregnated her in a flash of lightning one evening when Philip was absent. Naturally enough this little revelation caused bad blood between Philip and Alexander; with Alexander being torn between his desire to be known as the son of a God, and his aversion to being classified a bastard; not of royal blood; and therefore not legally entitled to his claim to the throne of Macedonia.

Philip and his 800 "Companions to the King" or Clans of Macedonia, built up a fantastic fighting machine of 10,000 men, divided into a Cavalry (a new venture in Greek Warfare and copied from the example of Syracuse) and an Infantry, dressed in protective coats of Mail and sporting Helmets; who carried spears, swords, shields, and catapults; and who, moreover, were provided with battering rams for the opening of gates of hostile and inhospitably inclined cities. Naturally these Macedonian soldiers were an odd sight to the southern Greeks, as it had been the custom for the Greeks to go into battle bearing a sword and a shield, but otherwise, to be quite unadorned (i.e. stark naked) and to spend much time, prior to battle itself, combing and brushing their long hair; in order to present a well-groomed appearance when in action on the field, and possibly also, to ensure that they were more attractive corpses at the finish of the engagement. Of course after Marathon the Greek men took to cutting their hair. But after Philip, Alexander, and the Macedonians had gotten through with them, they took to shaving their moustaches as well!

Now, back to our story!

After much bloodshed, Philip finally managed to unite all the Greeks under his captaincy, although they strongly disliked this move, and the Athenians in particular, were extremely vocal in their opposition; and felt most hard done by, having a babarian in charge of them. But Philip had the force, and the Macedonians were not decadent, effete, butter boys —but hardy warriors — and there was no stopping them; so, Greece fell under Macedonian control.

Unfortunately for him, Alexander was compelled to come rather prematurely to the throne at the tender age of twenty years, as his father Philip, was slewn in rather suspicious circumstances, which could probably have indicted many people, including the Queen Olympias, along with half the Athenian Assembly! And what Philip had started, Alexander was then called upon to continue, and to fulfil.

All in all, Alexander was simply a boy put in a Man's job — a clever, energetic child, addicted to Myths and Heroics, who, (had he been given more years on this earth) could no doubt have developed his natural intelligence and to have attained some wisdom. But he was too young; and unfortunately for him, completely unable to deal as cunningly with his

Generals, as that French Maker-of-Empires, Napoleon, was able to deal so competantly with his Directory later on in History.

But, Alexander threw himself into battle so uncaringly, and so courageously, that his soldiers worshipped him; and he advanced on the East; freed all Greek cities from Persian invaders; and then went on to subjugate the Persians; and even to advance into India. But no matter what freedom he gave the Greeks; nor what bounty and loot he poured into their outstretched, grasping, and greedy hands; or even what lands he opened up for their trade and colonization — they always regarded him as a spurious upstart; a barbarian; an abomination; and an enemy. "O ye Athenians, will you believe what dangers I incur to merit your praise?" Alexander wailed in complexed confusion, completely certain, (his teacher Aristotle had probably implanted this idea most firmly in him) of his Macedonian inferiority, and of the pure Greek **superiority**.

One time in fact, at a banquet that was being given in his honour, he is reputed to have asked some disparaging Greek guests, with startling frankness and devastating honesty, "Do you not feel like demi-gods among savages when you are sitting in company with these Macedonians?" It is not so recorded, but doubtless the Greek guests sniggered as such disarming child-like openness of thought and character, and considered him provincial putty in their worldy-wise hands.

Yes, Alexander had been well-trained into proper respect for the Greek Citizen, and into equally proper contempt for all others not Greek; and his policy in the taking of cities, and in the treatment of their vanquished inhabitants; had been dictated by Aristotle's attitude, which was that "all Asiatic people were natural slaves." So Alexander savagely and systematically burned, looted, and executed barbarians — like the good student that he was — and remembering his teacher's words, he treated all his Greek enemies and armies with old world courtesy and tremendous respect. Alexander the great conqueror only began to throw off a little of his brain-washing, as he reached the age of thirty; when sciolist that he was; (having no time to plumb the depths of the many subjects which interested him;) he began at last to solidify his position in the East by marrying himself (and encouraging his men to do likewise) to the Persians; and thereby creating a scheme for assimilation between the various races, which a Celt would thoroughly understand and approve of, but, which, (horror of horrors!) a Greek never would! A civilized person to marry a barbarian? Enjoy her in bed, yes! But marry her? DEFINITELY NOT! "Bad blood will always tell," the Athenians muttered to themselves, sniffing disdainfully down their Greek noses at this Macedonian's carryings-on in the East.

And Alexander adopted Eastern dress as well — Again, more acquiring of barbarian habits! — Also-took to shaving (but as he was doing this strange thing even before he went to Persia, it really couldn't be blamed on the barbarans — simply another strange quirk of this peculiar Macedonian, said the Greeks!) And then, the most intelligent thing which he did (and the one which really annoyed the Greeks) was to have himself declared a God, and thereby manage to sanctify himself, and to make his personage inviolate. Some historians claim that this action of Alexander's proves that he was actually going off his head; while others attribute this deification, to megalomania on his part, and to primitive superstition, on the part of the Easterners. But what better way was there, to protect his life from scheming Greek generals and traitorous Macedonian Chieftains; and the shrewd, ever plotting and planning intelligentsia in Athens? Anyway, how can we ever know for sure what Alexander thought, or why he did as he did? It is certain however, that Alexander was the centre of innumerable plots and assassination attempts from his Generals; and his eventual death due to over-drinking (or so it is attributed) is very strange; as in his youth he had always been most abstemious in both food and drink.

With his demise in 323 B.C., the Greeks began the last stage of their final descent into quarrelsome oblivion; and Aristotle lost his most royal student; if not his most philosophic or intelligent one. The experiment with the Philosopher King, which had been blue-printed by Plato, and adapted and put into action by Aristotle, was finally over; and the Athenian, 'Indian Summer' had passed, leaving only the Winter of Stoicism in its path, with a little leaven of Epicureanism, for those who could afford more light and heat in their lives.

And now that our small pen picture of Alexander — this Macedonian shooting-star has been completed; let us proceed to his teacher, Aristotle, who was a very slow and steadily burning sun; and whose radience has enlightened our world, for over two thousand years now, and, who, strange to relate, (or possibly not really strange at that) was more interested in the workings of this mundane Planet, Earth — rather than in any of the computations and circumvolutions of the Heavenly Spheres.

Aristotle 384-322 B.C. came from Stageirus, a Greek settlement to the north, in Thrace; and his family, as we have seen, had a firm background in connection with the leadership of Macedonia. He was first taught anatomy, before being sent to Athens to study under Plato for about twenty years, and this early tuition probably helped to make him more scientific, and less idealistic, than his teacher. He was renowned as the most assiduous of students in the Academy. (Aristotle sat through lectures **without** falling asleep, it is recorded!) And he left Athens, and went to live in the Court of Hermeias, after Plato's death in 347 B.C.

Hermeias was a fellow student of Aristotle's from the Academy, who had raised himself up from slavery, to become the Dictator of Atarneus and Assus, in Upper Asia Minor; and we may imagine that this was no mean feat; and that this Hermeias must have been a most interesting person. Unfortunately, this 'self-made King' was crucified by the Persians, shortly after his rise to stardom, because they suspected him of aiding and abetting Philip's proposed invasion of Asia. And although one may damn the Persians for their cruelty to Hermeias, one must admire them for their intuition; as they were probably quite right about the situation all the time! Meanwhile, Aristotle had married Pythias, the niece and adopted daughter of Hermeias, and now following the death of this proto-type Philosopher-King or Dictator (obviously Plato would have loved Hermeias — or he should have!) Aristotle and Pythias fled to near-by Lesbos, where Aristotle spent his time studying Nature, (and in particular Marine Biology) and where Pythias bore a child, (a daughter) and in consequence, died from this ordeal. Although in later life, Aristotle took up common-law residence with the Hetaira Herpyllias, he always remembered Pythias with great love and loyalty, and on his deathbed, he asked to have his bones laid with hers; so we may presume that Aristotle and Pythias, did indeed share a 'grande amore'.

Perhaps this early passing of Pythias was actually a blessing in disguise, as in point of fact most disadvantages are; because Aristotle could always remember Pythias in the first bloom of love, before the petals of passion had begun to wither. And also, not having a wife to nag him; he was more able to get to grips with life, and to really observe and to analyse every little thing, to his heart's content. Aristotle is a **real** Scholar — there is hardly an avenue of life or thought, which he passes down, and on which he does not have something to say, or to remark on. An astoundingly analytical brain had Aristotle — and if you had put a bowl of breakfast cereal on a table in front of him, he would immediately have begun to compound and devise theories on the types of people attracted to each different type of cereal — the effect variously shaped bowls had on the mastication and digestion of same; the staying power of each individual cereal; the vitamin, protein, and mineral content of each variety of grain —the psychological affinity felt by some people for some types rather than for others; and the origins of these cereals; their places of growth; the ways of improving growth; and so on and so forth, ad infinitum! As I said, Aristotle was a real scholar; an observer; a biologist; and a philosopher —and he had something to say; and a deep interest in everything he came across. Now how can a man like that, ever have kept a wife happy, I ask you? It's probably just as well that poor Pythias died when she did, or else he would have driven her mad. Or else (perish the thought!) she would have cut short his gallop, and the world would have lost one of its very finest thinkers — Albeit, Aristotle approved of slavery as an institution — or rather he couldn't see anything functioning without it — but that was his only sin — in my eyes at any rate! Whatever anyone thinks of Aristotle, this philosopher must be admired for his tremendous hard work and his over-all diligent scholarship; and he certainly knocks his teacher, Plato, into a cocked hat!

Aristotle included in his writings, numerous works on the following:- Biology, Metaphysics, Physics, Ethics, Psychology, Politics, Sociology, Rhetoric, Literature, Poetry, The Form of Tragedy and the Art of Writing, Philosophy, and Thought and Logic. Now do you see what I mean? Aristotle runs rings around Plato!

And besides the above, he made innumerable detours into the effect geography and climate have on the development of Life, and on the Human Character. He was surely the true father of Sociology (and not that dreadful Spencer!) and along with that title, there must be an equally strong claim for the Paternity of Biology. A great man, but quite obviously poor husband material, and Pythias was lucky not to have lived longer than she did, and not to have had to endure his cluttering up her kitchen table with his books and treatises, as poor Mrs Marx had to, with old Karl. All great men (and women!) are very difficult to live with, and are seldom truly appreciated by their closest relatives.

In 343, Philip, the father of the "enfant terrible" Alexander, invited Aristotle, whom he had known as a child, to undertake the education of his son and heir. This then Aristotle attempted to do — as any, and every teacher, attempts — and with probably about the same degree of success! But he did definitely manage to imprint his racist attitudes on Alexander at least — but whether that can be termed a success, or not; it is difficult to judge!

In 340 B.C. Philip next commissioned Aristotle to direct the restoration and re-population of Stageirus; which had been destroyed in a war with Olynthus; and he also authorised the Philosopher to draw up a Code of Laws for the new modernised city. All of which Aristotle accomplished most satisfactorily, and thereby earned himself not only praise, but, also, the commemoration of his name in an annual town holiday from then on.

In 334 B.C. he returned to Athens and opened a school of Rhetoric and Philosophy known as the Lyceum; so named because the buildings in this green and shady place had been dedicated to Apollo Lyceus (the God of Shepherds), and Aristotle now also became a Shepherd; an Intellectual one — and gathered into his scholastic sheep-fold, students, coming mainly from the Middle Class of Athens.

In the Lyceum, he then set up a large library; a museum of natural history; and a zoological garden; all of which accoutrements were the envy of less well-equipped schools such as the Academy (Plato's school for the Aristocrats), and Isocrates' school for the colonial Greeks. Aristotle, incidentally, could not buy this school of his, as he was a foreigner; and the laws regarding non-Athenians strictly forbade full citizenship rights; therefore, he rented it! Truly, the Greeks compounded needless problems for themselves! — Excluding a person such as Aristotle from full citizenship rights in Athens, seems to be the very height of stupidity; and definitely proves the utter fallacy of the doctrine of Individualism of the Greek City-States. One imagines that the Romans would have jumped at the chance of having Aristotle in **their** home town! They were always much more pragmatic than the Greeks.

While Isocrates specialized in Rhetoric, and the Academy taught mainly Maths, Metaphysics, and Politics; Aristotle however, set his students to work on Natural Science; and to the gathering of data on:- the Customs of Barbarians (very helpful in setting-up the New States which Alexander was winning on the battlefield, me thinks!) the Constitutions of Greek Cities (also helpful — and very necessary for the attempt to unify the Greeks into a large all-embracing Empire and pluralistic society) the Chronology of Victors in both the Pythian games and the Athenian Dionysia, (useful for stirring national pride and building broader citizenship in Alexander's New Hellenic Empire) plus, the origins and habits of animals; and the character and distribution of plants; (most necessary for the creation of the *new* Greek Empire on a firm agricultural and animal husbandry foundation). And, in general, a type of survey of the Greek World began there in the Lyceum; a survey which would supply scientific data and statistics for the new governing body.

All in all, this research, which was carried out by Aristotle and his team of assistants, must have been of immense value to Alexander, and probably taught him skills in the diplomatic handling of the Barbarians —hence his adoption of their dress, and the attempted assimilation of cultures by the Macedonian/Persian marriages. Also the knowledge of the habits, thoughts, and ways of life etc. of the people he meant to conquer; and the distribution of the fauna and flora in the far flung fields he traversed; must have been of tremendous benefit to his army in their military campaigns. Aristotle, it must be noted then, was not only a Philosopher, and a Sociologist, but he was a great scientist as well; and that is why in years to come (when he was better appreciated in Europe) he became known as **THE PHILOSOPHER**. (Plato *naturally* must have been stirring in his grave!)

But let us now take a look at some of Aristotle's work, so the Reader can see for himself why this Philosopher deserves so much praise.

Having such a mania for definition, Aristotle therefore decided, that there were ten basic categories into which a thing — **any thing** — might be placed for consideration. And these categories were:- substance, quantity, quality, relation, place, time, position, possession, activity, and passivity — and quite possibly, this list may aid you, when next you are considering whether or not, to buy yourself a new television, or washing-machine — or indeed, whether or not, to marry the object of your affections!

Aristotle was also a sensualist; and, unlike Parmenides and the Eleatic School, he accepted the senses as the only **true** source of all knowledge. He is famous for his Principle of Contradiction; which is very meaningful (if a little difficult to get the hang of, unless read and muttered to yourself six hundred or so times) and it goes as follows; — "It is impossible for the same attribute at once to belong and not to belong to the same thing in the same relation", so says Aristotle matter-of-factly, and wondering at the sloppy thinking of others, "and universals are generalized ideas, not innate, but formed from many perceptions of like objects." No doubt, you now see what I mean with my quip about the six hundred times!

Imagination is not necessary, says Aristotle — but patient observation end experiment are always called for; and Poor Pythias and her Woman's Intuition would have been thrown right out the door! — Most definitely, Aristotle was a firm believer in Male Logic, and he thought that Women and their Feelings were not to be trusted, and that any ideas entertained regarding Female Logic or Intuition, were completely erroneous. In all of which he was later proved to be completely erroneous himself by the German physiologist and physicist Hermann Helmholtz, in the late nineteenth century — but then none of us is perfect!!

Despite all his mistakes, and incorrect assertions in Science and Biology (and especially those regarding Women!) Aristotle is still the father of scientific method and research, and his use of deduction and induction in logic, (even if a trifle over-done) at least demonstrates the birth of the scientific formula for the proving of theories, without relying on either tricks or faith. Aristotle accepted nothing on faith alone, and it almost seems that he lived only to prove, or to disprove everything and anything. Unlike Plato, he did not try to fit the truth to suit the theory; but painstakingly sought to discover the theory which was built on the truth —no matter how much time it took him, nor what criticism it brought him.

With Aristotle, Science is once again taken up from where it had lain after Democritus the Materialist had left it years before. And he sought to define the terms of matter, motion, space and time; and discussed the geological time clock of the world, with the seas retreating, or advancing over the land; and old areas dying and new locations opening up; and he likened these geological phenomena to the old civilizations which were decaying, and to the new, which were continually coming into being. And for a thorough understanding of his brilliance, the Reader really must avail himself of Aristotle's "De Caeto", and "De Generatione et Corruptione." Most of Aristotle's works it will be noted, are given with Latin names, as he was more appreciated by Medieval Europe for the scope and depth of his thought, than he was admired in the Classical World of the Mediterranean, as being a friend of Alexander's, had completely finished him off in most Greek eyes — Alexander was never Greek as far as they were concerned anyway, and Aristotle was almost as bad; and, as *barbaric* — to their way of thinking.

Wisely, Aristotle announced that, "Probably every Art and Philosophy has been repeatedly developed to the utmost, and has then perished again." And the wisest word in that sentence, in this Writer's opinion, is the word "probably." Not a dogmatist like Plato, Aristotle continually sought the Truth, but was always ready to confess his inability to be absolutely sure; and even with the problem regarding the Slavery issue, he announced, that until such time as Man would develop mechanical means for doing unpleasant and servile work, he (Aristotle) could not see any way past the drudgery and indignity of slavery as a state of life. Perhaps this is why the Writer personally favours Aristotle so much, as it is his quality of Truthfulness; or, honest openness, and sincere wisdom seeking, which she finds most endearing. And we must observe that he was extremely far-sighted for this particular time in history, because it is true that it is the Machine which has now released Man from some of his most soul, mind and body destroying labour. And that it is industrialism which has brought a smoother, more comfortable, and more just life to most people, in general. And if the Reader is not prepared to believe this, then I suggest that he, or she, undertake the experiment of ignoring the modern plumbing system for only one day, and then perhaps he or she will see what havoc results only from this. It is an extremely difficult task to nuture a lofty soul or mind, in conditions which continually degrade and exhaust the body. It can be done; but it is difficult. And sometimes I feel that it is really the inventors of the Wheel, the Water Pipe, and the Flush Toilet, who should really be idolised in Society and History, for they perhaps, have done more for the general Freedom and Happiness of Mankind, than have most of the Philosophers, Leaders, or other romantic figures whom we admire so much, from the Past.

The main and essential difference between the Classical Philosophers Plato and Aristotle, is that, whereas Plato denied the changing forces of life; Aristotle assented to them; and he then tried to work within the boundaries of reality; in order to fashion something better. Aristotle was naturally influenced by his study of Biology and he attempted to **Comprehend** Nature, in order to use her forces; while Plato tried fruitlessly to **Apprehend** Nature, and to deny her movement in our lives. The Aristotelians of this world are Life-Assenting people, who go with the natural tide and flow, and who are therefore, progressive; but the Platonists of this world, are by their nature, reactionary and Life-Denying; and fated always to lose in the end.

The very first Classifications and Definitions of life forms in the Animal Kingdom, were begun by Aristotle, and he collected, and researched, thousands of species of life in the Aegean areas, and throughout the Greek World; (with help from Alexander who was ordering his hunters, game-keepers, and soldiers to keep their eyes open, and to supply his teacher with whatever he requested.) Truly, a respectful and devoted student was Alexander, and Aristotle should have been well pleased with him — but he wasn't! At least not towards the end of their relationship!

Aristotle and his scientific team not only classified thousands of species, but they also compiled information regarding the sleep habits of animals; their reproduction; digestion; excretion; menstruation; sensation; and abortion — as well as observing how they reared their young; and, noting down copiously, their general behaviour and psychology. Most scientists of today should, by rights, give (at the very least) one minute's daily silence, in memory of Aristotle and his Lyceum for all the work they did. Aristotle in fact, even laid the groundwork for modern psychology, with his discovery that the two main drives, or motivations, of all animals are; 1. Eating (that is the preservation of the life instinct for survival, by feeding the body) and 2. Procreation, (a more advanced form of the instinct for survival). So the two main drives of all animals, are for the survival of the individual; and the survival of the species. — Therefore I eat, in order to live, and to survive myself; and I bear young, so that my particular group or species may also live, and survive.

Aristotle was fascinated with all aspects of reproduction, and he established massive records concerning multiple births; and made exhaustive studies of the embryo and its formation; and although it is thought fashionable nowadays to criticise him for the errors he made, it would possibly be more fitting for modern scientists to be a little more grateful and also more humble; **AND** — to bear in mind, what future generations may perhaps have to say, regarding them, and their mistakes, and their ignorance.

Although he rejected Empedocles' notion of Natural Selection of accidental mutations, Aristotle decided that there was no fortuity in evolution, but that the lines of development of each form, specie and genus were determined by an inherent urge to develop itself to the fullest realization of its nature. There was a design to life, but it was not really a guidance from without, but, rather, a drive from within; or, an "entelechy", as he named it. (Derived from the Greek word, 'echo' meaning I have; 'telos' meaning my goal or purpose; and 'en' meaning within.) So this "entelechy" was like a 'life force' or 'elan vital'; and something similar to that formulated later by Bergson. Or it could also be more simply expressed as an inner driving survival instinct, and this definition should suit best those who distrust anything except cold, hard reality, and scientific commonsense.

Aristotle's "History of Animals" is deemed full of errors by today's standards and superior knowledge; which is in turn due to our superior equipment, and to the abundant means at our disposal for study. But even bearing all that in mind, Biology had to wait some twenty centuries, for its equal, in either thought, or content. Aristotle once said — in order for people to understand his apparently crazy interest in animals — (the Greeks thought it crazy anyway!) "In all natural objects there lies some marvel, and if anyone despises the contemplation of the lower animals, he must also despise himself". And this statement alone, makes Aristotle worthy of the title of Philosopher, I think.

The Soul of Man, or his Psyche, Aristotle defined as "the primary entelechy of an organism"; therefore the Soul — the Survival Instinct or the Vital Force (or Élan Vital of Bergson) is really the organism's inherent and destined form; its urge, and, its direction of growth. The Soul to Aristotle was not something added to, or residing in, the body. It was co-extensive with the body. It was the body itself in its "powers of self-nourishment, self-growth, and self-decay. "All natural bodies are organs of the Soul," said Aristotle.

According to this great biologist, the Soul had three grades:- Nutritive, Sensitive, and Rational. Plants, Animals, and Man, all possessed the Nutritive Soul; that is, a capacity for Self-Nourishment, and Internal Growth. But, animals, and Man, had; in addition; the Sensitive Soul; which signified the capacity for sensation. The Higher Forms of Animals, also shared with Man the 'Passive Rational' Soul; which meant that they had a simple form of Intelligence. But Man alone, had the 'Active Rational' Soul; and this meant that he had the capacity to generalize, and to originate.

And just as the Soul was the form of the body, so God was the form, or "entelechy", of the world — its inherent nature, function, and purpose. But this God to Aristotle was not a Creator — but an Energizer. God was the First Cause and the Prime Mover; and the source for all motion, and power, in the world. This Prime Mover was the main energizing form, and catalyst; and which was 'Within' — i.e. the 'inner essence' of everything. And this inner essence, or energizer, he named the "Quintessence", that is, the fifth essence; which he saw as necessary to add to the essential four main materials of life which the Milesians had discovered and named as air, water, earth and fire. And this "Quintessence" he thought, might also be the fifth element of the Heavenly Spheres, that is Aether; and quite possibly it held the Heavens together. Being aTeleologist;(believing everything existed for an end) Aristotle therefore rejected Plato's DivineDirectory Intelligence ruling the world, and replaced it with the Inner Natural Drive of all Life Organisms towards perfection and order; and he also refuted the pre-destination of Plato's Cyclic Succession, and decided that there were alternative future events possible, which were bound only by our freedom of choice as humans. (And we will look more deeply into his theories on 'Choice' and Morality, a little further on) Therefore, Aristotle, is at all times, much more optimistic than his teacher; who was obviously a born pessimist, along with all his other faults! (It will no doubt not have escaped the Reader's attention that the Writer has a positively irrational hatred for Plato and his fore-runner Parmenides!)

The main problem though was that Aristotle was as honest a man as George Washington is reputed to have been; and just as that distinguished gentleman kept cutting down cherry trees, and then admitting to his guilt; so did Aristotle keep discovering new knowledge about the Heavenly Spheres, which led him to cut down his one great Prime Mover, and to divide it up into many. And in the end, instead of having only one; he ended up with fifty-five! And this just confused everyone! Oh, dear, if only Diogenes the Cynic had been around at that time, he could have found his really honest man, and completely without the aid of a lantern either! Nobody actually appreciated such a multiplicity of 'Unmoved Movers', or, 'Intelligences in the World'; and it certainly did nothing to enhance Aristotle's reputation with the Greeks. He was quite possibly, actually trying to define the laws governing the attraction of objects; as he had decided that the 'Movers', or 'Causers', of motion, were objects of love or desire in others; and perhaps, he had been influenced by his study of the insect world as well; and maybe he had come across the 'activity centre' ant, which in a way, can be likened to a 'Prime Mover' in his nest. But the result of all this scholastic veracity was that most people took an intense dislike to Aristotle — as people are in general, lazy beings who like simple monic explanations which save them from thought.

Every effect, said Aristotle, was produced by Four Causes (and the Reader is probably muttering to himself that we just do not seem to be able to get away from all these "Causes" and "Movers" — but a little patience is necessary sometimes, and it is definitely one of the pre-requisites for developing a philosophical disposition!) anyway, Aristotle decided, that all things–and all movements–were caused by the following:-

1. The Material Cause — the stuff out of which the thing is made
2. The Efficient Cause — the agent or the act itself
3. The Formal Cause — the nature of the thing making it
4. The Final Cause — the goal or the necessary reason

And in order to illustrate the above and to make it more understandable, let us examine Aristotle's own definition of Man, as based on these Four Causes. So we have

1 The Material Cause of Man, which is the Menses, i.e. the provision of the Ovum.

2. The Efficient Cause, which is the Semen, i.e. the act of insemination.

3. The Formal Cause which is Nature, and

4. The Final Cause which is the purpose in view.

So you see this system of definition worked quite well for Aristotle, and if the Reader is still gasping in incomprehension, then he or she must simply go back and study the whole thing again!

Being a great man for Definitions (and possibly that was his Achilles' Heel) Aristotle defined Art; the purpose of which, he said, was to capture the essential form of things; and **not** merely to produce a mechanical copy (unlike some people who fancy themselves to be painters!) Art should imitate, or, represent life, and the soul of matter; said he, so that even though this intuitive mirroring of essence might be of an ugly object, the ugliness would in fact be beautiful. Therefore Degas and the Impressionists were definitely Aristotelians! "Beauty is Truth, Truth Beauty, — that is all ye know on earth, and all ye need to know," so said the poet Keats, also consciously, or unconsciously echoing the words of Aristotle. And this beauty, Aristotle further defined, as Unity — or the co-operation and symmetry of all the parts into one whole. In Drama this Unity was essentially, or basically, a Unity of Action — the Plot had to concern itself with one Action mainly, and only permit other Action to advance, in order to illustrate the central theme. (All writers or would-be writers, would do well to study a little Aristotle!) He also defined Tragedy and its development in such a way as to provide a fool-proof blue-print for all writers of this persuasion, including the greats, Shakespeare and Eugene O'Neill. And he paid special attention to the psychologically corrective aspects of Tragedy as well, — and, of how we are nefariously able to enjoy the spectacle of other peoples' violence and pain; as a way therefore, of discharging our own; or, of vicariously converting; or emotionally compensating — or even, of experiencing, (and enjoying) that which is not within our own life style, or experience range. Aristotle thought it a mark of civilization to produce great works of Art for, "nature requires not only that we should be properly employed, but that we should be able to enjoy our leisure in an honourable way." And the key word in this sentence here is surely 'honourable', and most nations with high unemployment policies and desultory soul-destroying Leisure Centres could afford to give Aristotle a read, as well!

As regards what constitutes a good life — Aristotle the Stagerite, decided that it is a happy one; and unlike his master Plato, he applied himself to considering the best ways to make a man happy — rather than to make him good! All other things, other than happiness, he mused, are sought with some other end in view; but happiness is sought for its own sake. And with these principles we perhaps discover a little of the influence of Aristippus the Hedonist, in Aristotle, just as we will discern a slight flavour of Aristotle, in the works of Epicurus, in the next chapter.

Realistically, Aristotle comes to the conclusion that in order to have lasting happiness, one needs the following:- good birth, good health, good looks, good luck, a good reputation, good friends, much money, and to be possessed of the quality of "goodness", itself! And, unfortunately, for anyone worried about their appearance, Aristotle is even further from comforting, because he says, "No man can be happy who is absolutely ugly." But then, according to Aristotle, even an ugly object in Art is beautiful if it be True; so therefore we may hoist Aristotle on his own petard, and say that an ugly man who is truthful and honest, must (like an artistic object) be a thing of beauty. So, take heart, all Readers!

Also he notes that, "as for those who say that he who is being tortured on the wheel, or falls into great misfortunes, is happy, provided only he be good; they talk nonsense" — and I think most people would agree with him on this point. He also passes comment on Simonides of Ceos, a poet, and his answer to the question as to whether it is better to be wise or rich. "Rich", was the reply, "for we see the wise spending their time at the doors of the rich," However, according to Aristotle, wealth is only a means to an end and not an end in itself and the true secret of happiness is action — and the use of energy — in a way suited to one's nature and circumstances.

All action, Aristotle proclaimed, was preceded by 'Choice' and Morality as such, did not really equal good will; but only the will, or choice, of the good. (This is rather a Sophisticated attitude for an ex-student of Plato's —I doubt if he ever spoke much in class — his teacher would probably have expelled him early on in the piece, if he had known what insubordinate thoughts his analytical and definitive mind was harbouring!) Virtue, he said, is a practical wisdom, and a wise practicality, and it is the golden Mean — "Everything in Moderation" — the Ancient Greek Motto. Man needs intelligence to discover the Mean, and he needs self-control, or discipline, in order to practise it — and Aristotle advocated "enkrateia" meaning 'inner strength' in the Greek language. All men aimed at "eudaemonia" or 'well-being,' and a state of complete satisfaction, and wanted (or needed) not only to *feel* happy, but to really have all well *within.* (The word "eudaemonia" is derived from "eu" meaning good, and "daemon" meaning the spirit within the body.) And Aristotle advocated the development of "arete", which translates in Greek, "to be good at something". Therefore, based on this definition, the "arete" of a liar, is to be a really good, and successful liar — like Odysseus in the Odyssey. But "arete" actually means, in Aristotelian terms, something akin to the word "virtue" in English; and this virtue is not so much an Act, as it is a Habit.

(Incidentally "arete" was actually derived from the word Ares, that is the God of War, who in Ancient Greece was deemed to be the most Manly or Virtuous fellow — as a good warrior was most admired by all, and was the 'ideal' most boys aimed for.)

At first this Virtue must be enforced by discipline, says Aristotle, but in time, this compulsion will become a habit, and second nature; and therefore something both pleasant, and desired. "The Virtues we acquire by first exercising them," he wrote. "We become Just, by performing Just Acts, Temperate by performing Temperate ones; Brave, by performing Brave ones. Men will become good builders by building well, and bad ones as a result of building badly." And there we have it in a nutshell! Habit makes slaves of us all, and Life itself is only composed of habits, good, or bad; and most Behaviour Therapists would agree that it is simply a matter of setting-up a certain pattern of behaviour, in order to build a particular personality; or, to change; or to formulate, a person's psychology. And Educationists would all benefit from a reading of Aristotle as well! In fact the whole world could probably do with a little more perusing of this philosopher, I feel sure! It is also worth noting in passing, that when Aristotle was presented with that old 'chestnut' on the exact value of Education to Man, he, unlike Aristippus, was able to reply immediately, briefly, and succinctly, with the definition that Educated Men, compared to the Uneducated were, "as the Living are to the Dead."

And in his work "Ethics", he sets out in his usual clear and definitive way, examples of both Virtue and Vice, in certain activities, and attitudes.

ACTIVITY

1. Facing Death
2. Experiencing pleasure/pain
3. Giving and taking money
4. Attitude towards honour/dishonour
5. Assertion
6. Giving Amusement

ATTITUDES. The Vices or Virtues associated with each of the Activities listed above.

Vice of Excess	**Virtue or Golden Mean** (i.e. what you should exhibit in your attitude)	**Vice of Defect.** (i.e. what you should not exhibit in your attitude)
1. Rashness	Courage	Cowardice
2. Self-Indulgence	Temperance	Insensibility
3. Prodigality	Liberality	Meanness
4. Empty Vanity	Proper Pride	Undue Humility
5. Boastfulness	Truth Telling	Mock Modesty
6. Buffoonery	Ready Wit	Boorishness

It is hoped that the Reader will bear the above attitudes in mind when Facing Death; Giving or Taking Money; or Experiencing Pleasure or Pain. The Author is definitely bearing in mind (and taking to heart) the Golden Mean Rule on the Giving of Amusement; and she is hoping that her writing has neither been full of buffoonery nor abundant in boorishness, as she feels the cold analytical breath of Aristotle on this page even now while penning these words. And perhaps the Athenians had a point in disliking Aristotle, after all. He really was, rather **too** definitive, and **too** analytical for comfort!

This noble and lofty definer of things, finally decided, that the best life lay in contemplation, and he announced that, "those who wish for an independent pleasure should seek it in philosophy, for all other pleasures need the assistance of men." Truly, Aristotle was a wise, if uncomfortable, man; and the above sentence should definitely gladden the hearts of all those alone, or friendless, or lacking in any type of diversion. And, for the practice of philosophy, one does not need pen, paper, or money; and neither is there need of a football team, nor a football. Nor, is there any great call for any object, person, place or thing. All that one needs, is one's thoughts; and, the companionship of one's own mind. "The most fortunate of men," says the dedicated scholar Aristotle, "is he who combines a measure of prosperity with scholarship, research, or contemplation; (as) such a man comes closest to the life of the gods." And he stresses that "the proper work of Man, is a working of the Soul, in accordance with Reason." And we have noted, that to Aristotle, the Soul of Man, is his Inner Drive, or motivation which is urging him on for the best conditions, and the fulfilment of himself.

There is some really fascinating material in Aristotle, about Sense-Perception and Memory, and about the link between Association and Image in the brain, and all modern psychology must surely be in his debt — Freud especially! And besides these lengthy treatises on psychology, he has defined and classified Logic, Types of Poetry, Types of Justice, Ethics, and Sensations, and much, much more. Always classifying, always defining —he would definitely have driven poor Pythias off her head. Or perhaps that comment of mine is only an example of my vice of excess, Buffoonery! However we will leave aside all this wonderful and interesting work of his (for the Reader will doubtless now be licking his lips in readiness to read it all for himself) and we will instead, turn to Aristotle's ideas regarding Politics, in which once again he shows himself to be the very antithesis to Plato; although, a great deal of his political theory had been developed from a Platonic foundation.

"Man is by nature a political animal", decided Aristotle, and as the word "politics" actually comes from the Greek word "polis", meaning the 'city', so it is true that the ability of men to live together in a city or 'polis' depends on the individual achievement of each person in mastering the Arts of toleration; respect for others; and courtesy; in dealings with all. The word "polite" is also derived from this word "polis", and originally described (perhaps a case of wishful thinking!) the chivalrous and gracious behaviour of people living in close proximity to each other in a city. As a matter of Etymological interest, it may be noted that the words "police" and "politician" are also derived from this same Greek root, but it does not necessarily follow however that either of these two categories of people are the most polite. It is also unfortunately to be observed, that seldom nowadays does one find a "polite" member of our modern version of the "polis" either. But then, words hardly ever retain their original meaning!

Aristotle came to the conclusion however that the function of the State was to organise, for the greatest happiness of the greatest number of inhabitants. "A State is a collective body of citizens sufficient in themselves for all the purposes of life," he said. And accordingly therefore, he collected and studied, one hundred and fifty eight Greek Constitutions, and divided them into three main types:- Monarchy, a Government by Power; Aristocracy, a Government by Birth; and Timocracy, a Government by Excellence. And once again, as with the virtues and vices outlined by him in his Ethics Doctrines, there is a Golden Mean; this time, a political one. All of these forms of Government, in Aristotle's opinion, can be good or bad, depending on how they are carried out. Monarchy can become Despotism, Aristocracy can develop into Oligarchy, and Timocracy can turn into dreadful Democracy with rule by the Common Man. (I feel sure that here he must have meant a very *common,* Common Man!)

Single rulers can become Tyrants, he thought, and Aristocratic Families tend to deteriorate into degenerates or maniacs. (Attention here, please, all titled people — ploughing through these pages!) But Democracy can also lead to suicidal chaos, with a rabble of mechanics and urban tradesmen. (Aristotle's choice of occupations — not mine!) So this philosopher whose name itself means "the best" (derived in Greek from 'Aristos') decided that a Government, needed specialized people with ability, and knowledge, and good character, judgement, and training — and all these qualities he thought, were quite impossible to find in a mechanic, or hired servant. (Some of Plato must have stuck — or maybe he was only expressing the general consensus of the Age itself!) All men are created unequal, says Aristotle; and one is unfortunately, forced to agree, as in truth we are all completely different in abilities, physical details, and mental and personal characteristics. "Equality is just," he announces, "but only between equals." And that is the rub! How to establish anEquality, in order to put Justice into practice? But he finally comes up with the idea of a mixed constitution, or Timocracy, and thinks that this might be the answer, as it is a system based on a combination of Aristocracy and Democracy; and in which the Suffrage will be restricted to landowners and a strong middle class, which will provide a balance for the whole. "It is plain, then, that those states are best instituted wherein the middle classes are a larger and more formidable part than either the rich or the poor... Whenever the number of those in the middle state has been too small, those who were the more numerous, whether the rich or the poor, always overpowered them, and assumed to themselves the administration of public affairs..." Hence his development of the system of Timocracy, and the preservation of a strong middle class, which later served as a model for the foundation of Society in the United States of America.

His system is more humane than Plato's Utopia, and he gives provision for the Poor from public land and funds; but the Aristocrats of Thought rule, just like the Philosopher Guardians, and they strongly regulate education, industry, marriage, property, music, and literature etc. The main difference from Plato, is that Aristotle allows a little glimmer of hope to pass through the system of regulations, and he provides for the rise of excellence as did Alexander in his Empire, and Napoleon in his also, much later in history. But this idea of the rise of excellence is very important to Aristotle for as he saw it, "All Men by Nature desire to know." Aristotle obviously could not get it into his head that the world was not full of philosophical seekers and definers like himself, and that the majority of people might just be happy to exist in blind ignorance.

Possibly this scholastic idealism was a remnant from his early Platonic education, and one cannot help pitying him for his naivety when reading —"Since the highest virtue is intelligence, the pre-eminent duty of the State is not to train the citizens to military excellence, but to educate them for the right use of peace." And whoever heard of a country being run on those principles? Or was Aristotle writing tongue-in-cheek?

On the subject of slavery we have already noted his attitude, but for the record, it must be observed that Aristotle is supposed to have made extremely good provision for all his own personel slaves in his last Will and Testament. However this alone is hardly good enough to excuse him. Why didn't he set them free before he died, one may ask? And even if people are not **born equal**, they at least should all be **born free**! And Aristotle, like every other Great Thinker, lacked the humanity, the rationality, and the compassion, necessary to understand and to identify with the slave in his servile position. If in fact Pythagoras is right, and we do all keep coming back, then I feel it would only be **Just** that such detached scholastic individuals like Plato and Aristotle (and some of the other philosophers as well!) should get a chance to enjoy a short life in some modern version of the Laurium silver mines — the experience (due to the type of work) would no doubt only be of brief duration, but it might open their eyes a trifle, to the condition of their fellow men. How strange indeed that Aristotle could realize that he was only a higher form of animal ("Man is a rational animal") and yet not identify with the slaves around him and say, "There but for the grace of good breeding go I." (Of course if Aristotle had actually freed all his slaves he would have been so occupied in washing-up his dishes and mopping his floors that he would never have had the time to define anything — let alone leave the world such a collection of multifarious and magnificent wisdom. There are always two sides to every coin, and I am personally inclined to forgive Aristotle for any attitude he had towards slavery, as he was such a brilliant 'brain' and he contributed so much wisdom and knowledge to the world.)

In 323 B.C., on hearing of the death of Alexander, there were anti-Macedonian riots in Athens, and even celebrations in the streets, over the passing of the head of the Empire, (the Athenians were never known to mask their true feelings!) and Aristotle was therefore accused of impiety by Isocrates (his professional rival) among other envious gentlemen; and he was charged with having offered honours to Hermeias, in the past. As Hermeias had at one time been a slave — (the Athenians were also known for their long memories — like elephants!) — he could not have been a God, and consequently Aristotle should not have honoured him. This of course was just another trumped-up charge like the earlier indictments of Socrates and Anaxagoras — but then who should look for either Justice or Logic in the Law — "Justice equals inequality," said Plato, and the Athenians had ALWAYS believed that!

The great biologist however, decided not to fight the charge, but to leave the city immediately, and remarked ironically, while tidying up his notes, that he "would not give Athens a chance to sin against philosophy a second time." He then went off to Chalcis in Stageira, and left his Lyceum and all its problems, to Theophrastus his most brilliant student, and of whom we shall hear more later.

The Athenians tenaciously succeeded in passing a death sentence on him, but were most exceedingly irked, when he beat them to the punch, as it were, by dying of natural causes, or stomach trouble, (possibly an attack of gastro-enteritis — or even poison self-administered) and Aristotle passed to his just reward at the tender age of sixty-three, leaving those ingrates, the Athenians, to deal with their problems unaided.

And so with the passing of both Aristotle and Alexander, the Indian Summer of Athens and the Greek World passed away also — and the bitter Winter of Defeat, Despair, and Stoicism, came howling in with a vengeance. And the Greeks, and the Athenians in particular, would now pay heavily, for having ignored Philosophy — and for having ignored the very lessons of Nature itself.

Winter

The Winter of Death and Despair in the Hellenic World.

The Final Break-up of the City-State and the Hellenic Empire. Alexandria shows the Flag — for a short time!

Epicurus and the Epicureans

Zeno and the Stoics

Theophrastus and the Peripatetics

Pyrrho and the Pyrrhonian Sceptics

Sextus Empiricus and the Alexandrian Sceptics

Arcesilaus and Carneades and the Academy Sceptics

CHAPTER 12

FINE WINE OR VINEGAR

The Epicureans and the Stoics. The Winter of Discontent in the Hellenic World.

The death of Alexander in 323 B.C. ushered in the final act in this Greek Tragedy, which possibly, should more fittingly be called a Comedy of Errors — for it was due to needless and senseless, and ignorant mistakes, (seemingly comical, when viewed from a distance of two thousand years or so, in a fervour of smug, self-congratulatory patronage and the wisdom of hind-sight!) that the Greeks eventually fell. They, (especially the Athenians), were of course, not aware that this was to be their end; and they therefore welcomed the passing of Alexander, and thought only that they were obviously much better off without him. And so, as the wars of succession, and the internecine rivalry, and fierce social antagonism began to arise once more, the majority of citizens foolishly imagined, that once the inconveniences of these bloody battles were over, then they would simply resume their old lives just as before. Barring a very few enlightened souls, the majority of the Greeks, failed completely, to grasp the *substance* of the Alexandrian Empire, and instead, fell to chasing *shadows;* and in consequence thereof, retreated into evolutionary darkness, as before. They had not been able to understand that the time of the City-State was over, and that the historic period of small and pifling nations and nationalities, and their various petty feuds, was over as well. There had been a Climatic Change. And they refused to accept the real challenge of the Hellenic Empire, which was to build a broader, more cosmopolitan world, in the Mediterranean. So therefore the Greeks refused the invitation to the dance; and threw down the gauntlet, which the ROMANS promptly picked up — and accordingly, went on to pursue paths of glory and splendour — until they in their turn, also experienced the rheumatism of winter and old-age, creeping into their bones. The truth, however, probably was, that the Greeks were just too old for such adventuring — and that's why they lost their empire. It takes youth and vigour to control colonies — and the Athenians were just not up-to-scratch, any more!

Not being able to comprehend that the times indeed were a-changing, the Greeks, and the Athenians in particular, found themselves embracing only the demons from their short season of Imperial splendour — and *not* the angels. Fastidiously they practised Selective Acculeration; selecting —seemingly — all the wrong elements from both East and West; and never understanding the real message of the era through which they had just passed — but grabbing at the material riches; confusing and befuddling themselves with the new gods, and the new religions entering their territory now; adopting the worst, and not the best from Asia — and steadfastly putting back all clocks — refusing to raise their eyes in order to read the writing on the wall — and burying their heads, in true Platonic fashion, in the sand. The Greeks were in fact, rather like a contemporary Third World country in which the people have no sanitation, and no proper legal, or educational system; but in which everyone is drinking as much Cola as possible; and the entire youth population sports blue-jeans. The conflict of cultures had occurred — Athens was at the head of the confluence; and she managed somehow — to end up taking the dirty water from both streams!

This was truly a time of trauma for the Greeks. Dispossessed, and displaced people wandered in every city of the Hellenic World. There was no really stable or common language; and the people shared no common unification in communication, customs, faith, or, Gods. The Greeks had invaded the East, but now the East had in turn invaded the Greeks, and the Athenians learnt reluctantly, and to their sorrow, that by conquering — one is in turn, conquered. And that the master, eventually develops the bad habits of his slaves! The new customs, habits, ideas, clothing, food, and religions flooding the Greek World at this period created such an overload in the system, and bewildered the people so much; that in the end, they were neither Greeks, nor cosmopolitans; neither European, nor Eastern — nor Hellenic. They were nothing. And when the Romans came along, many of the Greeks were only too happy to adopt their citizenship. The relief of actually finding a nationality, and of being able to define themselves, sociologically, was immense; and the common latinization of names which was popular at this period, is a fairly good example of this psychological and sociological crisis of theirs. Socially speaking the Greeks had always been inclined to 'cannibalism', but now this capricious tendency of theirs had become a permanent vice, and they took to the streets and took to each other; and, between themselves, managed to achieve their own destruction in a manner which would even have done credit to their enemies, the Persians — and which surely must have made old Darius turn happily in his grave and laugh.

Immediatcly following the demise of Alexander, the Empire split into three main sections:- the Macedonian Kingdom, the Seleuceed Empire, and the Ptolemy Dynasty. The various Greek City-States of the area, plus the 'half-Greek' States in Epirus, Judea, Pergamum, Byzantium, Cappadocia, Galatia, Bithynia, India, Syria, and Bactria, thereupon became very confused about the autonomy issue. Did they belong to anyone, or not? If they didn't, then how to enjoy their freedom? So, as the Empire fell; the City-States fell also. And on the edges of the Greek World, the barbarians gathered like packs of hungry wolves. In the West, Greek Italy and Sicily began being attacked by both the Romans, and the Carthaginians; and in the East, the Gauls were most inconsiderately, depriving everyone of a good night's sleep. Sniffing disunity and vulnerability, their enemies closed in; and the Greeks; instead of strengthening their defences, and coming to grips with the situation; turned in on each other, biting and scratching; (and generally getting themselves into as bad a condition as they could) and accusing each other; and debilitating themselves; until, such time, as they in turn, could be conquered, and mercifully, put out of their misery, by a final blow on the head, from Rome. Perhaps Imperialism sat too heavily on the Greek Head! Perhaps; as such freedom loving people, they had never really wanted an empire in the first place. The City-State is what they had invented — they were happy with it — and they didn't want to change! And the Athenians were the most conservative of them all.

By 321 B.C., having waged continual bloody war between each other, the Greeks had succeeded in further dissolving their trust from Alexander, until it was finally partitioned into five chief areas. Antipater was the head of Macedonia and Greece; Lysimachus ruled Thrace; Antigonus held the reins in Asia Minor; Seleucus entertained in Babylonia; and in Egypt, the Ptolemy and his descendents held sway. Ironically, the Greeks had now over-whelmingly succeeded in establishing the Monarchy, and even, in 'institutionalizing' it, in Europe — and the Greeks had always loathed monarchies! But then, people should take better care of their Democracies when they have them — and should also remember that we generally get the type of Government that we richly deserve!

This particular period of violence affected every class, in the Greek World, and until the Romans came, in 168 B.C. there were unceasing foreign and civil wars between the City-States; with hundreds of generals contesting for the various thrones; and with coups, and counter-coups, and Juntas being formed at night-fall; only to be dissolved again rapidly, at first light. War had become a way of life, and like all habits, it seemed very hard to break!

Athens in particular revolted many times after 323 B.C. and the inhabitants, anxious to be free of foreign rule and occupation, kept insisting on counting their chickens long before they could ever be hatched. And after the first revolt, the Macedonian General Antipater, established a Macedonian Garrison in Athens, in order to keep the peace; and thereby began a traditition for the stationing of foreign troops in Athens which has continued until this day! Interestingly enough, the only time that the Athenians actually managed to rid themselves entirely of foreign bases, (and only for a very short period) was just prior to the final take-over by Rome.

Antipater also forced the Athenians to pay reparation for their little insurrection, and all citizens who possessed less than two thousand drachmas worth of property were immediately compelled to emigrate (actully this was more in the way of a deportation order) to the colonial settlements which the Hellenic Empire of Alexander had opened up. This was an extremely clever strategy for spreading Greek influence in the East, as well as for ridding Athens of extreme social discontent, and Antipater should doubtless be congratulated. The degree of social discontent was rather high though, and the number of citizens deemed below the poverty belt was also far from modest, for it is recorded that 12,000 people, out of a total population of 21,000, immediately left for pastures fresh and green in Asia. People with less than two thousand drachmas were quite obviously, natural Anarchists, in Antipater's eyes!

In 318 B.C. Athens went up in flames again (there was just no stopping the Athenians in their pursuit of individual City-State liberty!) and again their revolt was put down; but this time, by Cassander, the son of Antipater. Meanwhile though, Antigonus I (known as Cyclops — due to his possessing only one optical organ) who ruled in Asia Minor; began to dream of re-uniting all Alexander's Empire under himself. Unfortunately for him, he not only dreamt about this, but he fell to scheming about it as well, and began assiduously attempting to make his dream a reality. But Antigonus was lacking not only in physical sight, but in military force as well, and during the wars which he initiated, he was roundly, and soundly beaten, by Seleucus I. And so, in 301 B.C., all of Asia Minor passed into the hands of the ruling faction of Babylonia.

Then, Antigonus' son, Demetrius Poliorcetes, in revenge for the loss of his father's estates, set about "liberating" Athens; and as a reward, was given the keys of the City, and comfortable pied a têrre there. However, this 'guest of the City', after taking up residence, began to drive both the Athenian men, and the women, mad with his attentions; and one unwilling male virgin even went so far in the protection of his honour, as to throw himself into a vat of boling water, in order to escape the "Liberator's" desires. Demetrius never allowed such little things to get him down however, and ignoring his lack of popularity, (and the number of suicides he was causing) launched himself into winning a naval victory over Ptolemy I at Cyprus in 308, (a few years after Zeno the founder of Stoicism had emigrated to Athens); beseiged Rhodes unsuccessfully for six years; crowned himself King of Macedonia in 294; established new garrisons in Athens; began a series of new wars in which he was defeated by Seleucus; and finally-died of drink! Demetrius was a real broth of a boy, and his life story makes for very interesting reading, however it is understandable that the Athenians were slightly less than happy with him.

Then in 279 B.C., tribes of Celts and Gauls, under the leadership of one Brennus, (not the same Brennus who invaded Italy in 390 B.C. and who would have destroyed the Roman camps except that some geese took exception to the arrival of these marauding Celts and gave the game away by cackling loudly, and thereby alerting the Romans!) marched down through Macedonia into Greece — (neither the Greeks, nor the Macedonians, kept geese around their cities it seems!) and he was helped on the way, by various dissatisfied Greeks, who had decided it was hightime indeed, to sell their Motherland. In the words of Pausanias, the great travel writer and topographer of the 2nd century A.D., "At no time was Greece wanting in people afflicted with an itch for treason." And so the Greeks turned traitor in great numbers, and helped the barbarians to find their way through the mountain passes into the cities. Therefore Brennus and his men availed themselves of this splendid opportunity, and helped themselves to large quantities of gold, and votive offerings from the temples, before continuing on their merry way thorugh Thermopylae to Delphi — where they butcheredall the males, raped all the women, and ate all the babies! At least that is the story according to the Greeks. We do not of course hear what the Greeks had done to them, in previous engagements in Asia, Italy, and Sicily! But Pausanias certainly poured forth on paper some very torrid descriptions of what barbarities the Celts inflicted on everyone they met. So torrid were these descriptions indeed, that it is no wonder that it is not yet considered fashionable to be descended from the Celts! But then, the history of that time was written by the Greeks and Romans, so one must expect a little bias.

These same blood-thirsty and booty-hungry warriors then crossed into Asia Minor and repeated their massacres there, while back in Macedonia, now that the Celts had left town, the Poor under Apollodorus, rose against the Rich, and commenced to show what neat tricks in slaughter they had just picked-up from the recently passing militia. But in Asia Minor the Greeks realised quite early on, that the only way to deal with these incredible fighters was to compromise, so accordingly, they bought them off with land grants, and Northern Phrygia became known as Galatia in consequence; and even in Thrace, and the Balkans, large tracts of territory passed over into their hands. For two generations the Celts were also paid 'fear tribute' by Seleucus I (the man who never began a fight he could not finally win!) and the Greek cities of the Black Sea and the Asiatic Coast supplied them with huge sums of money — just to stay away, and leave the occupants in peace. Byzantium was another area which later paid large amounts of money every year, just to convince the Celts that city-life was not worth bothering about. And the Celts took their money, and hung around on the fringes of society feeling decidedly miffed about the whole thing, and probably wondering why nobody seeemed to like them. Quite possibly they were really only intent on getting "civilized", and therefore wanted to drop into the local "polis", in order to see how things were done, but — the Greeks would have none of it! The Greeks had no desire, (and no intention either) of carrying the Classical Man's Burden — at least not back in their own home ground! And so the Kings of Pergamum, Seleucia, and Macedonia, spent both time and money in liberal quantities, repelling continuous waves of undesirable Celtic *tourists,* and as this was hardly a cheery way to manage their affairs, this stress of constant invasion was one of the factors which caused the tremendous upsurge in Stoicism, in the Greek World. The Greeks, in fact, were Stoics beause they needed to be —unhappy endurance was about all that was left to them!

The Author (due to her name and colouring) being forced to claim direct descendency from the Celts (whether fashionable or not) is in fact wondering if this monetary arrangement with her ancestors might still be considered lawful. She would love to receive a payment of filthy lucre every year in order to vouchsafe her absence from the areas of Thrace, the Balkans, and Byzantium; and she feels that in all fairness, this matter should be brought to the attention of the governments concerned. Unfortunately the Celts left no magnificent pieces of architecture and sculpture behind for their descendents to make any money out of, but it seems only logical — that like the modern Italians and Greeks–the Irish and Scots should also be able to live off their ancient forebears — and what they lack in the way of Parthenons and Colosseums, they could make up for in legal hassles regarding old treaties. Celtic Readers might care to take note of this information, and to begin filing suit for 'fear tribute' at the earliest opportunity!

There is another interesting aspect to the story of the Celts and their battles at Pergamum, and it concerns the magnificent statuary which the Greeks later erected showing the valiant fortitude of these barbarians while in battle. The Author was in fact very impressed with the tortured lines of her ancestors who were depicted preferring to kill themselves rather than to surrender; and she especially admired the Stoic thrust of their heads, the gritting of their teeth, and the flexing of their muscles in attitudes of proud and honourable death. (The Reader may sometime come across such examples in pictures of the Pergamum Acropolis, and the famous "Dying Gaul".) As previously noted, the Author was exceedingly admiring, and proud, of her people's stamina and heroism, until one day when informed by a friend of hers in the medical profession, that in fact, the bodies of the dying warriors were not twisted in noble heroism, but in the torturous pains of TETANUS, the greatest killer in the battles of those days — when people did not bother unduly about keeping their swords, or other instruments of war, free from rust! Ah! another illusion destroyed, you sigh. But then — education itself, (like Hedonism) never promised to make anyone actually happier — only more knowledgeable!

Anyway, with all this chaotic mess in the Greek World, a strong man was called for, and the times produced such a one, in Antigonus II, a son of Demetrius Poliorcetes. And he drove the Celts and Gauls out of Macedonia, put down the revolt of Apollodorus, and succeeded in ruling, not wisely — but firmly — from 277 B.C. to 39 B.C.

During this period of wars and invasions there was also money to be made by some, and very big money at that. Small factories arose in Athens, and there was a tremendous increase in Slave Labour there, as well as in other cities of the Hellenistic World. Slave dealers in fact joined the various armies of the day, and unransomed prisoners of war found themselves reluctantly joining in the hustle and bustle of the huge Slave Marts which were held in Delos and Rhodes. The merchandise generally sold for approximately $100 to $200 per head, and Rhodes also began a large and comprehensive insurance scheme in order to protect slave owners against the loss of their property.

This was a time for new Greek cities to flourish, and for oldones to die. Athens felt the pinch, but managed to keep her head up somehow, while Piraeus, the old lady of the sea, developed chronic arthritis due to the new movement of merchants all over the Hellenic World, who took their trade and their ships elsewhere. Speculation increased, and the Traders came into their own, and became **really** wealthy, and a life-style was seen in the Greek World which had never been dreamt of before, with palaces, orgies, abundant slaves, servants, and new luxurious furniture; and seemingly almost in preparedness for the Roman opulence which was still yet to come.

The wages were low, and in consequence made for depopulation as people left for the colonies, or took to pauperism, celibacy, or abortion; in order to release themselves from the strain of providing for new life. Hardly anyone could afford to marry anymore — they couldn't even afford to live! There was in fact little difference between the poor Freeman and the Slave, and many people became mercinaries in order to earn their bread and olives. The Athenian Government became so worried about the conditions (in case there were fresh revolts) that free dispersal of corn was begun, and tickets were supplied liberally to the people of the streets, in order to keep them amused and acceptably occupied at the games. The Poor however started to form Unions, and turned towards socialistic doctrines, which shows that the whole movement didn't begin with the French at all; and they (the Poor) demanded the cancellation of debts; the redivison of land; the confiscation of large fortunes; redistribution of property, and, the liberation of slaves. This last grievance was certainly a cause of great concern to the Authorities, because there were by this time, more slaves in Athens, than the entire population of Freemen all told.

The conditions were such that in 300 B.C. when Zeno the Founder of Stoicism brought out his initial publication, "Republica", he became immediately and immensely popular. This romance of his inspired many Greek rebels with its depiction of a Utopia in some Blessed Isle in the Indian Ocean (possibly meant to be Shri-Lanka) where all men were equal in ability, as well as in rights; and where there were no poor, and, no wealthy; and where all shared the work, and the governing of the place. This Utopia was a land of perfection, with no wars, and no classes, and in which men lived in harmony and universal love. And with this book, the founder of Stoicism made himself an over-night success, and completely gained the people to him; before he cut them all down to size with his development of the 'Acceptance Dogma' in Stoicism. And like the grand old Duke of York, who had 10,000 men, Zeno marched the people of Athens up to the top of the hill, and then, marched them, just as swiftly down again!

In every Greek city, class conflict with accompanying massacres, suppressions, demonstrations, and the destruction of property became the order of the day. Some cities fell completely as people raced away to escape each other. Polybius the historian, writing in 150 B.C. was most distressed to note the greedy mob reign of violence everywhere, with its attendant massacres, banishments, revenge killings and enthronement of new despots and oligarchies. Foreign wars and class wars weakened Greece until Rome finally managed to surround and invade her. Crops were destroyed, property razed, captives sold into slavery, and the Greeks, (and those Athenians in particular) proceeded to bite and scratch at their social psoriasis until they were raw and bleeding. The strife; the deforestation; and the erosion of the land continued so, that the Trade in the East grew (as the Merchants couldn't trust the Athenians anymore) and old Mainland Greece suffered even more. Ionia and Asia Minor experienced an Indian Summer of their own economically speaking, for their cities were not in the same depth of chaos which was now current in Athens. So, with this second Spring which had been granted to them, Greek power, literature, art, and general creativity, (which always accompanied the trade,) passed back again into their hands. And from them, the centre of civilization reverted even further afield to Asia, and to Egypt — the new colony of Greece — and from which Greece had originally taken most of her first culture. The old school-mistress from whom Greece had originally learnt her first words, in fact.

With the rise in foreign merchants, and with foreign slaves flooding Athens, there came a decay in orthodox religion, and skepticism spread. New exotic divinites were entering from the East and jousting for position with the old Olympians. Isis, Ammon, Atys, Bendis, Cybele, as well as other imported gods from Asia (and in particular from Egypt) caused great confusion in the minds of people, and there was also a great revival of the old attachments to Orpheus, and Dionysos, and — Drink! The Olympian Gods of the Mythology now only lived, and were only respected, in the country. In the city areas, the educated alone, gave them lip service, and then only in matters of art and literature. Nobody though actually believed in them anymore, and philosophy struggled to find, and to define **not** a civic loyalty (as in the days of Plato) but a universal reasoning, in order to hold these divergent Hellenic people, and places, together.

And due to the confusion; atheism and agnosticism had grown so greatly that by 300 B.C. Euphemurus of Messena in Sicily was not afraid to publish a most scathing and satirical attack on the Greek Gods with his book "Hiera Anagrapha". And these new cults from the Alexandrian conquests were such exotic new faiths and they all promised Heaven, and threatened Hell, and were so multitudinous and bewildering, that Epicurus the philosopher, denounced **all religion** as bad for the"peaceof the mind." There were also built new temples in Athens, to Isis, Serapis, and Bendis (and various other imported aliens) and these new Cults welcomed all men and women, slaves, or freemen — and even foreigners! The Olympians had only been gods for the Greeks, but these new deities now crowding the Acropolis, were for everyone!

These new cults, which met and merged with the old Greek cults of Orpheus, Dionysos, and Demeter, promised Eternal Life to all men, be they alien, bonded, or free; and superstition flourished and grew, with the number 7 becoming renowned for both holiness and luck. There were 7 Days in the Week, 7 Wonders of the World, 7 Ages of Man, 7 Heavens, 7 Gates of Hell, and so on. Interestingly enough, this pre-occupation with the number seven has persisted down to this day, and many of our Twentieth Century brethren also deem it a figure of great fortune. The ancient science, or superstition, (depending on how one views it) of Astrology was also rejuvenated at this time by renewed contact with Babylon, and the Stars became gods and ruled the destinies of people; and characters were formed or decided by the position of Mercury in orbit etc. Truly, when Man is desperate enough to find an answer to his problems, he can come upon the sign of Truth in all sorts of the most unlikely places. The tenacity of Man is indeed marvellous and should never be underestimated! The whole Hellenic World now became Astrology-mad, and though the Peripatetics, of whom we shall read in the next chapter, fought to save the sciences of Astronomy and Biology, people preferred to believe in the Stars instead. The answer, everyone thought, must lie in the Heavens, and so they spent their time searching the skies in order to find a sign — in the fashion of some of our own Generation who have currently taken to searching for U.F.O.s and who endeavour to spot a race of Space "Supermen". When Man becomes throughly disgusted with himself and his animal, earthy conditions — he always looks upwards in desperation and supplication. And this traumatic condition in Athens had not only been affected by the loss of their national gods, but by the superfluity of deities who swept in to take their place. Choice is fine, but not when it is bewilderingly diverse. And perhaps; Man doesn't really like freedom —**not** complete freedom, anyway. He only finds it stressful to have too many decisions to make, and would welcome some type of dogmatism or despotism in order to take the whole weary business of choice off his shoulders. This period of great transition in the Greek World though, was really a repeat of the earlier era of turmoil at the time of the Hedonists and Cynics, but by now the illness of the Greeks had become a terminal one. With no faith they floundered, and in consequence they suffered from a lack of pride, patriotism, hope, and morality. How could they reconcile the natural Epicureanism of the individual with enough necessary Stoicism of the group? The crisis the citizens underwent was like that of a combined attack of adolescence and middle-age; and it was enough to break the spirits of a much more Spartan people.

Education spread, but it was not an 'in-depth' education, and the citizens moved continually from city to country areas, and back again. Athenian life became full of triviality, seduction, adultery, and homosexuality. Prostitution was at its zenith, and women took to dancing naked at parties and dinners, in the oriental tradition.

Abortion was now legally permissable, except in cases where the husband refused the right; and it became such common practice that only one family in every one hundred had more than one daughter. In Miletus, the fertility ratio in 200 B.C. was such that out of 79 families, 32 had one child, and 31 had two children; and altogether there were 118 sons, and only 28 daughters. Therefore this tendency to bear only male children caused an imbalance in the sexes and probably helped promote the cause of homo-sexuality. There was no common Statesmanship of this period, and no philosophy, nor religion which could help to bind the people together; and on the whole, the philosophers tended to condone infanticide and suicide as an answer to the population explosion and pressure — and finally the Death Rate over-took the Birth Rate, and the population began to decline alarmingly.

In Macedonia in particular, Phillip V. became so upset about this tendency (where was he to get his soldiers from, if things went on like this?) that he forbade the limitation of families, and succeeded in raising the population by 50% in the space of thirty years. And by 150 B.C. the extremely grave situation is shown by Pausaunias, who wrote that, "the whole of Greece has been subject to low birth rate and general decrease in population owing to which cities have become deserted and land has ceased to yield fruit..."

The Greeks had once and for all, finally given up the struggle; lost their instinct for survival, as well as their will to live; and sat patiently waiting for the Romans to come down and finish them off.

And now — having painted a suitably gloomy and dismal picture of this period in order for the Reader to understand the sociological background to this historical time, let us finally turn to the two most popular philosophies of that fateful Athenian Winter — Epicureanism and Stoicism.

The philosophy of Epicureanism was actually a philosophical mutation; or perhaps hy-brid would be a better word to describe it; and it came about as the result of a combination of the Materialism of Democritus, and the Hedonism of Aristippus. The Founder of Epicureanism, was a gentleman by the name of Epicurus, and he formulated a new doctrine from the pleasure-loving individualistic Greeks of the Asiatic coast, designed for the use of the educated Upper, and Middle Classes of the Athenian Mainland. This was a philosophy of detachment and impeccable taste, and unlike Stoicism, it was never meant to appeal, or to apply, to the masses, or, to the Universal State.

Epicurus was born at Samos in 341 B.C. (or thereabouts — as some people say that he first appeared on Earth about 342 — but a year or two can hardly make much difference to our story) and he died, we are reliably and firmly assured, in 270 B.C.

At the age of twelve he is reported to have fallen in love with philosophy, and one may wonder why he didn't turn his attentions to some pubescent female instead; but philosophy is what claimed his heart; and the Western World is all the richer for this vagary of his.

At the age of nineteen he went to Athens and spent a year in the Academy of Plato, but preferred Democritus to either the Puritan, or his student the great Biologist, and accordingly he returned to Asia to lecture, and to learn more from the Cynics, Hedonists, and Sceptics of the day. The Hedonists taught Epicurus the wisdom of pleasure; then the Sceptics gave him the doctrine of tranquillity or 'ataraxia', which he was later to introduce into his own writings and theories; and the Cynic Theodorus of Cyrene, showed him the error of preaching atheism openly — and thus he understood from early on in his career, just how careful he would have to be in practising Philosophy in public.

Epicurus lectured at Colophon, Mytilene, and Lampsacus, and it is reported that the people of Lampsacus were so pleased with him that they raised the money in order to return him to Athens, and even, to buy him a house and garden there. This surely is a bit of a tall story, as who ever heard of anyone giving anything to anyone completely free of charge, or free of strings? Quite possibly the people of Lampsacus were so anxious to get rid of the philosopher that they decided to buy him a house elsewhere, but it is highly unlikely that if they had truly admired him as a teacher, they would have wanted him to leave them! Or, could it have been, that the citizens of that city were so philanthropic in disposition, that they felt it their duty, to allow Athens to drink in the knowledge which they themselves had so recently and fortunately acquired? If this tale is true, then it is a great shame about the Greeks and the fall of their Empire, and one can only wonder how it could possibly ever have come about — with such unselfish and generous people like this! Also, this story is rather similar to that little anecdote concerning the real-estate which was handed over to both Plato and Aristotle, and personally, the Author is exceedingly sceptical about the whole thing!

Anyway, whatever the truth of the matter, by 306 B.C. Epicurus, at the ripe old age of thirty-five, took up residence in his house and garden in Athens, and began his Epicurean School. It must be noted by all would-be-followers of Epicurus, that the possession of a garden seems to be absolutely essential for practising this particular philosophy, and all those who seriously wish to join this sect, are therefore advised to get themselves some type of area containing a modicum of shrubbery and greenery, at the very outset — *if* they wish to do the thing properly that is!

Into his garden Epicurus then invited everyone who wished to come (and he even included women!) but most of his disciples however, like himself, were the sons of colonists from Asia Minor. And in between spraying his rose bushes, and pruning his hydrangas, he held forth on the horrors of Religion, and denounced it as hostile, to peace of mind, and as a thief, to the joy of life. Philosophy and Religion, Epicurus thought, were only other forms (or variations) of Politics; and in his opinion, Politics was a complete waste of time, and, moreover, political troubles were like nasty eruptions on the skin (Epicurus and I are in agreement on this point it seems) and they were external sores on the body which represented the internal disorder of the whole organism. Therefore, Epicurus would have none of them (no politics, religion or philosophy!) — and he cast such miseries from him; devoted himself to the quiet pleasure of contemplation; cultivated the art of elegant conversation; and in between times, wrote voluminously — three hundered rolls or so — all of which have unfortunately perished — apart from a few letters, and statements — plus the inevitable fragments.

The main philosophical theory of Epicureanism was based on a comfortable and sensual Hedonism, combined with a crude Atheism; and it was the detached, quiet, and academic answer to the social ills of Greece, which, seemingly, no one was able to cure. The Epicureans themselves were an exclusive and refined group of staunch moral character (we are assured most firmly!) and devoted to their founder; and they were bound together in friendship by tremendously strong bonds of loyalty. People who once became Epicureans, **never** left the movement. There weren't many of them, it was true, but they never lapsed in their faith. Once an Epicurean, always an Epicurean — and very few religions, or philosophies, can say as much of themselves, or, of their members.

They were very unpopular as a movement in Greece though, because their teachings ran completely counter to the Stoics, Platonists, and Aristotelians of their day, although they were more accepted in the Roman World at a later date. Unlike the Stoics, Platonists, or Aristotelians, however, the Epicureans did not unduly affect Christianity; in fact, none of their doctrines or ideas ever entered it, as Christians will doubtless be very pleased to note.

But like the Stoics however, the Epicurean philosophy was divided into three main parts:- Canonic, Physics (including Psychology and Theology) and Ethics. Epicureanism, like Stoicism, was a philosophy of the Hellenistic Age, and accordingly therefore, it dealt with, 'How *not* to deal with Life', and thus provided an escape from the hideous reality which was facing everyone. Their prime rule of life was based on Reason — but on reason tempered with "ataraxia" — and the Epicureans symbolized the wisdom of an old man living secure unto himself, in utter tranquillity, and completely safe from the troubles of the world, or — immune from the slings and arrows of outrageous fortune. Which is something even Hamlet found difficult to manage — but then maybe that's because he didn't have a proper garden in Elsinore. (The Danish climate was probably too prohibitive for the growing of lemon trees and sweet magnolia!) Like the Stoics, also, the Epicureans sought absolute, and imperturbable serenity, but while the Stoics wanted to identify with Divine Providence or Fate, the Epicureans denied any Divine 'Hand' in their affairs. Tranquillity in their eyes equalled freedom from pain and from fear, and accordingly it spelt a type of Negative Hedonism. The worst pain, according to Epicurus was firstly, Fear itself — and then, there came, fear of the Gods; fear of the Unknown; fear of Death; and fear of Life after Death. Therefore, he proposed to do away with all Fear, by the simple process of ignoring it. And this is a nice theory, but very difficult to put into practice, as I know from my own sorrowful experience while sitting in the Dentist's Chair. How often has that good and capable man (perhaps a secret Epicurean!) told me sadly, "There is a great deal of difference, Madam, between the fear of pain, and the actual pain." But no matter how philosophic **he** is, the fear — the pain — and the general misery — seem to go on forever; and I always wonder how Epicurus felt at the Dentist's, and how **he** managed to endure the ordeal; and, if he did so, with the correct amount of tranquillity, and 'ataraxia', befitting his station in life!

And still on the subject of teeth, I always personally find that Stoicism stands me more in good stead on such horrendous occasions, as outlined above, but Epicurus and Epicureanism were the very antithesis to Zeno and Stoicism; and Epicureanism held that man had to free himself not by enduring doggedly; but by totally accepting the material world, and by understanding the rational theory of Nature. The Epicureans were not however really very scientific; nor were they overly interested in phenomena. Theirs was not so much a philosophy, as, 'a way of life'; and it was solely directed for the enjoyment of the Middle and Upper Classes.

Their Canons were the criteria, or tests of Truth, and included the following:-

1. All feelings of pleasure and pain equal the ultimate critieria in Ethics. (Which means that if you don't enjoy doing something, then don't do

it! And this is a fine and dandy doctrine, but a little lacking in moral direction for those who are involuntarily forced to do something which they don't enjoy!)

2. Sensations, and

3. Concepts, both equal forms of immediate physical experience, and represent ways in which our material Souls are physically affected by other material things. (Even Epicurus felt compelled to bow in the direction of the increasingly ever-popular Soul, but he decided therefore to make it a 'Material' one.) Sensations in particular, are infallible said the Epicureans, and error only comes from incorrect judgements made concerning the senses, and what they show us. (There will be more on this torturous doctrine later!)

4. Acts of Intuitive Apprehension are those by which we can grasp certain sorts of concepts.

As we see, Epicurus' ideas regarding sensations and concepts were built upon an extreme form of the Atomism of Democritus —and possibly proves Socrates' theory that all extremism is bad! Epicurus decided, that the atoms given off, are in fact the outermost layers of an object, and that the object itself kept the original shape; but that the atoms floated off as 'images', until they finally came into contact with the perceiving subject. Ah! ha! the Reader sighs, back to these wretched atoms and the void again! But unfortunately, the Reader may indeed sigh, and sigh heartily, because Epicurus is not half as scientific, reasonable, *nor* logical, as was Democritus; and his rather spurious theories are certainly tiring.

However, we must just plough through these atoms and get on with it, as the study of philosophy never promised to be simple, and the attainment of wisdom is seldom a thing of ease. But Epicurus might have done us all a service if he had spent more time on his rhododendrons. and less on concocting this Atomic Doctrine.

Larger and less subtle atoms, according to this indifferent gardener, made direct physical impressions on the sense organs; and very fine and subtle atoms produced mind pictures; and in particular, visions during sleep. Furthermore these 'images', he taught, could get mixed in the air sometimes, and in a dream, the atoms representing a man, and a horse, could combine to equal a centaur. Hallucinations and delusions in people's minds came from the mixing of images, said Epicurus; thereby vouchsaving his precious theories on sensation and concept from confutation. In fact his third and fourth criteria depend exclusively upon this image supposition, so he had great need to make the 'image' doctrine infallible. (Of course this theory of his could really have been the beginning of primitive psychological understanding of learning; and of the distorted mental pictures which assail some sufferers of mental illness. And possibly Epicurus was attempting to analyse the phenomena of schizophrenia, and maybe he was very far in advance of his day!)

Concepts of things, to his mind, equalled the immediate result of physical experience, and therefore he rejected Logic entirely. Words, said Epicurus, were always used in the first and most obvious meaning; and possibly the great man has a point here, for how much do we really convey when we speak? And how much of what we say, do we really mean? And for those people who distrusted his theory on the infallibility of the Senses, and who wished to shoot holes in it, he gave the example of a tower in the distance appearing to be small, but which on approaching, proved to be big. This, said Epicurus, was not a fault of the Senses, but a fault of judgement, and therefore the Senses never lied; only people misunderstood them, and hence, made incorrect assumptions. I am inclined to agree with him about the indubitability of the Senses, but I do think he could have given us a better example of proof than his tower in the distance. Perhaps on the day he formulated this example there was green-fly in his cabbage patch, and he found it rather difficult therefore to concentrate deeply on his Atoms.

All things consisted of Atoms which were perpetually moving in a Void, said this gentleman of refinement and elegant taste, and there was no Divine Ordering Intelligence existing in our world, and there were in fact many worlds (cosmoi) *not only one* — and they were the chance collections of 'nebulae', which continually came together, and then just as continually broke up. All this of course was a direct slap in the face for the Stoics, who insisted on claiming most dogmatically, (and even more loudly) that there was only one world — a divine universe.

As there was noDivine Providence, so there was complete human Free Will,and only the power of Impersonal Fate ruled everything. And in case the Reader feels that we may have finally done with these Atoms forever, then I must inform him, or her, that unfortunately we still have a long way to go, as Epicurus seemingly never knew when to stop, and he was obviously far more fond of his Atoms than of his early spring blooms.

The base of Epicurus' doctrine of Human Free-will rested on his Atomic Doctrine of "swerve", or "parenklisis", or "clinamen" — it really matters not what you call it, it is just as plaguy and difficult to understand under any name, and the Reader must really hold on to his hat here, for we are entering into some very rough territory now.

The doctrine of 'Swerve' equalled the following:- Everything was composed of Atoms, and these Atoms were moving up and down; and generally–due to their weight–they were falling down in straight lines. But, out of chance, sometimes these Atoms swerved, slanted, and collided with each other; and these collisions and counter-collisions, gave rise to new worlds and contents. Therefore we have a "Philosophical Leap" here, with the indetermined movements of Atoms, being likened, or rather, linked, to the indetermined movements of Humans — and hence we have Free-will and Chance; and Development and Change in our world, and in our lives. And thus Epicurus has accounted for the Physical Necessity of Life, which the Materialists believed governed everything; and he has also introduced Indetermined Chance, which affects our lives and upsets the rigid pattern of it all. All this is quite logical, and not really as fanciful as it appears at first glance, but it does need a mind as keen as that of a Nuclear Physicist in order to comprehend it most fully — plus a little of that scientific breed's intellectual appreciation, in order to completely come to grips with it. Epicurus is not an easy man to read — or to follow!

Of course he went absolutely crazy about these dreadful atoms and even found them in the Soul, (as we have mentioned) but he aggravated the problem by giving these the name of "anima" — and in the body, (that is, the soul atoms in the body) they were also called "anima" — but the soul atoms of the logic in the mind, and of the emotions in the breast; were known by the name of "animus" — and this is just too much for any mere plebian or member of the proletariat to even grasp — let alone swallow. And it is no wonder that the majority of people turned towards Christianity so joyfully! Even that religion's most nonsensical doctrines are child's play; and easily understood — compared to stuff like this!

The properties of these atoms, which are all completely different and individualistic are :- size, shape, weight, and solidity. But colour, savour, or odour, are not atomic in themselves, and are only the product of atomic arrangements. The number of atoms of each shape is infinite; although the shapes of atoms are not infinite in number; and the sensed qualities are produced by combinations of atoms of various shapes, sizes, and weights. Finally, the Soul is composed of atoms; hence at death; the soul dies with the body — obviously the Atoms passing on into the Void! And that is a final summary of Epicurus's Atomic Theory — as it is not this Writer's intention to split the Atoms of the Reader's mind by anymore of this tortuous hypothesis. Epicurus was probably just too far in advance of this day, and possibly — even in advance of ours! And it would probably be better for us to concern ourselves with the more mundane portions of his life, and writings.

As we have seen, Pleasure to Epicurus, equalled the Freedom from Pain, and also, the Freedom from Desire itself. Pain, Fear, and Desire, all created unhappy tensions in people, and unnecessary stress, and suffering in the world. And I must admit that this philosopher does grow on one, the more one reads about him. And more than likely, if he had only left those atoms alone in the void, then he would most probably have become more popular, and much more well-known. The greatest fear, as we have seen, is the fear of fear, and after that, the fear of pain, or of death — but, for the moment, let us turn to the business of dealing with desires, so that those pesky little emotions will not be giving us any more trouble either.

Desires, says Epicurus, must be natural and necessary, and therefore an ascetic life is called for, (rather a Stoic view-point in fact!) and these desires must be reduced to the very minimum. Certain natural desires are very necessary though, as the gratification of such desires is preferable to the gratification of **unnecessary** natural desires — or, to desires attaching to artificially cultivated tastes — so put that cocktail glass down at once! In order to understand the fine distinction between necessary and unnecessary I think we have only to consider the meal table, and the conflict which generally occurs thereon. When exactly do we reach the point at which we stop eating, from hunger; and continue eating — due to greed — or, for the flagrant gratification of our taste buds? Feeding our hunger is necessary, but gratifying our greed is unnecessary, and in bad taste (yes, a pun is intended!) And this little example might also have better suited Epicurus — in his attempts to demonstrate his theory on the infallibility of the senses — rather than the one which he gave concerning the tower in the distance. And as with our faulty judgement, and incorrect use of our Senses, as in the analogy given above, so, at the dinner table, we also often make the rather vulgar, but singularly apt comment — that, "our eyes have been too big for our bellies." It is not that our Sense of Hunger is in any way impaired, but our Judgement of the situation is wrong, and there has been a conflict between the Sense of Hunger, and the Sense of Taste. (And in Platonic terminology, the wrong horse has obviously won!)

Continuing on this same gastronomical note, it may be observed that Epicurus claimed that the foundation of all happiness equalled the pleasure of the belly, that is, a good digestion; although poor man he seldom managed to achieve that state for himself — and that is quite possibly what drew him towards philosophy in the first place. (And all those suffering from gastro-enteritis, or, from spastic colons, would doubtless agree with this doctrine of digestion, and should possibly get themselves gardens as soon as possible, and take up Epicurus seriously!)

Pleasure, he said, is the standard by which every good and every right action is to be judged, and no pleasure is really bad in itself (although how this doctrine deals with sadists who like whipping others for pleasure, beats me!) and all pleasures are alike in quality — (Try telling that to a child when you give him a piece of bread and he's screaming the house down for cake!) But, Epicurus insists, there are only three essential needs of man, in order to live happily; and these are:- Equanimity; Bodily Health and Comfort; and the Exigencies of Life. And this is probably where Epicurus loses a great deal of his first-flush-enthusiastic following — because it is the very exigencies of life that constitute the most trouble for the majority of us, and paying the rent, and buying the food, and clothing and shoe-ing ourselves — not to mention buying the odd chapeau or two — generally takes all of our energies. And quite obviously Epicureanism is too rich for our blood, and should be left to those for whom it was meant — the well-to-do Upper and Middle Classes suffering from 'ennui', 'angst', and Bleeding-Heart-Liberalism. I don't really think that the ordinary 'hoi-polloi' can afford it. Like Despair and Depression, it is a luxury which the poor and the desperate cannot entertain, and which they must regretfully leave — until such time as they too reach that blessed state and enter the Upper-Middle Class — whereupon they will then be able to develop all sorts of sensitive and moralistic susceptibilities, which are unfortunately, totally uncalled for and unappreciated, in their present situation in life.

To have a good life, insisted this refined and comfortable Hedonist, Man had to cultivate both prudence and philosophy in his life; and the other virtues could also afford a quick brush-up, at the same time, so he thought. Death was not anything to be feared, he said, because while we are alive, then we are not dead; and when we are dead; then we experience nothing. You see, it's easy really, and probably just as natural, and enjoyable, as falling off a log, as they say.

And besides adopting such a philosophical and fearless attitude to death, Epicurus advocated that a wise man should not seek to lengthen his days on this earth, and he gravely articulated, "Just as with food, he does not seek simply the larger share and nothing else, but rather the most pleasant, so he seeks to enjoy not the longest period of time, but the most pleasant." But this little homily didn't stop Epicurus from hanging on in there by the skin of his teeth, all through a pain-racking attack of gall-stones, and right up until the bitter end, when the Void finally claimed him unto itself. But it must be admitted that he was an extremely tolerant, honest, and wise man, in his pronouncement that it was more foolish to become "a slave to the destiny of the natural philosophers", (meaning the strict scientists, who denied anything in life except harsh, cold, materialistic, and comfortless reality) than to follow whole-heartedly the myths about the gods. The best thing and the wisest, to Epicurus' way of thinking, was quite obviously to be calm and happy, and to believe, whatever made one feel that way. And that is why he criticized all the other philosophers, as he didn't feel that at any time they had ever made anyone either calm, or happy! On the whole though, he had not very much to say regarding the religion of his state and time, and although he took part in religious rituals, (after what he had seen happen to some atheistic philosophers, he decidedly knew which foot to put first!) he held that the gods didn't really care about Men; that they existed — but that they were not interested in what Man was doing, and in fact never even bothered their celestial heads about him. Of course Epicurus not only admitted to the gods in order to keep on the right side of the Authorities, but also because due to his theory of atomism, and the truth of sensations and concepts, he had more or less worked himself into an intellectual corner, and therefore, he **had** to admit to their existence. He had said that the images which came to men in dreams were true; although they were sometimes slightly confused; and, as man sometimes dreamt of the gods, therefore there had to be gods for men to perceive them in these images and visions — as all images, so Epicurus said, were of material things. Therefore, he finally decided that there were indeed Gods, but that they were uncaring of the universe; that they lived in the "intermundia" or, between worlds; and that they gave off subtle images like any other atomic bodies. However, generally, only the wise and philosophic élite, were able to actually perceive these beatific images. So therefore, Epicurus advised everyone, that they should practise meditation, in order to be able to properly discern these divine images. And the theories of this philosopher range so greatly from the probable to the impossible, and the Author has become so very confused; that like Epcurus' very mysterious atoms in their "swerve", she finds herself swinging to and fro in admiration one minute, and in disgust and incomprehension, the next. And if his gardening was anything at all like his philosophizing, then it must have been an amazing sight, and possibly the only time the weeding ever got done, was when his disciples were down on their hands and knees in the dirt, trying desperately to memorize the Master's Principal Doctrines, or forty articles of Epicurean Faith.

Regarding Justice, that much sought after abstract quality on which everyone seems to hold different ideas, Epicurus decided that it is originated in "a pledge of mutual advantage to restrain Men from harming one another, and to save them from being harmed". Which definition is really quite sound, when one dwells sufficiently long upon it — but, this sentence is hardly likely to catch the ear of the "mob", and seems to lack somewhat in sufficient verve or sparkle; and is not really likely to become the slogan or catch-phrase of any group or government that I can think of. Epicurus was quite right to stay away from politics; he obviously didn't have the demagogic rhetoric, and personality, necessary to make a success of that profession! Furthermore, he said, Justice did not exist among primitive tribes, and what was considered "just" in one country, was not necessarily considered "just" in another; and the Justice of a Law, ultimately depended on its being to the mutual advantage of both parties to the contract. So we are now back again with Aristotle and his supposition that Justice is only possible between Equals.

The only reason that Epicurus could actually come up with (in order to support the *good,* as opposed to the *bad)* was that the one who did bad, would be subject to the fear of being discovered and shamed publicly; and therefore his wrong doing would disturb his inner tranquillity. And accoridingly therefore, the wise did not committ bad actions **if possible**. "The just man is most free from trouble, the unjust most full of trouble," said Epicurus — but personally I know of any number of unjust men (and women) who are completely tranquil and untroubled by any fears, or pains, or remorse whatsoever — and I really don't think this theory of his holds altogether any better than did his pronouncement on the existence of the Gods. And it was comments and statements like the above that caused the Sceptics in Athens to descend like angry wasps around his poor old head as he sat musing in his over-grown garden. The Sceptics decided that he was really running a narrow, quasi-religious organisation there among the tulip beds, and that it was a dogmatic and absurd sect, whose Creed was built on very shaky intellectual foundations — and that if they could have gotten to his petunia patch — why, then, they'd have showed him, what for! But while these wasps of wisdom contented themselves with merely swarming over Epicurus' hedges, and making a lot of noise in his bourganvillia; they concentrated most of their attention, and venom, on the Stoics — whom they loathed even more; and whom they considered it their duty — to sting to death!

For thirty-six years Epicurus lived and taught in his green garden, over which there hung the sign, "Guest thou shalt be happy here, for here Happiness is esteemed the Highest Good." (Obviously Epicurus was the right sort of person to visit as a house-guest!) And during this long teaching period he was always more interested in the subject of Ethics, rather than in Cosmology. And for him and his devotees, all governments were the same, although he is said to have preferred monarchy to democracy — as in his opinion, it was less inclined to persecute heretics. (Surely though — this depends exactly on what the heresy actually concerns!) All Epicurus really asked for in life, was the freedom of the body from pain, and the freedom of the soul from disturbance; and in consequence therefore, he did not get married; but spent most of his non-gardening and non-philosophizing hours with his mistress (an ex Hetaira) Leontium, who went in for a little bit of philosophizing herself, and who wrote some tracts on "Marriage". Although what she knew about the institution it is difficult to say, as her lover was so very loth to put the marital noose around his own neck.

"Everything natural is easily procured, and only the useless is costly," said Epicurus, and this is a nice little statement to mutter to yourself when standing outside the window of an expensive shop. "Lathe biosas" (Live unobtrusively) he also said, and urged his students to decrease the pain factor by decreasing the desire; and to ignore the world completely, as the individual was powerless to change it in anyway — and furthermore, had **no obligation** to do so, whatsoever! (Perhaps I was wrong in describing them as Bleeding-Heart Liberals, for there was nary a breath of Reforming Zeal among them!) Eating and drinking, he declared, were dynamic, or restless, pleasures, but reading, talking, and friendship, were passive pleasures, and more comforting in general. And his religion or philosophy, or whatever it was, seemed to demand a great deal of solitary courage, and intellectual resourcefulness; plus self-control, and refined taste. The Epicureans were a very groupy sect, and bound together with lots of meetings, and by constant letter writing. The wise man, they believed, did not burn with ambition, lust for fame; or envy the good fortune of others — nor did he fret his life away, in any emotion whatsoever! Instead, he laughed at Destiny, and sought a companion like himself, in order to share his thoughts, and to "live like a god among men." Now perhaps the reader really understands why it was necessary for the Epicureans to have a group, and, a meeting place in a garden. They were really rather like a syndicate of retired Major-Generals, and the only companionship they could tolerate, was, each others. But it is nice to know that the few true men of peace and intellect in Athens, had at least this safe haven to escape to, far from the storms of invading Romans and Gauls; and seeing as how it was open to slaves and women, as well as to Freemen, it served a very democratic purpose. Although Epicurus would probably not have liked to have heard it described in that way.

Some enemies of his, said that Epicurus spent his time gorging on fine food, and that was why and how, he developed his enternal problems. But he insisted however that he lived mainly on water, wine, bread, and cheese, and the historian Diogenes Laertius confirms that this is correct. And whatever the diet of this first Epicurean, the fact remains that he made a strong and obviously moral impression on his pupils, for, after his death, their motto became, "Live as though the eye of Epicurus were upon thee" —and perhaps it was some emigrant Epicurean who first gave the idea for the lyrics of the Texan song which appeared at a much later date — and which warned the residents of that mighty State that they should also be morally on their guard at all times.

He died stoically, and agonisingly in 270 B.C., willing his property to his school, and hoping, "that all who study philosophy may never be in want... so far as our power to prevent it may extend." And all philosophy students are probably sighing, and saying that it is a great pity there are not any modern Epicureans ready to do the self same thing, as we would all appreciate a little quiet joy, and gratis greenery in our lives,even today.

His basic equation of Happiness = Pleasure — Pain; was ably demonstrated to the Roman World, by one of his most devoted students, Lucretius 98-55 B.C. who, (as you will no doubt have noticed) lived a long time after the period of Epicurus, but who is said to have faithfully continued the philosophy of the old Gardener, and without the slightest divergence of doctrine. Perhaps the record-keeping of the ancient period was more efficient than we have ever realised, or perhaps, as Epicurus' writings were lost, everyone finds it a whole lot easier, to say that Lucretius has set down an exact exposition of the theories of a man, whom he **never** knew. Be all that as it may; the Epicurean Movement was really introduced into Rome by Lucretius, and I can forgive him any inconsistencies which he might have made, for one extremely wise statement of his own, and which he was fond of quoting — (As the Author is also!) "Tantum religio portuit suadere malorum" — "So much evil has religion been able to put over." And when one thinks of the Holy Wars right down through the Ages, and the number of people slaughtered in the cause of proclaiming and advancing the **true** God, and the **true** Religion, then one is forced to agree with Lucretius, and to admire his style — whatever his memory or scholarship were like!

Even before Epicureanism became popular in Rome among the educated people in the 1st century B.C. (and we can include Virgil the Poet among those) the Hellenized Jews of Alexandria had accepted it as being the only religion or philosophy viable for them, after having renounced their own in an effort to assimilate. (And as the Greek choice available, they found rather lacking in appeal!) Epicureanism tended to attract most, the Detached (and fairly wealthy) Intellectuals of the Hellenistic Period, during the break-up of Alexander's Empire; and to answer the needs of the Educated and Liberal Romans, who were to come later. Philosophy of course, is not really something which one freely adopts, but, by which, one is involuntarily adopted. One's philosophy really depends on one's environment, and the conditions of life; and anyone rich enough, and educated enough, to become an Epicurean, does so. The rest of us have to remain Stoics!

Epicureanism has not passed from the world, but still exists wherever there are detached, and financially comfortable intellectuals, who are in possession of gardens; and in the 16th century, the world enjoyed the writings of the famous Frenchman and Essayist, Montaigne, who was a combination of Sceptic, and Epicurean, and who decided that Ethics, equalled a matter of custom; and that Religion, equalled a matter of geography; and whose motto was, "Rejoice in your present life; all else is beyond you."

But now we must pass from this genteel philosophy of ignoring pain, and get on with a study of that rather nasty, and totally pessimistic philosophy of *accepting pain.* Zeno the Stoic stands impatiently outside Epicurus' garden, and unfortunately, we must now descend with him, into the truly agonising circles of his philosophical inferno. And during this tour, the Reader may care to bear in mind, that most of our present-day Christian Religions are jam-packed full with the tatty remnants of this unhealthy, and unnatural creed — and probably Stoicism also accounts for many of the psychotics, and guilt-ridden neurotics, so abundant in the 20th century.

From Epicureanism and the connoisseurship of fine wine, we have now been reduced to Stoicism and the imbibition of extremely sour vinegar. But before partaking of this bitter beverage, let us examine again the reasons why one particular religion or philosophy tends to flourish over that of another, and why Stoicism 'took-off' as it were, far more readily than did Epicureanism.

All socio-political movements or protests — and we may include religions and philosophies in these categories — arise out of Need. Necessity, as Democritus said, is the key to everything, and the prime motivator of all Human (and animal and plant) actions. These are not of course the exact words of Democritus, but his meaning is definitely contained in them. I believe, because I need to. I believe this particular belief, because it seems to be the only answer available to me (at the time!) People, all through history, have done innumerable things, and committed countless actions, out of need. People change Governments out of need; they work, due to need; begin to think, from a need; adopt, or abandon, religions, because of a need — in fact, the whole struggle of life and evolution is based on Need. So long as people have no needs, than they will not struggle. When they do have a need, however, they will fight until they achieve it, and then go on to achieve some other need. The need must be there though, and we all know quite well (although hardly any of us from first-hand experience in the matter) that you may lead a horse to water, but that you can not make him drink! A philosophy, like a religion, if it is to be truly popular, must answer the needs of the people. When it ceases to do that, it is no longer useful; it is then discarded; and a *new* one if found. We are all motivated to achieve what we need — or perhaps, more importantly — to achieve what we **think** we need! And it is because of this rather fine distinction between needing, and thinking about needing, that Stoicism was first born in Ancient Greece.

Stoicism, like Spartanism, was produced as a completely unsuccessful solution to what seemed to be an insoluble problem. The Spartans were frugile (or Spartan) in their life-style, simply because they had to be — at least, so their Leaders had convinced them. The land of Sparta was in general poor; being both hard and mountainous; and there were a large number of Helots, and Serfs to feed — and, to keep in subjection! There was no trade to speak of; no development of business, as in the Athenian City-State; so, in order to keep the status quo, and to preserve the society from any evolutionary, or revolutionary change, the State Collective System was introduced, in which the individual mattered not one iota, and in which each member gave his life and work for the good of the whole. This was the only way for them to survive, (without a drastic change of systems) given the prevailing conditions of the time — and like the bee in the hive, each individual was bound in mental, physical, and spiritual communism into working for the ideal of their integral and indivisible world. All for one; and one for all — but the 'one' was virtually **unimportant.**

The Athenian City-state, on the other hand, was the very antithesis of the State Collective ideal. It was Individualism gone mad; rampant Selfishness; and Free-Enterprise to the point of rabidness. In Athens no one sacrificed himself for the whole, or even thought that it might ever be necessary to do so. The thought of working together as a group, and enduring mutual hardship, in order for the state to survive, and for the good of the whole, never really crossed anyone's mind. But now that the City-State had failed, and the eleventh hour experiment with the strange new Hellenistic Empire had also floundered! — what with the confusing multitude of ever-changing monarchies, and the constant pressure of Roman and Gaul invasions; plus the proven bankruptcy of the Olympian God System and the totally bewildering choice of foreign deities — the economic depression — the defeated state of agriculture; and the loss of trade; (probably to the Athenian Merchants, the most decisive point!) some solution would **have to be found**. Some new philosophy would have to be adopted, in order to see the Citizens of Athens through their darkest night; to help them to endure their sufferings; and to support them in this hour of their greatest need. Stoicism — the acceptance of suffering — was therefore offered them. Like Spartanism, it was never meant to make anyone happy, but it was meant to occupy their minds, and to give them a reason for the awfulness of life. And the Athenians were in terrible need of a reason for all that they were enduring, in those grey days prior to the Birth of Christ — and the Birth of the Roman Empire.

Zeno, the founder of Stoicism, was born in Citium Cyprus, in 336 B.C., and he died of self-strangulation in Athens in 264 B.C. And that little piece of information should set the scene rather well for this truly miserable doctrine. Probably the reason why the Author feels so strongly about this particular philosophy, is, because, in her youth, she had the misfortune to be thoroughly indoctrinated in it, and in consequence it took a rather long time for her natural Hedonism to raise its bloody, but un-bowed head, and for her free spirit to finally take flight and to come unto its own. Stoicism is a bitter creed; and it makes for miserable people.

According to legend, Zeno was either of Phoenician, or, of mixed Hellenic and Semitic parentage, and he was a tall, thin dark person, with a bent head, and weak legs — not an attractive picture certainly, and I am personally wondering if the 'bent head' part, could possibly have been a description of his customary carriage and deportment when walking, and not have been meant as a reference to any physical malformation. Whichever the case, Zeno, in the early part of his life, managed to make up for any lack in beauty of body, by an outstanding ability to amass money, and when he first visited Athens (so it is reported) he was a very wealthy merchant indeed. Later, however, in 314 B.C., after being ship-wrecked on the Attic coast, he arrived back in the Big Apple for the second time — but on this occasion he was penniless.

Sitting himself down by a book-stall, so the story goes, Zeno began to read a brochure about Socrates. (I personally find this most suspicious, as most Book-sellers do not encourage people to spend their time browsing in perference to buying, and this humble Author has often been turfed out on her ear from many such an establishment for attempting to do the self same thing. But this is what the myth of Zeno purports, and so we will let it ride!) Then, according to this fairy-tale account, Zeno asked this Book-Seller (to whom he had not paid so much as a drachma) where he, Zeno, could find a man such as this Socrates. (Obviously Zeno was a little out-of-date, and didn't know that *that* gentleman had been dead some eighty-four year or so! Or maybe he was still suffering from shock from the ship-wreck, and his mind was not working too well!) However, the Book-Seller replied smartly, that Crates, the great Cynic philosopher, was just at that moment passing by to collect his laundry from the near-by laundromat, and that Zeno should immediately jump to his feet, and give pursuit. (And that last part is really stretching the imagination too much, for it is highly unlikely that the Book-Seller would have bothered to be so helpful to such a parsimonious customer — unless of course **he** was really the **original Stoic**; and was trying to suffer, and to make his life worse than it already was!)

Anyway, Zeno hopped to, and acted on this advice, introduced himself to Crates at the entrance to the laundromat, and offered to carry his parcels of clean clothing home. (I sincerely hope it is understood by The Reader, that the Author is having a rather sardonic (and possibly uncalled for) joke, with all these references to the laundromat and clean clothing —although Crates must have had his washing done somehow, and probably he actually had some little woman tucked away round the corner somewhere in Athens, just to fulfill that very purpose.)

The outcome of all this, however, was that Zeno found a home with the Cynics, and being now fed, and bedded, (comfortably, or otherwise!) he was at least one up on what he had been while sitting on the ground at the foot of the Book-Stall. And having achieved some security, and so to speak, having chased away the wolf from the door, he then settled down to a study of philosophy, and probably became Crates' oldest first-year student, as Zenon was then about thirty years of age.

Although a mature student (or perhaps, because of it) Zeno was a fast learner, and in no time at all he had trotted out his very first publication, "Republic", with the title stolen from Plato, and the information and ideas in it, plagiarised from every passing philosopher he had ever come across. On the whole it was a very Cynical book (after all Zeno was making his living from them at the time he wrote it) and it proposed a type of anarchistic communism, and blisteringly opposed slavery, money, (the use of, as a form of manipulation and exploitation of others) private property, religion, laws, and marriage — the Cynics it must be remembered (among numerous other philosophers) only believed in Common Marriages, or, in sharing their common women! Anyhow, this book earned Zeno immediate popularity with the poor who could read; and even more popularity with those who couldn't, because they had to rely on word-of-mouth accounts of what his great and philanthropic thoughts were (and stories always improve in the telling!) Then having established himself in the hearts of the unhappy, Zeno decided that the time had come for him to leave the Cynics (possibly the diet of lentils so loved by them, was proving difficult to bear with) and he moved on to pastures new, and studied for a while in the green fields of the Academy, under the direction of Xenocrates, and even ventured to inquire into the Delphian mental recesses of Stilpo, of Megara. After this, having read a little Heracleitus, and an even lesser amount of Socrates (after all, there was really nothing to read!), he proceeded to open his own Thinking Shop in 301 B.C., and at the ripe age of forty-three, became a merchant of ideas — for a merchant is what Zeno had always been, and he was *most* successful at it. In fact this guy had a definite talent for the making of a fast buck! And not only did Zeno have an extremely good economic attitude, and business brain, but he was (like Napoleon) very aware that it was Religion which kept the Poor from murdering the Rich, and therefore it was Religion (in one form or another) which Zeno gave them!

In this new school of his which he set up, Zeno had the habit of walking up and down under the 'Stoa Poecile', or 'Pointed Porch', while he was giving out his dreadful soul-destroying propaganda; and in consequence, his school, for want of a better name, and because the philosophy coming from it was such a confused collection of everyone else's, became known as the 'Stoic'. Probably even this walking while teaching idea, Zeno had pinched from the Peripatetics! This man had no shame whatsoever! And it may be of interest to the Reader to note that the Author's dislike of Zeno and Stoicism was shared and also volubly expressed by Plutarch, the Historian, who couldn't stand the sight or sound of this philosophy either.

To the Stoa, Zeno welcomed both rich and poor alike. (How things had changed from the time he wrote the "Republic"!) But he generally refused all young men, as he thought they usually **talked too much**, and didn't **listen enough**! Of course, he could have been right in this matter, as anyone who deals with the "Young" would be more than likely to admit; but possibly the real reason he didn't care for them was because they had the nasty habit of asking difficult questions — and insubordinate questions also! To one youth in particular, who asked too many questions for his own good, Zeno informed him pointedly, that the reason Humans had been given two ears, and only one mouth, was so that they could hear more, and speak less! Zeno was obviously a man well used to dealing with hecklers. One can hardly imagine a phrase like that coming from the lips of either Plato, or, Aristotle, but then neither of them came from such a crude and vulgar mercantile background as did Zeno. This Cypriot was 'a man of the people', and he knew how to deal with the 'mob'!

But, if Zeno was heartily disliked by the Youth of Athens and the other philosophers of the time, he made up for this lack of philosophical and youthful friendship by being the 'golden-haired boy' of both the Assembly, and of Antigonus II of Macedonia.

Being actually liked by the Athenian Assembly was of course enough to give any man a bad reputation; as, from all the records of the day, it is quite obvious that there was not a more corrupt bunch around; and absolutely none who could compete with this crowd of legislators, for absolute skull-duggery, and deviousness. Phocion (402-317 B.C.) an Athenian Statesman and General, was so suspicious of the Assembly in fact, that when one day they applauded a speech of his, he asked a friend in great distress and concern. "Have I not unconsiously said something bad?" Phoicon knew those assembled for what they really were, and even though they had put their hands together for him that day, he was quite right in distrusting them — because they put him to death, only a few years later! And the Assembly that was around in Zeno's time was just the same; different members, but with the identical ideals (if one can use the word 'ideal' in the same breath as the Assembly.) The people might have changed, but the spirit of the place was undeviating, and these very people who were persecuting Theophrastus, (and passing legislation against all other philosophers) were allowing Zeno unlimited licence, and even giving him the keys to the Walls of the City! And he a foreigner from Cyprus! And besides the keys, they voted him a statue; and a crown; and even built him a tomb, at the public expense! And all historical detectives are now asking themselves feverishly — what exactly was this man doing for them, that they should honour him in this way? Well, we will come to that, a little later.

His friendship with Antigonus II of Pella, is also most suspicious, especially as Antigonus was not well liked in Athens; and although historians have described Aristotle as the "pensioner of a king", they generally neglect to investigate Zeno's connections with the highly placed. And Zeno is a most suspicious character, who was not a fraction of the scholar that Aristotle was.

Zeno finally died in his ninetieth year, (having lived off the fat of the land, and at the expense of Athens for a not inconsiderable time) and, according to reports, his death occurred as he was coming out of his Stoa one day, when he suddenly tripped and broke his toe. Perhaps broken toes were a great tragedy in Ancient Greece; unfortunately the Author, really cannot say for sure, but in Zeno's eyes, they were obviously on a par with broken legs in race-horses, so accordingly, he proclaimed aloud, a line from a famous tragedy then currently popular in Athens, and as the last word left his lips, he neatly strangled himself. Rather an extremist action, to committ because of a broken toe, but then possibly it was correct for Zeno, given his life-style and philosophy — and the Peripatetics and the Sceptics probably thought that it couldn't have happened to a better man!

The work of his Stoa though, was carried on by the Asiatic Greeks mainly, and especially by Cleanthes of Assus, and Chrysippus of Soli. The first of these gentlemen was an ex-pugilist and common labourer who had studied under Zeno for a period of nineteen years, and who had often worked as an assistant-teacher, and, who probably found that his fists were just as useful to him in his philosophical employment, as they had been when he was in the ring. Chrysippus was the more learned of the two, and he expounded the Stoic Doctrine (and expanded it also) into a gigantic seven hundred and fifty volumes — which only goes to show the extent of the Stoic talent for plagiarism.

Stoicism then spread through the Hellenistic World, and was especially popular in Asia, and Panaetius of Rhodes, eventually took it to Rome about 143 B.C. Other famous Stoics of the period included Zeno of Tasus (Saint Paul's hometown) Beothus of Sidon, Diogenes of Seleucia, and of course, the most famous of all, Marcus Aurelias, the Roman Emperor– of whom more will be said later.

And now the Reader is probably wondering exactly what the Writer is getting so steamed up about, as this Stoicism doesn't seem too malevolent, and probably is no worse than any of the other half-baked, and harebrained notions, which the Reader has already had to hear about! So, in order to illustrate the sheer psychological depths and depravity of Stoicism, let the Reader be aware from the outset, that the Stoics were firm believers in Fatalism, and that one of their more cheery analogies regarding this belief, was, that "Man was like a dog which had been tied to a moving cart, and which could either trot along cheerfully, in submission to this movement; or be dragged along, uncomforably instead." Either way, he could not win. He was fated to suffer, and he should just get on with enduring it. And that is why the Stoics were such firm believers in suicide as well. (There were of course a few sociological reasons why they were so keen on advancing this idea to the general public, and we will come to those later.) And that little example is just a taste of the pessimism yet to come. Practically the whole of the Christian Church's Doctrine on Hell, and of the suffering therein, originated with the Stoics; and the blame for all those terrible dreams which the Reader endured as a child, with visions of the Devil, and fiery pitch-forks in eternal damnation, can be safely layed at the door, or the Stoa, of Zeno.

One of the last, and most well-known sayings of the Roman Emperor Marcus Aurelius, 121-180 A.D. was, "You are only a little corpse, carrying a soul about." And that can hardly be termed a comforting thought, and it shows quite definitely that the poor man couldn't even enjoy his position as Emperor, and that was a dreadful shame, considering all the other attendant miseries of his life. Stoicism in fact bred this attitude of 'Apathy', that is, no feelings, (especially not any HAPPY feelings) whatsoever, and the good Stoic, or pure Sage, was supposed to accept everything and anything; and to continue doggedly accepting, and enduring — until death! And if things really got on top of him, then he was advised to suicide, as the Stoics maintained that leaving this life was just like quitting a room, and when one got tired of the conversation, as it were, or, if the air pollution were too great, then one should just move out! And during this historic time in the Classical World, many people did just that, having earnestly and faithfully, taken the advice of Zeno and his Associates. Stoicism in fact, was a combination of all the worst elements of the Pre-Socratic philosophies, plus diverse aspects of Plato's and Aristotle's theories; and having been hastily thrown together into one bowl, was presented as an indigestible, and coarsely chopped Stoic Salad. Of course Zeno, like all the other philosophers, was able to trace the roots of his movement right back to Socrates — and everything —began, and ended, with that philosophic saint — otherwise it didn't stand much chance of being taken seriously!

It was probably Chrysippus who first divided Stoicism into three main parts, (after all Zeno was too busy just making up the doctrine, and didn't have the time to get it into any sort of order!) and these were:- 1. Logic —including the Theory of Knowledge. 2. Physics — Theology and Psychology (similar to the Epicurean divisions) 3. Ethics.

Logic dealt with the Art and Science of Expression of Thought, and with Rhetoric, and Dialectic Argument; Grammar, Formal Logic, and the Theory of Knowledge. All of these subjects; baring the Theory of Knowledge; were simply re-writes of various works of the Sophists, and Aristotle; and eventually the Greek Grammar passed on into the Greek schools, where Zeno is either praised or damned for the invention of it, (depending on how the individual student feels about this complicated law of syntax) Strangely however, the Sophists and Aristotle are never even considered when compliments are being passed on the authorship of Greek Grammar and Syntax. The Logic of Zeno eventually passed into, and affected, the Mediaeval European attempts at that skill, and has even influenced our modern understanding of this art; or is it a science? But Zeno's Theory of Knowledge, however, was mostly stolen from his rival Epicurus, and leads us to think that Zeno must have had someone stationed outside the wall of that gastronomic gentleman's garden, busily taking down all the Epicurean lectures in short-hand! And possibly it is for the invention of shorthand, that Zeno should truly be honoured, as he must have invented *some form or other of it,* because his theories contain practically every syllable of the Epicurean Doctrine —only Zeno's version is even more confusing, and much less optimistic.

The Stoics were Materialists (like Democritus and Epicurus) and they believed that only bodies acted and caused action; and that God and the souls of men were bodies (as in the theories of Epicurus) and that immaterial things equalled a space, void, or 'lekta', such as, the things we say about them — (Democritus and the Atoms and Void theory again!) The Soul was one body, which was both fiery breath, and part of the all-pervading Divine Principle, and it was affected by other bodies, that is, the things which we know. And here Zeno has borrowed the fiery breath of the Soul from Heracleitus, plus the 'aether' of Aristotle, the 'pneuma' of the Milesians, and the Divine Principle, or Craftsman, of Plato (with a little of the Prime Mover idea of Aristotle, thrown in for good measure.) And if you are confused about Zeno's theories, rest assured that your are not the only one — hardly anyone in The Classical World really understood what he was driving at!

The sense organs were the normal channels of knowledge according to the Stoics (as they had heard it over the garden wall!) and sense perception, was achieved on the soul, in the same manner as a seal made an impression on a piece of wax. The soul had to give assent to the impression in order to attain a firm mental grasp of it, and this impression, or image, had to be a 'gripping representation', in order to be forced onto the mind and to compel its assent. All this psychology of learning they had discovered by reading some Aristotle, as he had gone into great detail neatly defining how impressions were made in people's minds. But the Stoics really applied this theory to practice, and instructed their disciples to bring up their children in such a way that only the 'correct' (by their standards!) impressions were made on the innocent wax of their young minds. The soul at birth, said the Stoics, was blank, (a 'tabula rasa') but gradually it received it's store of impressions, and so general notions were formed; and one of the first things which the Stoic Epictetus advised all guardians, or teachers, of children to do, was to embrace the child each day, while dolefully whispering, "Tomorrow, you will die!" In consequence, Stoic children in the Classical World were well-known for their general hysteria, and deep melancholic depression, and could be easily identified in any crowded street in Rome or Athens. They were the ones who walked along the road as though the Sword of Damocles was about to descend on their heads at any moment! And of course these theories stuck — the Stoics paid great attention to making their education courses into 'gripping representations'; and children brought up in a Stoic atmosphere never really had a chance — from the word go.

The really big Stoic doctrine, and the absolute 'must' for all believers though, was the 'Pneuma', which they had developed from the thoughts of Heracleitus, the Milesians , Aristotle, and various Eastern Religions. This 'pneuma' was the vehicle of the immaterial soul, and the instrument through which it acted on the body; and, as the body dead, was both cold and unbreathing, so the conclusion come to by everyone, was that whatever life was, then it was both hot and airy; or, that it contained breath! Probably if in point of fact the Ancient Greeks had known more about medicine in general, then they wouldn't have kept coming up with so many different religions and philosophies, and consequently would not have given so many scholars and writers such terrible headaches, just trying to understand their theories! Anyway, this Constructive Fire of Life permeated all passive matter, and it was the Active Principle which formed and ordered, and ruled the whole universe — shades of Aristotle and his active and passive principles here! And God was the Divine Providence and Immanent Nature (both Aristotle and Plato here!) and parts of this Divine Universal Providence (more or less like pieces of God, if you can imagine it) were the "seminal logoi", or seeds of Divine Fire, which were implanted in the world, and were the origin of all growth.

If the Reader is having some trouble understanding this idea, then he, or she, has only to cast his, or her, mind back to the most ancient of all myths — not only to those myths of the Greeks, but to those myths of primitive man everywhere. In all these stories there is generally some attempt to explain the birth of the world, based upon a very crude and rudimentary sexual knowledge, and in which some male figure impregnates some female figure, with the 'seed' of life. The Greeks had similar stories to this originally, and the Aborigines in Australia also had a legend about a Female Goddess who plucked some babies from her belly, and who then planted them in certain areas so that the first tribes were begun. What is also very interesting, although slightly away from our point of 'seminal logoi' or seeds of life, is that most primitive people also had stories about women, (sometimes the Female Goddess herself) cutting off the sexual organs of the Male God, or, the sexual organs of any other males who happened to be around the place. And one begins to wonder if this was actually a common custom in ancient times, and if it might have been an early form of Birth Control, or, of Female Revenge upon the Male, for general ill-treatment. But this theory certainly would account for the over-anxiety, and the almost neurotic light in which Men in general regard their genitalia, and it quite possibly might also account for the theory of "Penis Envy", which Male Psychologists subscribe to. Personally the Author doesn't feel that women really care about actually possessing this portion of a man's anatomy, and as it is Men, who through the ages have organised the building of Phallic Symbols in every country, it is surely the Male who is more pre-occupied with this organ — not woman. But probably to the ancient people, this "sperm" of life was thought to be the only important part in the birth process, or the creation of life, and as Man was considered the active giver, or planter of the seed, so woman was only thought of as the passive taker, or holder of the seed of life — and men obviously felt very superior, and therefore guarded their gentitalia with great care, and probably regarded women most contemptuously, because they, poor things, did not have any! So rather than "Penis Envy", it might be said that there is some type of "Penis Superiority" complex, which would also account for the strange desire in men to accentuate this part of their bodies by the use of 'cod-pieces', 'sporans', and other fashionable forms of clothing over the years. And although, all the above may have seemed slightly off the track and away from the main discussion of the Stoic theory, it is actually connected, because Zeno felt that this Divine Fire, or "seminal logoi", was definitely both Active and Male, and that all Passive Matter in the world was Female; and that this Passive, Female matter was generated by the Active, Male Fire, and periodically re-absorbed into it. Therefore the universe was eternally destroyed and re-constructed in endless cycles (which was very like Pythagoras' ideas, and very tiring indeed) and at the end of a cycle, there was a universal conflagration, or 'Apocalypse', or destruction of the world, (the Final Last Day of Earth in the Christian Doctrine) and then an 'Apokatastasis', or, 'Restoration', where-upon there would be a complete renewal, and the whole process would be repeated exactly the same as before. And that is the really heart-breaking hopelessness of this theory, because the world would simply repeat itself, with another Socrates, another Zeno etc., and we would all merely come back only to suffer as before — and where is the Justice in that, I ask you? It was this theory of Pythagoras' about life cycles, which Zeno had taken and turned inside out, with a lot of Middle Eastern, and Far Eastern pessimism as well, which really transformed the Stoic Doctrine into such a hideous creed, and into such a depressing one as well. There was just no hope at all! At the Conflagration, the soul was absorbed back into God (like Atna into Brahmin) and then the whole dreary thing had to be endured again and again. No wonder so many Stoics killed themselves. The only possible way out for them was to jump their cycles; like a worn out and non-serviced washing-machine with an over-load. They probably thought if they kept suiciding, or averting misery that way, they would manage to be free of it also, in the *next* programme. Virtue was definitely its own reward, because no matter how much you tried, you could never manage to escape Fate, and this idea of Predestination travelled on into many extremist and Puritanical divisions of the Christian Church, and gave rise to all sorts of obnoxious and psychologically sick individuals. And the Stoic was advised to resign himself completely, just as some forms of Christianity abjure their members to practise total resignation and acceptance of suffering and persecution. And to illustrate this unhealthy attitude; and how one could really never compete to advantage with Zeno; there is a story about a slave of his, whom he caught stealing in the Stoa one day. As Zeno beat his slave, the poor captive (who had been thoroughly indoctrinated in Stoicism in the process of his daily work) cried out, "But, Master, why do you beat me? I was fated to steal. That is what the Stoic doctrine of Predestination says." But Zeno answered smartly," And as you were fated to steal, so I was fated to beat you!" And that goes to show that one just couldn't win with that man!

The Stoics however, believed that religion was so necessary for the good of the people that they advised them to hang onto their Olympian God System in addition to joining the Stoics, because in Zeno's eyes the State Collective good came foremost. Marriage, like religion, was also deemed necessary for all people, and marriage, and the bearing of children,were both regarded as a duty to the State. The Stoic accepted the laws of the State, and of the Monarchy in particular, but did not care for the idea of independant City-States, or individualism, in any shape,form or size. And the ordinary citizen, he considered to be only a dangerous simpleton — and quite possibly, he might have been right there!

It was not wise to pursue pleasure, or learning, or any sciences, said the Stoics, as they were fiercely anti-atheistic — hence we see the reasons for the mutual dislike between the Stoic group, and the other philosophers of the time. They (the Stoics) completely accepted Astrology and the superstitions regarding the movements of the stars, while at the same time roundly and soundly denouncing Astronomy. They countenanced superstition and State conventional morality, and the Government of the State (whatever it was!) and they did their best to eradicate all science — and any interest in it!

The good Stoic should live according to Nature; shun luxury, economic, or political strife; content himself with little; accept without complaint the difficulties and disappointments of life; suppress all emotions; and **never question fate!** Now, perhaps we can better understand why the Stoics were so popular with the Assembly and with Antigonus, and even later with the Roman Establishment. If the System could have people believing this sort of rubbish, then it would be so easy to rule them. Indoctrination in Stoicism was like carrying out a massive 'collective lobotomy' in the State. The population would give no trouble at all, after imbibing such ideas and dogmas as these. And now the historical detective can finally understand why Zeno was receiving such 'red-carpet' treatment in Athens from the Authorities.

The Stoics were completely indifferent to the issues of Slavery, Freedom (or the lack of it!) Sickness, or Pain. And they advocated that teachers should be very hard on their pupils, and that administrators should be very stern. And that EVERYONE was responsible for his every action, and that, the most important task of every citizen, was to **fulfill his Duty** —

which is why this philosophy proved so popular in Rome during the building of the Empire.

Chrysippus, whom we have mentioned before, said that Wars were in fact very useful in correcting the over-population problem (a forerunner of Malthus!) just as bed bugs were useful in preventing us from over-sleeping. That man definitely had a nice turn of phrase! He also wanted to limit the size of funerals, and to make them very quiet affairs. Or, it would be even better yet, he thought, to eat the bodies of our dear departed; in order to avoid costs and to save on protein. And this very utilitarian lad really implemented the sense of individual guilt and sin in Stoicism — which in due course passed on to us in the Christian Religion with the Doctrine of Original Sin. And when he wasn't pouring brimstone and fire down on everybody's heads, and generally making them feel just awful; then he was savagely attacking, and prosecuting Aristarchus of Samos, for his ideas on Astronomy; as indeed he was busy persecuting anyone, anywhere, who had any ideas on anything at all! The Stoics were completely against education, and Aristo, another student of Zeno's, defined Logicians as people who spent an inordinate amount of time, trying to pull minute morsels of meat from the crustaceous shells of lobsters. (Actually I quite like this definition myself, even though it was composed by a Stoic; and I have a lingering suspicion that Aristo might also have been some type of 'closet' Hedonist, and only masquerading in Stoic sack-cloth and ashes!)

Although both Epicureanism and Stoicism purported to be Materialistic Doctrines, and to be philosophies designed for the Detached; Epicureanism, equalled a recipe for a natural ethic for the individual, and for the obtainment of his individual salvation. Stoicism however, equalled a disciplined call to Duty for the entire collective, and it attempted to become the guiding morality (if not the religion) of the entire State. The Stoics actually wanted to build a strong selfless group of collective workers, —but, unfortunately for them however, the Greeks were just too pleasure-loving and individualistic, for this to succeed. In later years though, the Northern Europeans really adopted Stoicism staunchly and passionately, and it has permeated their nations ever since — to the detriment of everyone, naturally!

Stoicism was designed for both the Rich, and the Poor, as it didn't tell anyone to give anything away, and consequently didn't frighten off the Rich — and those (Rich) with a melancholic disposition, or a sad life-style, were probably even quite attracted to it. The first Stoics believed that one was either completely good (that is a Sage or a Saint) or completely bad. There was absolutely no half-way measure of morality for them! Later Stoics however, (especially those in Rome) brought out a theory of 'preferred' and 'deprecated' actions in order to judge morality; and there was even a convenient third category termed 'absolutely indifferent'. Need we say, that to the Stoics, those commmon or garden matters of Life and Death, were placed immediately and unhesitatingly into the 'absolutely indifferent' category! But they still adhered to the ideas (more or less) of attaining saint-hood like Socrates, Antisthenes, and Diogenes the Cynic, whom they had now claimed to have all originally been STOICS, and to have been the first Witnesses to the Living Truth of their Church!

The Stoic was admonished to perform actions, or to take the role, or part, on the Stage of Life, which were appropriate to him — "Life is but a Stage, and the men and women merely players." Shakespeare must have done some heavy reading of Stoicism, in conjunction with his Platonism. And to achieve a good life they were admonished to master desires; to perform their duties; and to think correctly (perhaps the hardest part of all!) Only what was within Man's power, should concern him, and he should not hunger for the unobtainable, but instead, he should fulfil his duty to others. Never to argue — always to accept! Lower his expectations, in order to be happy. And build habits of self-mastery, and discipline!

According to Epictetus, (the gentleman who believed in fully preparing children for death!) one could work towards this discipline by daily writing and meditating upon the experience of being tortured! And when the Stoic actually found himself enjoying anything, then he should immediately conjure up mental images of the opposite — in order not to fall prey to pleasure-loving, or to the seeking of happiness. The Stoic should also daily study, not only how to die, but how to endure torture, exile, and scourging; plus the foregoing of anything in his possession which might give him any pleasure; as one needed constant practice in order to face the trials of life. He should also daily committ to paper all his sins, and occasions of anger, (one imagines that the average Stoic must have had a great deal of frustrated anger bottled up inside him!) and any other **unStoic** emotions; and he should not consider a man who treated him badly as unjust, but rather, as a brother — and therefore he should bear with utmost equanimity all bad and cruel behaviour. And here we have the outline for the Christian Resignation Doctrine, and a brief browse through Epictetus is rather like a reading of some of the advice offered by Saint Paul in his epistolary letters to his various missionary groups in the Mediterranean and Middle East. "Everyman's life," said the Stoics, "is a kind of warfare, and it is long and diversified. You must observe the duty of a soldier, and do everything at the nod of the General." The question which the Stoics seemed very intent on begging though, and which the Author would have liked to have asked them; is,"Exactly who decides whether one gets to be the General or the soldier?" But naturally the Stoics would only have replied that one couldn't question Fate — much less fight it!

Poor Marcus Aurelius was almost destined from birth to be a Stoic, and perhaps there is something to be said for their Predestination Theory after all, because he had a lamentable child-hood, and then spent a pretty terrible adult-hood as well. What is most strange however, is that he spent so much time and effort persecuting the Christians in his empire, when they, poor things, believed almost the same dreadful doctrines as Marcus himself — especially after Paul had gotten through with them! Marcus had been brought up to refrain from passion (especially sexual passion), and he had been given a thorough religious training; a sparse diet; and lots of discipline. He was also advised constantly, to live as though each day were his last, and never to rely on anyone at all; for there were few true friends in this world, (and unfortunately this proved to be correct advice for this most miserable of men.) So while his wife betrayed him in the bed-room, and his children all died, (except the one who later became a tyrant) and as he battled against the treachery of the colleague with whom he shared his empire; and put up with famines, floods and plagues; and *put down* rebellions and roving bands of hysterical Christians; he was often moved to comment to himself, "That which is not good for the bee-hive, cannot be good for the bee." Which hardly seems to be an answer (not even an approximate one) for all the problems which were facing him at the time — but the Historians, and the Writers of Philosophy, generally state that Marcus was a good man (I'm afraid that I can't see it myself — but then my sympathies are with my Christian ancestors who were being branded and burned; fed to lions, and crucified; which punishments I consider just a little extreme, no matter how annoying they were to the authorities!) and they, the Historians, give the credit for all his goodness to the Stoic philosophy! So, perhaps I am biased, and perhaps there was some good in the Stoic doctrine after all, and *perhaps* I have unfortunately not been able to fathom it sufficiently well — in order to fully appreciate it.

Stoicism, as we saw, existed to a certain extent naturally, in the life-style of the Spartans, and it later entered the Christian Religion in order to play a very important role in certain churches of a more puritan character. It also exists in Puritanism, Fascism, and in certain forms of Communism (such as when the State needs building on the bones of the masses, and when the word 'Individual' is considered 'dirty', as it was in the time of Stalinism in the U.S.S.R.) Happily, it is generally only a transitory stage, and pleasure-loving man soon gets the better of it, the moment the economics of the situation have been improved; as Stoicism is more a disease than a philosophy, and is most inclined to break-out in depressed areas – and a little of it goes a long, long way! Certain ages or times in history tend to be more Stoic than others, and during the 1930's and 1940's, the entire world resounded to a lot of Stoic Doctrine from politicians and Leaders in every country. And Zeno, either in the Void, or in the 'Divine Pneuma' (or maybe back on earth — perish the thought!) must have been very pleased to see how popular his creed had again become. Unfortunately we will probably never witness the complete eradication of this fascistic dogma, but we must just think of Heracleitus and wait for the flowing waters of change to reach us. Sooner of later there is always a Climatic Change — and we can always work towards attempting to bring it about more rapidly. Stoicism is never the answer; it is only a miserable stop-gap, and it is completely against the Life Forces and the vital spirit of Human Hope and Endeavour — as both the Greeks and the Romans discovered long ago. As a philosophy, it flourished in the Winter of the Greek World, drawing upon the despair of a people who knew not where to turn. With Stoicism true philosophy died, as Intellectual Thought had fallen to its lowest superstitious depth — to its Nadir! — And the Greek Philosophers had all passed away — as had passed the glory of their people. Our last chapter though, will consider the Sceptic and Peripatetic post-scripts to this era, and the new, and exceedingly glorious hy-brid culture, which now burst into blossom in Alexandria.

CHAPTER 13

THE DANGEROUS WALKERS AND THE NAUGHTY TALKERS
ALEXANDRIA — And the Peripatetic and Sceptic Post-Scripts

After the death of Alexander in 323 B.C. Ptolemy, the son of Lagus, a Macedonian General, brought the body of the great conqueror to Memphis in Egypt, and placed it (for public veneration) within the confines of a golden sarcophagus. Later Ptolemies however, removed the gold, melted it down for more practical use; and placed the remains of Alexander in a glass coffin, where doubtless, they would be more accessible to viewers. —For how short a period indeed, does respect, or fame, last? No wonder it is said, that heavy is the head on which the crown sits; for the moment the crown is gone — so is the respect! But perhaps, Alexander should actually have considered himself fortunate that the Ptolemies didn't think to put the theories of Chrysippus, the Stoic, into action, and to have his body consumed as a form of nutrition; instead of being buried in any manner — fitting or otherwise. And many a man of less social standing in his Hellenic Empire endured a far more disrespectful interment than did the Great Alexander.

This historical anecdote however, sets the scene for, and it helps to explain, the rise of Alexandria in the Classical World, as the behaviour of the Ptolemies was at all times extremely down-to-earth, and pragmatic. And it was, to some extent, because of this very attitude of expediency, that this Hellenic area flourished economically, and produced such a bounteous scholastic harvest. This smallest, but richest morsel of Alexander's legacy comprised a Greek Egypt which also included the control of Cyrene, Crete, the Cyclades, Cyprus, Syria, Palestine, Phoenicia, Samos, Lesbos, Samothrace, and the Hellespont. So that in this collection of small gems, we see gathered into one thrilling combination of talent, and expertise, the genius of both Old Ionia, and Old Egypt — and together they united to create the most intellectually fertile centre in the Greek World, ever to be witnessed in history.

The great majority of the people of Alexandria might not have been all that happy with the System of Government which prevailed there, but it was definitely a most productive one. And future generations can only stand in awe and admiration of how much it managed to achieve — especially in the Sciences. Although of course, this great mental development was built upon great physical exploitation of the mass of people.

Ptolemy I promoted agriculture, commerce and industry in Egypt, as well as creating a stupendous fleet for both the protection of the State, and for the development of trade; and in 290 B.C. a Museum (that is a House of the Muses for Arts and Sciences) and a Library, were also established in Alexandria by him. Philosophy, and Learning, and Art, have always depended on a strong economic foundation in order to be able to prosper abundantly — and Alexandria was to prove no exception to this rule.

Then in 285 B.C. Ptolemy II came on the throne. He was a real Hedonist, who ate to the point of obesity; married his sister Arsinoe; and perpetrated many other terribly immoral acts which would only distress the Reader to learn of; but who, for all his vices can be forgiven, because during his reign, he invited to Alexandria, all the famous poets, scientists, philosophers, and artists of the Mediterranean and Aegean World. And for creating such a nursery of culture, he must surely be exonerated of, and absolved from, *all* his sins of the flesh!

The newly established University of Alexandria sheltered these scholars, and this building included a refectory, and a library; living quarters for the academics; and an amazingly well-equipped astronomical observatory. Astronomers, Writers, Mathematicians, and Physicians all took up residence there, and were paid a wage from the Royal Treasury — which itself was supplied with the 'necessary', out of the taxes paid by all the Greeks who were making so much money from their participation in commerce in Egypt. The functions and duties of these scholars were to research, study, and experiment, which included the dissecting not only of animals, in the cause of medicine — but also, for the very first time, the surgical segmentation of human bodies. And the Ptolemy it must be said, never stinted either himself, (or them,) in this scientific work; but liberally suppplied countless slaves and criminals to aid in their laboratory experiments. As I remarked earlier, possibly not everyone was completely overjoyed with the way things were run in Alexandria — and doubtless the slaves and criminals were not very impressed with this Greek addiction for discovery and knowledge. But the Greeks thought it was a marvellous idea — after all, none of them was either a slave, or a criminal!

Ptolemy III took over Alexandria in 246 B.C. and managed to add Sardis and Babylon to his territory, at the same time as he was vigorously knocking the foundations out from under the Seleucid Empire, so that it fell more rapidly into the out-stretched hands of the Romans. The Ptolemies, it will be observed, were tending to become more predatory and aggressive in disposition, and the old-hand at history reading will probably now begin muttering wisely to himself, "Ah, ha! Pride comes before a fall — they're on their way down a slippery slope from now on!" And of course, he will be completely right, as that is exactly what began to happen.

Ptolemy IV then arrived on the scene, and gave himself over to bacchanalia completely, and in 205 B.C. his mistress killed his wife, and soon after this little malapropos, the Ptolemy himself died. Nothing could be categorically proven against the mistress over his untimely death, but

Alexandrian detectives were never really satisfied about this case, and in consequence, filed it in the draw marked 'Unfinished'. And Alexandria was now teetering on the brink of catastrophy, and open to attack. Macedonia and Seleucid (who had been licking their wounds all this long time, and plotting bloody revenge) were just about to avail themselves of this golden opportunity to own a Museum and Library of their very own, (Alexandria was a most attractive piece of real estate!) when the Romans beat them to the punch, by marching in; taking down the For Sale sign on the front lawn; and making Egypt a Protectorate of Rome, in 205 B.C. After this of course, it was down hill all the way in Alexandria. The scientists and artists went on working diligently, but the State itself was evolutionarily damned.

But how was this, the **true** cradle of Western Civilization fashioned? And how did the Ptolemaic System (the most efficiently organised government in the Hellenistic World) actually work? We should perhaps look more closely into the economics of Alexandria, in order to have a better understanding of how, and why, the Museum and Library were able to function; and of how this city managed to present to the world (and to future generations) so much knowledge. For it was here in Alexandria, that the diameter of the world was successfully calculated to within fifty miles of what it actually is; and here also that Hero devised the very first steam-engine; and Euclid compiled the standard geometrical text-books which are still in use in our schools today. The entire world is still in debt to Alexandria and its scholarship, and consequently, in debt to those corrupt Ptolemies who supported this academic hot-house, by the use of a most ruthless economic system which spelt dreadful misery for the poor. But then, sighs the poet, a lily may grow on the top of a dung-heap, and its beauty and scent will in no way be diminished by the rancid material at its roots — and so as the dung-heap is to the lily, so the Ptolemies were to intellectual advancement and may be described as having been a type of necessary evil — if there is such a thing!

In Greek Egypt, the Ptolemies owned all the land, lock, stock, and barrel, and they oversaw all farming and land operations which were carried out by the "fellah", or, "Fedayeen", who were all bondsmen, or, in simpler terms, slaves. Therefore the Egyptians worked the land for the Greek Pharoh-God-King, and while this procedure functioned quite well at the beginning, the people did eventually begin to realise that their idols had feet, (not of clay) but of flesh and blood, just like themselves — and then naturally, they began to feel very resentful about the whole affair.

The Ptolemy also controlled all the mines and the industries, and employed Greek engineers to work on these systems and ventures. In fact, the Government (that is the Ptolemy) controlled every section of production, and the system was rather like that of a State Capitalism, or type of

Pharoh State Capitalist Socialism. All commerce and handicrafts were under the direction of the State; all caravan routes and waterways were also owned and run by them; and even Banking was a governmental monopoly.

The Greek population equalled about three hundred thousand people, who mainly occupied beaurocratic positions; enjoyed a luxurious social life; and had access to tremendous economic opportunities. The three major population groups in Egypt at this time were the Greeks, the Egyptians, and the Jews. While the Greeks were principally centred in administration and trade, and the Egyptians laboured on the land; the Jews, who had been especially brought to Egypt, by Alexander; were mostly involved in commerce. The Ptolemies had also encouraged this Jewish migration to Egypt, and to Alexandria in particular, because they saw the Jews as useful allies for the Greeks against the Egyptians. However, the Jews never really assimilated Greek religion and culture, and only paid obligatory lip-service to the Hellenic Ideal. In 200 B.C. the total population of Alexandria was about five hundred thousand souls, and it comprised Greeks, Macedonians, Egyptians, Jews, Persians, Anatolians, Syrians, Arabs, and Negroes; with the Jews making up one fifth of the whole amount.

There were taxes on absolutely everything, and on every item, under the Ptolemies; and an enormous number of tax-collectors were employed, who were continually on the move up and down the country, gathering in the dues of the Pharoh-God-King. This tax collection was most burdensome to the "fedayeen" naturally, although it was the beaurocrats and merchants who were most bitterly vocal about it, (but then that is always the way with taxation!) And even though taxed so very highly, the city of Alexandria was the most wealthy in Egypt, and architecturally (for its day) was a fantastically modern, beautiful, and luxurious metropolis.

The growth of commerce led inevitably to the emergence of a large Lower-Middle Class, and to a very cosmopolitan atmosphere; and naturally also to a decline in morals. "Alexandria is the house of Aphrodite", decried the Writer Herodas, in great despair, and Polybius, the Historian, confirmed that the finest private houses, all belonged to Courtesans! One good point about this laxity of morals though was that women moved freely in the streets with men, and the Greek women of Alexandria were probably the happiest, and the most progressive (for their time at any rate) in the entire Greek World. Of course the Greeks as usual, went to extremes, and adopted the worst of the Eastern customs (such as contracting marriage with their sisters), as well as retaining most of their own bad characteristics-such as their habitual, and vicious, arrogance, to all non-Greeks.

In the gold mines of Nubia, as in the Silver mines of Laurium, there were eventually bloody strikes and revolts, such as those in 216 B.C. and 189 B.C. — because the Rich as usual, could not learn to treat those unfortunates in their power, with anything approaching humanity, or, benevolence — (let alone Justice!) It seems that the Alexandrian elite had never heard the Aesopian proverb regarding the inadvisability of killing the goose which layed the golden egg! There was also trouble due to the racial mixtures in the country, and the inequality on which the whole system was based, and inevitably there began to occur revolts, and riots of priests, Jews, and Egyptians against the Greeks who were in the ascendancy. And so the place was wide open for the taking in 30 B.C. when Caesar strolled in, to have a look at Cleopatra, and to have Augusta make it a Roman Province. Whereupon this jewel of the Ancient World was then promptly snatched up and placed in the diadem of the Roman Empire.

But all the while that Alexandria had been growing up from ugly duckling to beautiful swan, Athens had been going steadily and even further, downhill. The Peripatetics, (the only scholars worthy of the name in that once fair city) had been enduring so much at the hands of the Stoics, and the Athenian Assembly, that most of them had as a result, migrated to Alexandria, and in consequence, helped to build her academic glory. Those few that remained however, now need to be spoken of, in order to round off this story of Greek Philosophy in a fitting fashion, and so we will return to Athens and the Peripatetics.

Firstly, an explanation of their name may be of assistance, as it was derived from the Greek word 'peripato' meaning, 'to go for a short walk;' and these philosophers, or rather, scholars, were exceedingly fond of taking physical exercise, at one and the same time, as they were limbering-up their minds. It is definitely true, the Author can categorically assure you (as she has carried out experiments in this herself) that walking is certainly conducive to the production of thought (great or otherwise!) and it therefore behoves us in the modern world to now start looking for our future philosophers among the many Marathon runners of today — for they, more than anyone else, have got the edge, as it were, in the movement towards philosophy.

Anyway, after Aristotle died, the work at the Lyceum was carried out by the Peripatetics, under the guidance of one Theophrastus, whose name, which had been given him by Aristotle, meant, "One who speaks like a God". As the original name with which he had been endowed at birth in Lesbos, had meanwhile been forgotten by everyone, it is therefore only as Theophrastus, that we shall ever know him — and it was said of him, that, "If there had been no Aristotle, then this period would have been called the time of Theophrastus." So we can see, that this gentleman was obviously no mean brain!

Aristotle had written the "History of Animals", but Theophrastus had written both "The History of Plants," and "The Causes of Plants," and like Aristotle, he was a Compulsive Definer by nature, and passionately loved order, facts, and science. A book without classifications, thought Theophrastus, was like a horse without a bridle — and probably twice as dangerous. Twenty centuries before Goethe, he recognized that the flower is in actuality, simply a metamorphosed leaf, a fact which the Author had never even known herself — until she dug up this amazing piece of information while reading. I am not suggesting that this discovery of Theophrastus' will in any way radically change your life, but it certainly is an interesting observation, and he was obviously an extremely intelligent person to have made it; especially at the time that he did!

He was a true Naturalist, who totally rejected the Supernatural, and among his writings was a learned work, "Superstitious Man"; showing how frail was the veneer of culture overlying our primitive superstitious societies — a fact which may still be observed today! And he wrote another work "On Marriage", in which he dealt rather harshly with that institution, and to which, Epicurus' mistress Leontium (probably with Epicurus holding her hand) penned a scathing reply. Even if Theophrastus was unduly castigatory towards the Female Sex, I think it is easy to forgive him, and to over-look this failing of his, when it is taken into consideration how much hard work he put into the Lyceum (in which he officiated for thirty four years from 322 — 288 B.C.) where four hundred volumes were published on every subject of possible interest, from Love — to War; and where specialist research was carried out in Zoology, Botany, Biography, History of Science, Philosophy, Literature, and Law. The Peripatetics incidentally, were helped in their medical and scientific discoveries by the information then becoming available to them from the vivisection being undertaken in Alexandria; and while the slaves, criminals, and other unfortunates who found themselves involuntary benefactors, and body donors to science, were less than enthusiastic about the matter; medical science, on the whole, made great bounds. During this time also, plant use for medicine was developed and encouraged and there was great enquiry into plant distribution, and the climatic conditions necessary for growth — as well as research carried out regarding their possible use in industry.

Theophrastus was an empiricalist, that is, a scientist who bases all his ideas on observation and experiment — and *not* on theory. And he led the Lyceum students in a firm committment to the continuation of the early trail-blazing of the Milesians; conscious of a need to know the real world — in order to understand what Life was all about.

Theophrastus was extremely popular with both the young, and the intellectualsof Athens, (although at this period, in time in Athens, there were not really all that many of either criteria on display,) and he often had up to two thousand students in attendance at his lectures, including

Menander the Comic Dramatist who lived from 350-277 B.C. This Larynx of a Diety also wrote a very interesting book entitled "Characters", which satirized the different Sociological and Psychological types in Athens, and noted the special faults and stupidities most prevalent in Man. And this book can't have made him very popular with any of the Athenian Assembly, — those who ever had the time that is, (away from their passionate, and all-consuming interests of money-making and political power-grabbing) to actually sit down to read.

In 307 B.C. Theophrastus was indicted for impiety by the Athenian Assembly, and a State decree was also passed by the Assembly, making their approval absolutely necessary and mandatory before the Head of any Philosophical School could be elected to office thenceforth. This was a flagrant attack on the general liberties of scholars, and ostensibly a law against philosophers, and their work of research. And yet, in 306 B.C. only one year later, Epicurus was allowed to open his school; and in 301 B.C. Zeno was also allowed to begin functioning behind his Stoa. Of course as Epicurus and Zeno were not real scientists, they were not deemed dangerous by the Assembly; and the study of philosophy itself had only ever been regarded as a threat, when it had involved new, and scientific, ideas, which had proved obnoxious in their freshness, and purity, to the stale, polluted (not to mention fetid) air, of the Establishment. Philosophers were deemed dangerous, and dangerous dissidents were not welcome in Athens. Anaxagoras had been punished not so much for his philosophy in Periclean Athens, as for his relentless determination to discover Truth; and Socrates, and the Sophists Gorgias and Protagoras, had been smartly rapped over the knuckles, as an example to all those other boat-rockers of that period; and in order that there should not be created a precedent in Truth Seeking. Now Theophrastus was also to receive the 'treatment.' Theodorus, the Hedonist of Cyrene, who had openly preached Atheism, had also been plainly shown the error of his ways; while Aristotle, on the passing of Alexander, had likewise been compelled to muse bitterly to himself on the disadvantages that true devotees of Apollo suffer. For Apollo, in the ancient Greek God System, symbolized the God of Truth. So while the Greeks may have paid lip-service to this deity (as the Jews of Alexandria paid lip-service to Greek culture) they rarely, if ever really respected the virtue which this God stood for, and never let any truth seeking philosopher stand between them and the pursuit of riches.

Anyhow, Theophrastus didn't wait around to receive his marching orders, but quietly left Athens at once, and his students went also. And then the shop-keepers began to complain — because they had lost their best customers, and business was bad, and the sellers of wine in particular, went bankrupt. And everyone began hollering, and shouting, and shaking their fists at the Athenian Assembly for having been so stupid in the first place. So the decree was annulled; the indictment withdrawn; Theophrastus returned to teach until his death at the age of eighty-five; and the shop-keepers smiled again, and stopped beating their wives and slaves in emotional compensation.

When Theophrastus died, the whole of Athens attended his funeral, it is recorded. And quite possibly that is because the Assembly and the Merchants were so glad to see the back of him that they went to the ceremony, more in a form of celebration than sorrow. And on his passing, Science began steadily moving to the more affluent, and more tolerant air of Alexandria; and the Lyceum and the Peripatetic School slowly dwindled into academic decay.

Under the influence of Theophrastus, the Peripatetics had abandoned the more Platonic elements of Aristotle, and had begun to stress his Naturalistic theories instead. Theophrastus, in particular, criticized Aristotle's Unmoved Mover — or, Movers; and later still; the Peripatetics abandoned this idea altogether. They believed in the immanent activity of Nature, as the first principle of the Universe; and they even wanted to represent the Soul more materialistically, than had their founder. The Peripatetics however, appealed to a refined, select, and silent minority only in the Greek World, but their thought influenced the work of scholars, and research students in Alexandria, which in turn influenced all later Western Scholarship. These Peripatetics were not outstanding personalities like the other philosophers whom we have met in this book, but they were true academics, and were dedicated to the search for truth — rather than to the declamation, and proclamation of theories.

As Philosophy and Science generally moves to where the money is —so the Thinkers of Athens moved to Alexandria, in much the same way that — even later in time — the Doctrines of Morality and Ethics (Epicureanism and Stoicism) would move from Athens to Rome — where they would then be more appreciated as a dogmatic religion of duty, and very necessary for the building of the young Roman Empire.

Gradually, the old Classical Schools, and the Scientists and Philosophers themselves, and who remained in Athens, gave way to Scepticism, and fell prey to doubt regarding everything. How could anyone know anything, anymore? they reasoned. The only thing they did know for sure, was that they didn't **like** what was going on. And there was not only one Sceptic Movement, but two major groups; and various off-shoots kept appearing in various sections of the Hellenic World for a great number of years, both prior to, and following, the Roman Conquest; and we shall examine the Pyrrhonian Sceptic Movement first of all, as it was probably the most famous of all these movements, and, 'Gorgon' like, kept growing new heads, and popping up in new places, no matter how many times it was cut down and decapitated.

Pyrrho of Elis, a Dorian by blood, (or possibly of more ancient and cultivated Aeolic or Pelasgic origin) and a Spartan by up-bringing, was born in 360 B.C. (some say 365) and he died in 275 B.C. — or therabouts! As a product of the Spartan system, it was quite fitting that he should have become a Sceptic, and have turned away in disgust from the ornate wordiness of Epicureanism and Stoicism, as the Spartans had always boasted that *Laconism* was the better way, and that it consituted a philosophy within itself.

During Alexander's imperialistic campaigns, Pyrrho followed the army into India, where, it is said, that for a period of time, he studied under the "Gymnosophists"; a nude, ascetic, philosophy movement in that land. As the Author has not carried out a great amount of research into this strange sect, she is unfortunately, unable to answer the burning question now doubtless uppermost in most Reader's minds: "Why were they nude? Did it have anything to do with philosophy as such?" — The Reader will just have to look into this matter for himself! But whatever the reasoning behind this peculiar lack of apparel, it doesn't seem to have affected Pyrrho all that strongly, because it is not recorded that his particular brand of Scepticism demanded the flinging-off of garments, and so possibly, the "Gymnosophist " nakedness, as such, did not really play an important role in the construction of their thought. Perhaps in fact, it was other experiences in Alexander's army which caused Pyrrho to become so taciturn and sceptical of his fellow man, and was not anything at all to do with these Indian ascetics — because most wars do tend, to make people a *little* philosophical. In fact, war does tend to cause a thoughtful, and a non-aggressive person to begin to ask himself, "Why are these people trying to kill me? Good Heavens! I don't even know them! What have they got against me personally, and what am I doing here, anyway?" War — like all misfortunes and sorrows — is the true creator of philosophy in Man, and possibly we should all have just enough of it (I am not suggesting bloody mayhem!) in order to get our mental processes working efficiently and up to scratch!

Anyway, Pyrrho — a contemporary of Epicurus and Zeno — found that war brought out the reflective side of his nature, and after returning from India he decided to spend his entire time in search of tranquillity of soul. He sought "Ataraxy", or "Apathy", and he felt, after due meditation, that it could only be achieved by belief in the following principles:-

1. The complete acceptance that all certainty was absolutely unattainable.
2. That Wisemen should suspend all judgement, and seek Tranquillity —rather than Truth.
3. That since all the theories are probably false — then one may as well accept the myths and conventions of each time and place.

Neither the Senses, nor Reason, can give us sure knowledge, Pyrrho decided, since the Senses distort the object in perceiving it, and Reason is merely the sophist servant of desire. As the Reader will have keenly discerned, this is not a very positive philosophy, but then Pyrrho was a complete and perfect agnostic, and his suspension of judgement concept, proves, that to him at any rate, all things were only indifferent, unstable, and indiscernable — and he certainly wasn't going to waste his time in trying to figure anything out. Possibly in India, during some of the fighting, he'd had such a quick shave with death, that he decided, since Life hadn't been snatched ungraciously from him, then he ought to start making the best use of it — and trying to discover the truth, was not, in his opinion, a good enough way to use it! Probably also, the Stoics and Epicureans were getting on his nerves so much that he just had to come out in opposition. Zeno, and his statements, were enough to drive even a Saint to drink — or a Spartan to speech!

Suspension of all thought, said Pyrrho, would eventually lead to utter tranquillity, and although I have on numerous occasions tried to do this myself — it has never seemed to work for me. Possibly true Sceptics are born — not made! Possibly, they are perfectly detached Human Beings who arrived on this Earth, already so fashioned; and possibly also, that is why this Sect, or Philosophic Movement, was such a very minor one, and with so very few adherents.

Everything is opinion, and nothing is true, said Pyrrho. Every reason has a corresponding reason opposed to it. Something may be ugly, or beautiful; good, or bad; depending on the mood, and the circumstances; he drawled through tight lips, determined to remain as reticent on this subject, as on all others. Morality and Deities are dependent on where we live, and everything is totally uncertain. Brusquely he observed, that Life is not a certain good; just as death is not a certain evil; and perhaps it is actually good, (as nobody who had experienced death had ever come back to inform us for sure!) but it was best, he decided in obmutescence, to calmly accept, and to be peaceful.

Being so much in despair of life in general (after his military experiences) Pyrrho therefore returned to Elis, where he formulated and practised his half-Hindu philosophy of detachment, and lived on, in grinding poverty, as a teacher. He conformed to the customs of life, and to the worship of religion in Elis, and so therefore, was not particularly victimized by the natives. He died at the age of ninety years without having written even a sentence, and probably the only reason posterity actually knows anything of his philosophy at all, is doubtless, because occasionally (like all teachers) he gave way to bouts of frustration in the classroom after the home-bell had rung, and burst into some type of monosyllabic soliloquy, which was probably memorised by the school janitor while occupied with sweeping up the litter of gum wrappers, and paper aeroplanes, which festooned the floor.

He made no attempt to prolong his life, it is said, and as he seemed on the whole, to have led such a passionless, and miserable existence, one must say that one is not really surprised. The truly strange thing though, is that he actually bothered to live as long as he did, and **not** to have done away with himself years before! However, the citizens of Elis liked him so much, that in his honour, they exempted all philosophers from the onerous task of paying taxation. Doubtless the real reason they had liked poor old Pyrrho so much was simply **because he didn't write anything troublesome**, and because he didn't rock the boat politically. And the children whom he taught must have been really happy, in having such an inconversable type for a teacher, as it is probably every child's dream that their tutor, and mental guardian, should become voiceless; and the child-hood of that particular group of youngsters in Elis, must truly have been the 'best days of their lives!'

Pyrrho's mute school of philosophical thought nearlydied out with Pyrrho himself, but he did have one or two pupils who must have visited him occasionally, and who possibly hung around with the Janitor in order to get those pearls of wisdom which infrequently dropped from his lips; and one of them was the Satirist, Timon of Philius, who wrote many satires, or "silloi," (possibly the true origin of the English word 'silly') and who made Pyrrho more famous than he had any right to have expected — or in fact, than he had even wanted to have become. Then in the 1st century B.C. Aenesidemus (100-40 B.C.) revived the Pyrrhonic Movement as it was then called, and under its flag, made a lot of nasty comments, and felled some very telling, and destructive blows, against the dogmatic Stoics and Epicureans, who were most decidely getting completely out of hand by then.

Later still, Pyrrhonism became a more positive and affirmative movement in Alexandria (where it was brought by Aenesidemus) and principally enjoyed support among the doctors of the town. The main proponent of this new Sceptical Movement in the 2nd and 3rd centuries A.D. was one Sextus Empiricus who claimed in true Medical fashion and terminology, that sceptical arguments were necessary in order to cure the dogmatists of the dreadful disease of supposing that knowledge was possible. The Sceptic, he maintained, relied on appearance, and avoided the error of passing judgement; and to suppose, as some poor fool dogmatists did; sniffed Sextus disdainfully; that it is possible to judge truth and falsity; is to ignore relativity of perception and judgement. It may be imagined, perhaps, that in Alexandria, in the 2nd and 3rd centuries A.D., there were many charges of medical negligence being brought to the attention of the Courts, and therefore, the medical practitioners had hit on Scepticism as a last-ditch attempt to save themselves from being struck off the Medical Register. A thoughtful doctor is a good thing it is true, and the word "skeptic" in Greek, actually means 'to think', but a Sceptical doctor is surely a horse of different colour entirely, and cannot have filled many hearts in that metropolis with either contentment, or relief, These new Sceptics in Alexandria were probably the new Sophists of their age, who were determined to throw out all the dusty, dogmatic, backward, and erroneous thinking of their forbears, and (more importantly perhaps) their elders and betters; and who were probably, *intellectually essential,* at that point in time — although not easy to live with. And Sextus insisted that the true Sceptic was in fact, a Lover of Mankind, who was seeking to cure the twin ailments of conceit and rashness. My word, these young doctors in Alexandria did take themselves, and their profession seriously!

By following this rule of silence and suspension of Judgement (the new form of Laconism!) Sextus insisted, that the mind would become perfectly balanced, and that tranquillity would follow as inevitably, "as the shadow follows the body." Sextus, who was both a doctor and a teacher (and having had such a large experience of the General Public, it is no wonder that the milk of Human Kindness had somewhat curdled in his breast!) then decided to interpret Pyrrho for the masses, and wrote "The Outlines of Pyrrhonism", and "Against the Mathematicians" — and yet another even more pugilistic manuscript, entitled "Against the Dogmatists." Sextus was definitely a boy not in fear of a fight, and with this attitude of "agin the World" and righteous indignation against injustice, so evident in his character, it would in no way surprise the Author to discover that he too (like Alexander) had some Celtic blood flowing wildly in his veins! It must be added however that Aenesidemus had started Sextus off on this dangerous game of crossing swords with the Establishment, by his article "Against the Logicians", and by creating such a furore that not only were the Sceptics against everybody, but, that Everybody was also against the Sceptics! Truly the new Sophists had arrived! And to illustrate the fact that Mathematics was a crazy and unreliable science in itself, the Sceptics proved that the number 6 actually equalled the number 15; for they said, (and showed by computation) that 5 4 3 2 and 1 added up to a total of 15, and therefore, they said, Mathematicians could put that in their pipes and smoke it! All those in Alexandria who found Mathematics unutterably boring, and unbearably painful to study, naturally, now joined the side of the Sceptics!

There were also some Academic Sceptics buzzing and stinging, and generally making themselves intolerable to the Establishment at this time, but we will finish off the Pyrrhonian Movement (before moving on to them) with some more extracts from the thoughts of Sextus. According to this busy iconoclast there were three main types of philosopher.

1. The Dogmatists, which included Aristotle, and Epicurus, and the Stoics; and all the rest who said that they had discovered the truth — (including, no doubt, the great Plato himself.)
2. The Negative Sceptics, like Carneades and the Academy, who said that the truth could not be found.
3. The Pyrrhonian Sceptics, who kept searching for the truth, no matter how hard it might be to find.

But any Pyrrhonian Sceptic readers may relax in their never ending battle for veracity for a brief while, in order to learn about the other main Sceptical School, which may prove even more to their taste, and possibly, less arduous as a philosophy to follow.

Plato must surely have been rolling in his grave, (and in a most unbefitting manner for such a staid gentleman) when Arcesilaus 315-241 B.C., became the 4th Head of the Academy, because he (Arcesilaus) then proceeded to lead the school of the great conformist into the destructive and negative criticism of anything and everything in Athens. Arcesilaus, who was head of the Middle Academy around 269 B.C., built upon (or demolished, might be a better choice of word) the famous Platonic dictum, "I know that I do not know" (which was actually attributed by Plato, to Socrates) and transformed it into the sceptical and sardonic, "We do not even know that we do not know!"

When the Athenians complained bitterly that his sceptical doctrine made life very difficult, Arcesilaus answered them smoothly, that life had long since learned how to manage with probabilities and difficulties, and that they shouldn't worry their pretty heads about it. And the Athenians went home shaking in their shoes at such bold-faced intellectual and moral nihilism. "Nothing is certain," shouted Arcesilaus at their departing backs, "and not even that!" And they threw themselves through the doors of their houses before their ears could be further polluted with such defamatory and frightening statements. This is possibly the reason why there were so few members of the Academy, and followers of Arcesilaus — Scepticism and Cynicism only appealed to a tiny minority of brave souls who had the stomach (collective!) for it — it was never meant to be a popular cause — and for everyone!

Arcesilaus wrote nothing (and that was possibly a good thing too — as there are far too many writers, and too much dashed writing in the world, at any time; and if anyone would like to offer the Author a couple of thousand pounds she would desist immediately, and cease from aggravating the situation still further!) but even though he wrote nothing, we still know something of him and his thoughts — possibly, due to another posterity conscious Janitor!

The Academy Sceptics were especially anti-Stoic, (which naturally makes the Author tend to side with them, and to consider them to have been an asset to Greek Society in general) and after the passing of Arcesilaus, they(the Academy,)found a new champion, and the Stoics found a new opponent, in a bright young man by the name of Carneades 213-129 B.C. At least the Reader can safely assume that Carneades died in 129, for the Author was able to turn up many references to this event, but there seemed to have been only a hazy understanding of when he first appeared on earth. Why is it, one wonders, that Historians, by and large, are always so sure of when people die, but not of when they were born? Can it be that people were as age-conscious in the Classical World as they are in the Modern? That everyone was attempting to conceal just how old, he or, she, really was? And that mere age itself was considered as some dreadful disease — then — as it is now?

Anyway, young Carneades arrived in Athens around 193 B.C and began studying Logic under Chrysippus and some other Stoics, and commenced making life distinctly bitter for them and therefore, truly stoical. He drove his teachers almost mad with his arguments in class, and he held them up to ridicule for all to see. As both Carneades and the Academy were thoroughly fed up with these dogmatic Stoics, they were only too happy to make fun of them, and they delighted in using intellectual humour at their stodgy colleagues' expense.

Carneades of Cyrene, (he had originally hailed from the African Hedonist Centre) used to state loudly and logically in the Stoic classroom (whenever they were attempting to shut him up, and to evict him from their monologues) "If my reasoning is right, well and good; if it is wrong, then give me back my tuition fee, for you have not taught me anything!" Certainly, he was a most annoying student, and it is only a wonder that the Stoics didn't think to put out a 'Contract' on him, among some of their members in Sicily.

Eventually Carneades set up a 'Thinking Shop' for himself, and thenceforth spent the morning happily arguing a point; and the afternoon, just as happily, disproving it! No one could ever discover his real views (or, even if he had any at all) but he was a brilliant rhetorician in the tradition of Protagoras, and he maintained that all conclusions were intellectually indefensible, and doubtless — for a price — he would take on any; just in order to prove it!

In 155 B.C. Carneades was dispatched to Rome by the Athenians, as one member of an Embassy, which was ostensibly sent to win the favour of these tough new Masters of the Mediterranean. But he completely shocked the old-fashioned, country boys of the Roman Senate by speaking one day in defence of Justice, and then the next day, by dismissing it as an impossible dream. He added that if Rome wished to practise Justice, then it would have to restore to the Nations of the Mediterranean, all that it had taken from them by superior force. Needless to relate, on the 3rd day of his visit, Cato had the Embassy (and Carneades in particular) curtly dismissed home to Athens — **never** to darken the doors of Rome again! The reason for this dismissal? Carneades was a danger to Public Morals, **So Cato said!**

Of course the real function of the Sceptic Movements had been to clear the ground, and the air, from the rubbish and pollution of decadent Stoicism and Epicureanism, and in doing this, they managed at least to hold aloft for a short period once more , the flag of Greek Intellectualism —and that was more than enough! They were the Reaction to the Action —the cold bright light of Enquiry piercing through the murky dimness of ignorance and dogmatism — and as Carneades said of himself, "If there had not been Chrysippus, than I should not have been either." There will always be Sceptics to attack the Dogmatists of this Life, and it is right that it be so. But we will leave the last word on the matter, with that great student of Philosophy, Mr. Will Shakespeare, who wrote into one of his dramas, this most sceptical of comments, — "Nothing is either good or bad — but only thinking makes it so."

And so we have completed our Cycle of Four Seasons in Greek Philosophy, passing from the Pure Scientists of the Milesian Spring, to the Winter of Stoic Discontent and Suffering and Superstition — And the Peripatetics, and the Sceptics — what exactly are they? Are they the last violent winds of Winter ravaging the trees and grasses in final necessary and climatic fury? Or are they in fact, the first hint of a new Spring, like the fresh winds of change — and therefore necessary to clear the cob-webs, and to stir the earth from its winter hibernation? The Cycle continues; and the Seasons die into each other; and they live on — in new forms. And so Greek Philosophy, or, the Thoughts of the Philosophers in our story, have continued; and are still continuing on today in our own thinking — ever changing — and yet always the same.

But the story of that new Cycle, and of those recurring Seasons, had best be left to another time, and–to another book.

INDEX

ILLYRIA
MACEDONIA
Pella
Olynthus
Potidaea
EPIRUS
THESSALY
Corcyra
ACARNANIA
Euboea
Delphi
PHOCIS
BOEOTIA
Plataea
Cephallenia
Megara
Zacynthos
ELIS
Corinth
ARCADIA
Argos
Mantinea
MESSENIA
Sparta
LACONIA

Athens and her allies
Sparta and her allies
Neutral states

0 150 km
0 100 mi

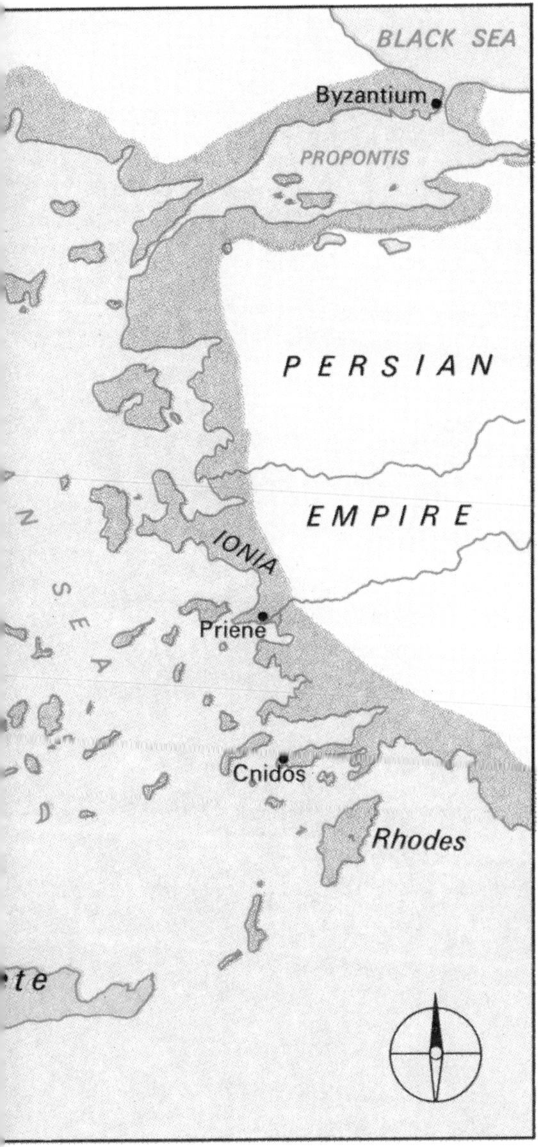

BLACK SEA
Byzantium
PROPONTIS
PERSIAN
EMPIRE
IONIA
Priene
Cnidos
Rhodes

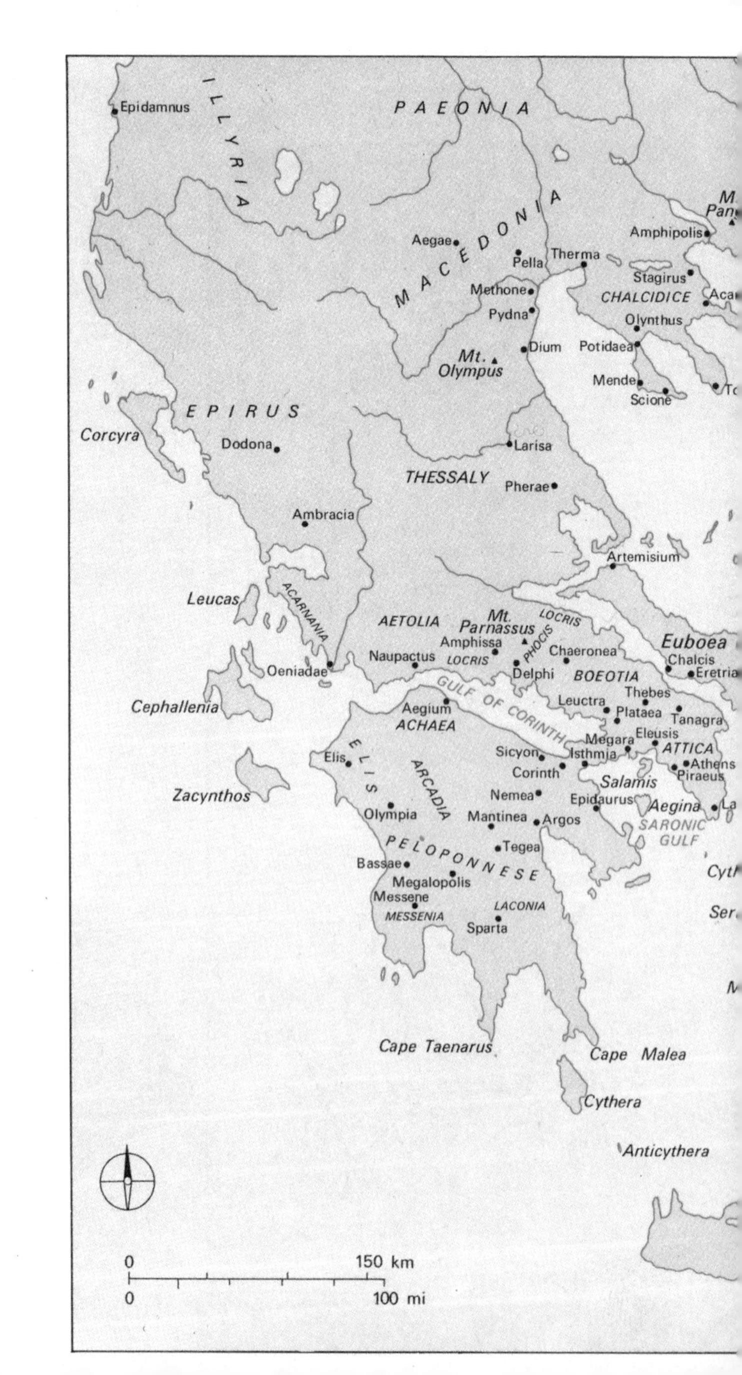
Epidamnus
ILLYRIA
PAEONIA
MACEDONIA
Aegae
Pella
Therma
Amphipolis
Stagirus
CHALCIDICE
Methone
Pydna
Olynthus
Dium
Potidaea
Mt. Olympus
Mende
Scione
EPIRUS
Corcyra
Dodona
Larisa
THESSALY
Pherae
Ambracia
Artemisium
Leucas
ACARNANIA
AETOLIA
Mt. Parnassus
LOCRIS
PHOCIS
Amphissa
Chaeronea
Euboea
Naupactus
LOCRIS
Chalcis
Eretria
Oeniadae
Delphi
BOEOTIA
Thebes
GULF OF CORINTH
Cephallenia
Aegium
Leuctra
Plataea
Tanagra
ACHAEA
Megara
Eleusis
ELIS
Elis
ARCADIA
Sicyon
Isthmia
ATTICA
Athens
Piraeus
Corinth
Salamis
Zacynthos
Nemea
Epidaurus
Aegina
Olympia
Mantinea
Argos
SARONIC GULF
PELOPONNESE
Tegea
Bassae
Megalopolis
Messene
MESSENIA
LACONIA
Sparta
Cape Taenarus
Cape Malea
Cythera
Anticythera
0
150 km
0
100 mi

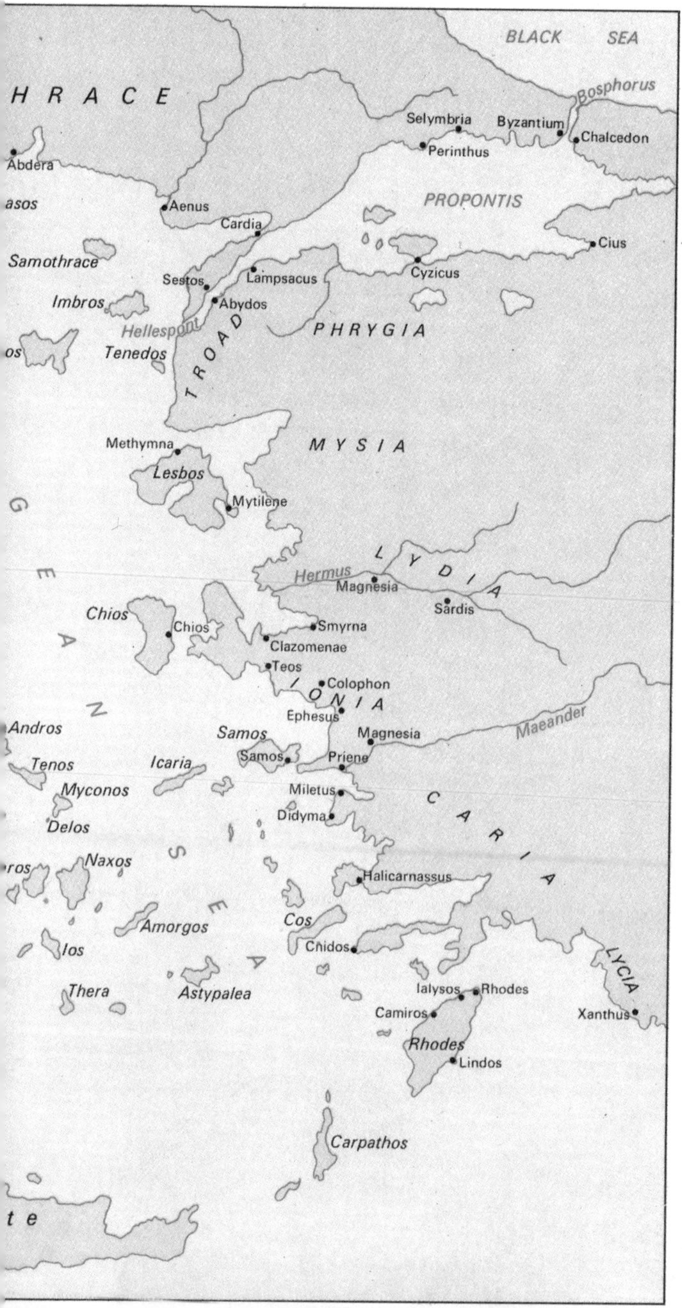

BLACK SEA
HRACE
Bosphorus
Selymbria
Byzantium
Chalcedon
Perinthus
Abdera
asos
Aenus
PROPONTIS
Cardia
Cius
Samothrace
Sestos
Lampsacus
Cyzicus
Imbros
Abydos
Hellespont
TROAD
PHRYGIA
os
Tenedos
Methymna
MYSIA
Lesbos
Mytilene
G
E
LYDIA
Hermus
Magnesia
Sardis
Chios
Chios
Smyrna
A
Clazomenae
Teos
Colophon
IONIA
N
Ephesus
Andros
Samos
Magnesia
Maeander
Samos
Priene
Tenos
Icaria
Myconos
Miletus
CARIA
Didyma
Delos
S
ros
Naxos
Halicarnassus
E
Cos
Amorgos
Ios
Cnidos
A
LYCIA
Thera
Astypalea
Ialysos
Rhodes
Camiros
Xanthus
Rhodes
Lindos
Carpathos
te

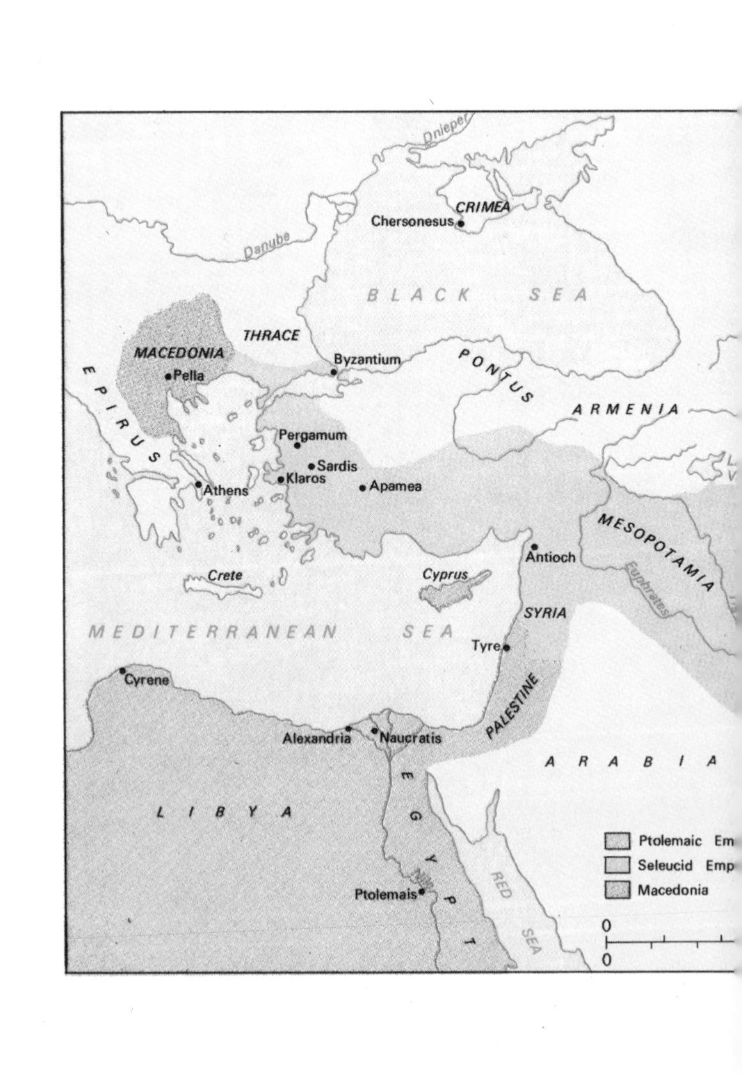

Dnieper
CRIMEA
Chersonesus
Danube
BLACK SEA
THRACE
MACEDONIA
Pella
Byzantium
PONTUS
EPIRUS
ARMENIA
Pergamum
Sardis
Klaros
Athens
Apamea
MESOPOTAMIA
Antioch
Euphrates
Crete
Cyprus
SYRIA
MEDITERRANEAN SEA
Tyre
Cyrene
PALESTINE
Alexandria
Naucratis
ARABIA
LIBYA
EGYPT
Nile
Ptolemais
RED SEA
Ptolemaic Em
Seleucid Emp
Macedonia
0
0

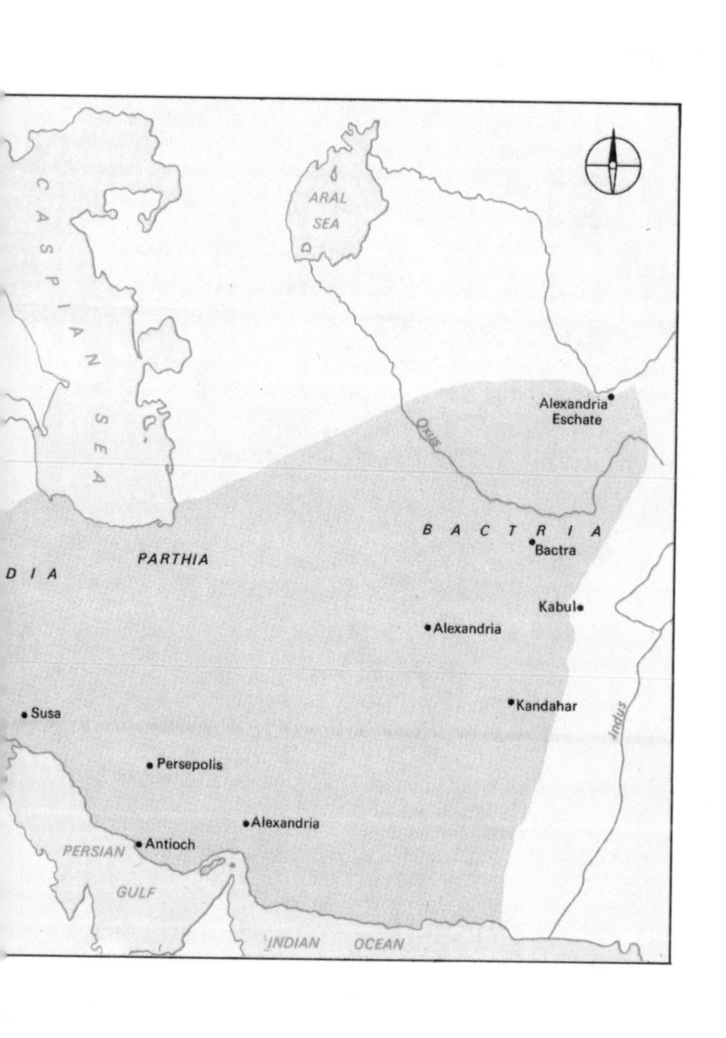
CASPIAN SEA
ARAL SEA
Alexandria Eschate
Oxus
BACTRIA
Bactra
PARTHIA
DIA
Kabul
Alexandria
Kandahar
Susa
Indus
Persepolis
Alexandria
Antioch
PERSIAN GULF
INDIAN OCEAN

SCYTHIA
Olbia
Tyras
LAKE MAEOTIS
Panticapaeum
Phanagoria
Theodosia
Chersonesus
Dioscurias
Phasis
Trapezus
BLACK SEA
Callatis
Odessus
Mesambria
Apollonia
Sinope
Amisus
Byzantium
PROPONTIS
Heraclea Pontica
Massilia
Rhodae
Emporiae
CORSICA
SARDINIA
ETRURIA
Neapolis
MAGNA GRAECIA
Taras
Metapontum
Thurii
Croton
Panormus
Messana
Locri
Motya
Himera
Rhegium
Selinus
SICILY
Catana
Leontini
Carthage
Acragas
Gela
Syracuse
Camarina
Athens
Sparta
RHODES
CRETE
Salamis
CYPRUS
Citium
Paphos
Aradus
Berytus
Sidon
Tyre
PHOENICIA
MEDITERRANEAN SEA
Apollonia
Barca
Cyrene
Naucratis
Pelusium
EGYPT